Federal Rules of Appellate Procedure

with Advisory Committee Notes

2017 Edition

Including Amendments Effective
December 1, 2016

HSE Publishing Co.

© 2016 HSE Publishing Co.

© 2016 HSE Publishing Co.

No copyright is claimed in any government work. This book has been prepared for general information purposes only and is not a substitute for and should not be considered legal advice. The publisher endeavors to ensure the accuracy and currency of this book's contents but makes no guarantee in either regard and cannot assume liability for inadvertent errors or otherwise.

Please send any feedback to hsepublishing@gmail.com.

ISBN-13: 978-9781537783253

ISBN-10: 1537783254

TABLE OF CONTENTS

PREFACE 5

TITLE I. APPLICABILITY OF RULES 6
    Rule 1. Scope of Rules; Definition; Title 6
    Rule 2. Suspension of Rules 7

TITLE II. APPEAL FROM A JUDGMENT OR ORDER OF A DISTRICT COURT 7
    Rule 3. Appeal as of Right – How Taken 7
    Rule 4. Appeal as of Right – When Taken 11
    Rule 5. Appeal by Permission 27
    Rule 6. Appeal in a Bankruptcy Case from a Final Judgment, Order, or Decree of a District Court or Bankruptcy Appellate Panel 30
    Rule 7. Bond for Costs on Appeal in a Civil Case 32
    Rule 8. Stay or Injunction Pending Appeal 33
    Rule 9. Release in a Criminal Case 34
    Rule 10. The Record on Appeal 36
    Rule 11. Forwarding the Record 38
    Rule 12. Docketing the Appeal; Filing a Representation Statement; Filing the Record 41
    Rule 12.1 Remand After an Indicative Ruling by the District Court on a Motion for Relief That Is Barred by a Pending Appeal 42

TITLE III. REVIEW OF A DECISION OF THE UNITED STATES TAX COURT 44
    Rule 13. Review of a Decision of the Tax Court 44
    Rule 14. Applicability of Other Rules to the Review of a Tax Court Decision 45

TITLE IV. REVIEW OR ENFORCEMENT OF AN ORDER OF AN ADMINISTRATIVE AGENCY, BOARD, COMMISSION, OR OFFICER 46
    Rule 15. Review or Enforcement of an Agency Order 46
    Rule 15.1 Briefs and Oral Argument in a National Labor Relations Board Proceeding 48
    Rule 16. The Record on Review or Enforcement 48
    Rule 17. Filing the Record 48
    Rule 18. Stay Pending Review 49
    Rule 19. Settlement of a Judgment Enforcing an Agency Order in Part 50
    Rule 20. Applicability of Rules to the Review or Enforcement of an Agency Order 51

TITLE V. EXTRAORDINARY WRITS 51
    Rule 21. Writs of Mandamus and Prohibition, and Other Extraordinary Writs 51

TITLE VI. HABEAS CORPUS; PROCEEDINGS IN FORMA PAUPERIS 53
    Rule 22. Habeas Corpus and Section 2255 Proceedings 53
    Rule 23. Custody or Release of a Prisoner in a Habeas Corpus Proceeding 56
    Rule 24. Proceeding in Forma Pauperis 56

TITLE VII. GENERAL PROVISIONS 59
    Rule 25. Filing and Service 59
    Rule 26. Computing and Extending Time 65
    Rule 26.1 Corporate Disclosure Statement 71

TABLE OF CONTENTS

- Rule 27. Motions 74
- Rule 28. Briefs 79
- Rule 28.1 Cross-Appeals 83
- Rule 29. Brief of an Amicus Curiae 86
- Rule 30. Appendix to the Briefs 91
- Rule 31. Serving and Filing Briefs 95
- Rule 32. Form of Briefs, Appendices, and Other Papers 96
- Rule 32.1 Citing Judicial Dispositions 103
- Rule 33. Appeal Conferences 104
- Rule 34. Oral Argument 104
- Rule 35. En Banc Determination 106
- Rule 36. Entry of Judgment; Notice 111
- Rule 37. Interest on Judgment 111
- Rule 38. Frivolous Appeal 112
- Rule 39. Costs 112
- Rule 40. Petition for Panel Rehearing 114
- Rule 41. Mandate: Contents; Issuance and Effective Date; Stay 117
- Rule 42. Voluntary Dismissal 119
- Rule 43. Substitution of Parties 120
- Rule 44. Case Involving a Constitutional Question When the United States or the Relevant State is Not a Party 121
- Rule 45. Clerk's Duties 122
- Rule 46. Attorneys 123
- Rule 47. Local Rules by Courts of Appeals 124
- Rule 48. Masters 125

APPENDIX OF FORMS 127

- Appellate Form 1. Notice of Appeal to a Court of Appeals From a Judgment or Order of a District Court. 127
- Appellate Form 2. Notice of Appeal to a Court of Appeals From a Decision of the United States Tax Court. 128
- Appellate Form 3. Petition for Review of Order of an Agency, Board, Commission or Officer. 129
- Appellate Form 4. Affidavit Accompanying Motion for Permission to Appeal In Forma Pauperis. 130
- Appellate Form 5. Notice of Appeal to a Court of Appeals from a Judgment or Order of a District Court or a Bankruptcy Appellate Panel 134
- Appellate Form 6. Certificate of Compliance With Rule 32(a). 135
- Appellate Form 7. Declaration of Inmate Filing 136
- Appendix 137

Other Books by HSE Publishing Co. 139

PREFACE

The Federal Rules of Appellate Procedure govern procedure in the United States courts of appeals. These Rules are amended periodically. The Advisory Committee generally prepares Advisory Committee Notes that explain the text of the new amendments and the reasons for them. These Notes can be extremely useful in interpreting the Rules. This book contains both the Rules and the Advisory Committee Notes.

Amendments to the following Rules of Appellate Procedure became effective December 1, 2016: Appellate Rules 4, 5, 21, 25, 26, 27, 28, 28.1, 29, 32, 35, and 40, and Forms 1, 5, and 6, new Form 7 and a new Appendix.

The Publisher
December 30, 2016

Rule 1. Scope of Rules; Definition; Title

TITLE I. APPLICABILITY OF RULES

Rule 1. Scope of Rules; Definition; Title
(a) Scope of Rules.
   (1) These rules govern procedure in the United States courts of appeals.
   (2) When these rules provide for filing a motion or other document in the district court, the procedure must comply with the practice of the district court.
(b) Definition. In these rules, 'state'1 includes the District of Columbia and any United States commonwealth or territory.
(c) Title. These rules are to be known as the Federal Rules of Appellate Procedure.
(As amended Apr. 30, 1979, eff. Aug. 1, 1979; Apr. 25, 1989, eff. Dec. 1, 1989; Apr. 29, 1994, eff. Dec. 1, 1994; Apr. 24, 1998, eff. Dec. 1, 1998; Apr. 29, 2002, eff. Dec. 1, 2002; Apr. 28, 2010, eff. Dec. 1, 2010.)

Notes of Advisory Committee on Rules—1967

These rules are drawn under the authority of 28 U.S.C. §2072, as amended by the Act of November 6, 1966, 80 Stat. 1323 (1 U.S. Code Cong. & Ad. News, p. 1546 (1966)) (Rules of Civil Procedure); 28 U.S.C. §2075 (Bankruptcy Rules); and 18 U.S.C. §§3771 (Procedure to and including verdict) and 3772 (Procedure after verdict). Those statutes combine to give to the Supreme Court power to make rules of practice and procedure for all cases within the jurisdiction of the courts of appeals. By the terms of the statutes, after the rules have taken effect all laws in conflict with them are of no further force or effect. Practice and procedure in the eleven courts of appeals are now regulated by rules promulgated by each court under the authority of 28 U.S.C. §2071. Rule 47 expressly authorizes the courts of appeals to make rules of practice not inconsistent with these rules.

As indicated by the titles under which they are found, the following rules are of special application: Rules 3 through 12 apply to appeals from judgments and orders of the district courts; Rules 13 and 14 apply to appeals from decisions of the Tax Court (Rule 13 establishes an appeal as the mode of review of decisions of the Tax Court in place of the present petition for review); Rules 15 through 20 apply to proceedings for review or enforcement of orders of administrative agencies, boards, commissions and officers. Rules 22 through 24 regulate habeas corpus proceedings and appeals in forma pauperis. All other rules apply to all proceedings in the courts of appeals.

Notes of Advisory Committee on Rules—1979 Amendment

The Federal Rules of Appellate Procedure were designed as an integrated set of rules to be followed in appeals to the courts of appeals, covering all steps in the appellate process, whether they take place in the district court or in the court of appeals, and with their adoption Rules 72–76 of the F.R.C.P. were abrogated. In some instances, however, the F.R.A.P. provide that a motion or application for relief may, or must, be made in the district court. See Rules 4(a), 10(b), and 24. The proposed amendment would make it clear that when this is so the motion or application is to be made in the form and manner prescribed by the F.R.C.P. or F.R.Cr.P. and local rules relating to the form and presentation of motions and is not governed by Rule 27 of the F.R.A.P. See Rule 7(b) of the F.R.C.P. and Rule 47 of the F.R.Cr.P.

Notes of Advisory Committee on Rules—1989 Amendment

The amendment is technical. No substantive change is intended.

Notes of Advisory Committee on Rules—1994 Amendment

Subdivision (c). A new subdivision is added to the rule. The text of new subdivision (c) has been moved from Rule 48 to Rule 1 to allow the addition of new rules at the end of the existing set of appellate rules without burying the title provision among other rules. In a similar fashion the Bankruptcy Rules combine the provisions governing the scope of the rules and the title in the first rule.

Committee Notes on Rules—1998 Amendment

The language and organization of the rule are amended to make the rule more easily understood. In addition to changes made to improve the understanding, the Advisory Committee has changed language to make style and

terminology consistent throughout the appellate rules. These changes are intended to be stylistic only. The Advisory Committee recommends deleting the language in subdivision (a) that describes the different types of proceedings that may be brought in a court of appeals. The Advisory Committee believes that the language is unnecessary and that its omission does not work any substantive change.

Committee Notes on Rules—2002 Amendment

Subdivision (b). Two recent enactments make it likely that, in the future, one or more of the Federal Rules of Appellate Procedure ("FRAP") will extend or limit the jurisdiction of the courts of appeals. In 1990, Congress amended the Rules Enabling Act to give the Supreme Court authority to use the federal rules of practice and procedure to define when a ruling of a district court is final for purposes of 28 U.S.C. §1291. *See* 28 U.S.C. §2072(c). In 1992, Congress amended 28 U.S.C. §1292 to give the Supreme Court authority to use the federal rules of practice and procedure to provide for appeals of interlocutory decisions that are not already authorized by 28 U.S.C. §1292. *See* 28 U.S.C. §1292(e). Both §1291 and §1292 are unquestionably jurisdictional statutes, and thus, as soon as FRAP is amended to define finality for purposes of the former or to authorize interlocutory appeals not provided for by the latter, FRAP will "extend or limit the jurisdiction of the courts of appeals," and subdivision (b) will become obsolete. For that reason, subdivision (b) has been abrogated.

Committee Notes on Rules—2010 Amendment

Subdivision (b). New subdivision (b) defines the term "state" to include the District of Columbia and any commonwealth or territory of the United States. Thus, as used in these Rules, "state" includes the District of Columbia, Guam, American Samoa, the U.S. Virgin Islands, the Commonwealth of Puerto Rico, and the Commonwealth of the Northern Mariana Islands.

Changes Made After Publication and Comment. *No changes were made after publication and comment.*

Rule 2. Suspension of Rules

On its own or a party's motion, a court of appeals may—to expedite its decision or for other good cause—suspend any provision of these rules in a particular case and order proceedings as it directs, except as otherwise provided in Rule 26(b).
(As amended Apr. 24, 1998, eff. Dec. 1, 1998.)

Notes of Advisory Committee on Rules—1967

The primary purpose of this rule is to make clear the power of the courts of appeals to expedite the determination of cases of pressing concern to the public or to the litigants by prescribing a time schedule other than that provided by the rules. The rule also contains a general authorization to the courts to relieve litigants of the consequences of default where manifest injustice would otherwise result. Rule 26(b) prohibits a court of appeals from extending the time for taking appeal or seeking review.

Committee Notes on Rules—1998 Amendment

The language of the rule is amended to make the rule more easily understood. In addition to changes made to improve the understanding, the Advisory Committee has changed language to make style and terminology consistent throughout the appellate rules. These changes are intended to be stylistic only.

TITLE II. APPEAL FROM A JUDGMENT OR ORDER OF A DISTRICT COURT

Rule 3. Appeal as of Right – How Taken
(a) Filing the Notice of Appeal.
(1) An appeal permitted by law as of right from a district court to a court of appeals may be taken only by filing a notice of appeal with the district clerk within the time allowed by Rule 4. At the time of filing, the appellant must furnish the clerk with enough copies of the notice to enable the clerk to comply with Rule 3(d).

Rule 3. Appeal as of Right – How Taken

(2) An appellant's failure to take any step other than the timely filing of a notice of appeal does not affect the validity of the appeal, but is ground only for the court of appeals to act as it considers appropriate, including dismissing the appeal.

(3) An appeal from a judgment by a magistrate judge in a civil case is taken in the same way as an appeal from any other district court judgment.

(4) An appeal by permission under 28 U.S.C. §1292(b) or an appeal in a bankruptcy case may be taken only in the manner prescribed by Rules 5 and 6, respectively.

(b) Joint or Consolidated Appeals.

(1) When two or more parties are entitled to appeal from a district-court judgment or order, and their interests make joinder practicable, they may file a joint notice of appeal. They may then proceed on appeal as a single appellant.

(2) When the parties have filed separate timely notices of appeal, the appeals may be joined or consolidated by the court of appeals.

(c) Contents of the Notice of Appeal.

(1) The notice of appeal must:

(A) specify the party or parties taking the appeal by naming each one in the caption or body of the notice, but an attorney representing more than one party may describe those parties with such terms as "all plaintiffs," "the defendants," "the plaintiffs A, B, et al.," or "all defendants except X";

(B) designate the judgment, order, or part thereof being appealed; and

(C) name the court to which the appeal is taken.

(2) A pro se notice of appeal is considered filed on behalf of the signer and the signer's spouse and minor children (if they are parties), unless the notice clearly indicates otherwise.

(3) In a class action, whether or not the class has been certified, the notice of appeal is sufficient if it names one person qualified to bring the appeal as representative of the class.

(4) An appeal must not be dismissed for informality of form or title of the notice of appeal, or for failure to name a party whose intent to appeal is otherwise clear from the notice.

(5) Form 1 in the Appendix of Forms is a suggested form of a notice of appeal.

(d) Serving the Notice of Appeal.

(1) The district clerk must serve notice of the filing of a notice of appeal by mailing a copy to each party's counsel of record—excluding the appellant's—or, if a party is proceeding pro se, to the party's last known address. When a defendant in a criminal case appeals, the clerk must also serve a copy of the notice of appeal on the defendant, either by personal service or by mail addressed to the defendant. The clerk must promptly send a copy of the notice of appeal and of the docket entries—and any later docket entries—to the clerk of the court of appeals named in the notice. The district clerk must note, on each copy, the date when the notice of appeal was filed.

(2) If an inmate confined in an institution files a notice of appeal in the manner provided by Rule 4(c), the district clerk must also note the date when the clerk docketed the notice.

(3) The district clerk's failure to serve notice does not affect the validity of the appeal. The clerk must note on the docket the names of the parties to whom the clerk mails copies, with the date of mailing. Service is sufficient despite the death of a party or the party's counsel.

(e) Payment of Fees. Upon filing a notice of appeal, the appellant must pay the district clerk all required fees. The district clerk receives the appellate docket fee on behalf of the court of appeals.

(As amended Apr. 30, 1979, eff. Aug. 1, 1979; Mar. 10, 1986, eff. July 1, 1986; Apr. 25, 1989, eff. Dec. 1, 1989; Apr. 22, 1993, eff. Dec. 1, 1993; Apr. 29, 1994, eff. Dec. 1, 1994; Apr. 24, 1998, eff. Dec. 1, 1998.)

Notes of Advisory Committee on Rules—1967

General Note. Rule 3 and Rule 4 combine to require that a notice of appeal be filed with the clerk of the district court within the time prescribed for taking an appeal. Because the timely filing of a notice of appeal is "mandatory and jurisdictional," *United States v. Robinson*, 361 U.S. 220, 224, 80 S.Ct. 282, 4 L.Ed.2d 259 (1960), compliance with the provisions of those rules is of the utmost importance. But the proposed rules merely restate, in modified form, provisions now found in the civil and criminal rules (FRCP 5 (e), 73; FRCrP 37), and decisions under the present rules which

Rule 3. Appeal as of Right – How Taken

dispense with literal compliance in cases in which it cannot fairly be exacted should control interpretation of these rules. Illustrative decisions are: *Fallen v. United States*, 378 U.S. 139, 84 S.Ct. 1689, 12 L.Ed.2d 760 (1964) (notice of appeal by a prisoner, in the form of a letter delivered, well within the time fixed for appeal, to prison authorities for mailing to the clerk of the district court held timely filed notwithstanding that it was received by the clerk after expiration of the time for appeal; the appellant "did all he could" to effect timely filing); *Richey v. Wilkins*, 335 F.2d 1 (2d Cir. 1964) (notice filed in the court of appeals by a prisoner without assistance of counsel held sufficient); *Halfen v. United States*, 324 F.2d 52 (10th Cir. 1963) (notice mailed to district judge in time to have been received by him in normal course held sufficient); *Riffle v. United States*, 299 F.2d 802 (5th Cir. 1962) (letter of prisoner to judge of court of appeals held sufficient). Earlier cases evidencing "a liberal view of papers filed by indigent and incarcerated defendants" are listed in *Coppedge v. United States*, 369 U.S. 438, 442, n. 5, 82 S.Ct. 917, 8 L.Ed.2d 21 (1962).

Subdivision (a). The substance of this subdivision is derived from FRCP 73 (a) and FRCrP 37 (a)(1). The proposed rule follows those rules in requiring nothing other than the filing of a notice of appeal in the district court for the perfection of the appeal. The petition for allowance (except for appeals governed by Rules 5 and 6), citations, assignments of error, summons and severance—all specifically abolished by earlier modern rules—are assumed to be sufficiently obsolete as no longer to require pointed abolition.

Subdivision (b). The first sentence is derived from FRCP 74. The second sentence is added to encourage consolidation of appeals whenever feasible.

Subdivision (c). This subdivision is identical with corresponding provisions in FRCP 73 (b) and FRCrP 37 (a)(1).

Subdivision (d). This subdivision is derived from FRCP 73 (b) and FRCrP 37 (a)(1). The duty of the clerk to forward a copy of the notice of appeal and of the docket entries to the court of appeals in a criminal case extended to habeas corpus and 28 U.S.C. §2255 proceedings.

Notes of Advisory Committee on Rules—1979 Amendment

Subdivision (c). The proposed amendment would add the last sentence. Because of the fact that the timely filing of the notice of appeal has been characterized as jurisdictional (See, e.g., *Brainerd v. Beal* (C.A. 7th, 1974) 498 F.2d 901, in which the filing of a notice of appeal one day late was fatal), it is important that the right to appeal not be lost by mistakes of mere form. In a number of decided cases it has been held that so long as the function of notice is met by the filing of a paper indicating an intention to appeal, the substance of the rule has been complied with. See, e.g., *Cobb v. Lewis* (C.A. 5th, 1974) 488 F.2d 41; *Holley v. Capps* (C.A. 5th, 1972) 468 F.2d 1366. The proposed amendment would give recognition to this practice.

When a notice of appeal is filed, the clerk should ascertain whether any judgment designated therein has been entered in compliance with Rules 58 and 79(a) of the F.R.C.P. See Note to Rule 4(a)(6), infra.

Subdivision (d). The proposed amendment would extend to civil cases the present provision applicable to criminal cases, habeas corpus cases, and proceedings under 28 U.S.C. §2255, requiring the clerk of the district court to transmit to the clerk of the court of appeals a copy of the notice of appeal and of the docket entries, which should include reference to compliance with the requirements for payment of fees. See Note to (e), infra.

This requirement is the initial step in proposed changes in the rules to place in the court of appeals an increased practical control over the early steps in the appeal.

Subdivision (e). Proposed new Rule 3(e) represents the second step in shifting to the court of appeals the control of the early stages of an appeal. See Note to Rule 3(d) above. Under the present rules the payment of the fee prescribed by 28 U.S.C. 1917 is not covered. Under the statute, however, this fee is paid to the clerk of the district court at the time the notice of appeal is filed. Under present Rule 12, the "docket fee" fixed by the Judicial Conference of the United States under 28 U.S.C. §1913 must be paid to the clerk of the court of appeals within the time fixed for transmission of the record, ". . . and the clerk shall thereupon enter the appeal upon the docket."

Under the proposed new Rule 3(e) both fees would be paid to the clerk of the district court at the time the notice of appeal is filed, the clerk of the district court receiving the docket fee on behalf of the court of appeals.

In view of the provision in Rule 3(a) that "[f]ailure of an appellant to take any step other than the timely filing of a notice of appeal does not affect the validity of the appeal, but is ground only for such action as the court of appeals deems appropriate, which may include dismissal of the appeal," the case law indicates that the failure to prepay the statutory filing fee does not constitute a jurisdictional defect. See *Parissi v. Telechron*, 349 U.S. 46 (1955); *Gould v. Members of N. J. Division of Water Policy & Supply*, 555 F.2d 340 (3d Cir. 1977). Similarly, under present Rule 12, failure to pay the docket fee within the time prescribed may be excused by the court of appeals. See, e. g., *Walker v. Mathews*, 546 F.2d 814 (9th Cir. 1976). Proposed new Rule 3(e) adopts the view of these cases, requiring that both fees be paid at the time the notice of appeal is filed, but subject to the provisions of Rule 26(b) preserving the authority of the court of appeals to permit late payment.

Rule 3. Appeal as of Right – How Taken

Notes of Advisory Committee on Rules—1986 Amendment

The amendments to Rule 3(d) are technical. No substantive change is intended.

Notes of Advisory Committee on Rules—1989 Amendment

The amendment is technical. No substantive change is intended.

Notes of Advisory Committee on Rules—1993 Amendment

Note to subdivision (c). The amendment is intended to reduce the amount of satellite litigation spawned by the Supreme Court's decision in *Torres v. Oakland Scavenger Co.*, 487 U.S. 312 (1988). In *Torres* the Supreme Court held that the language in Rule 3(c) requiring a notice of appeal to "specify the party or parties taking the appeal" is a jurisdictional requirement and that naming the first named party and adding "et al.," without any further specificity is insufficient to identify the appellants. Since the *Torres* decision, there has been a great deal of litigation regarding whether a notice of appeal that contains some indication of the appellants' identities but does not name the appellants is sufficiently specific.

The amendment states a general rule that specifying the parties should be done by naming them. Naming an appellant in an otherwise timely and proper notice of appeal ensures that the appellant has perfected an appeal. However, in order to prevent the loss of a right to appeal through inadvertent omission of a party's name or continued use of such terms as "et al.," which are sufficient in all district court filings after the complaint, the amendment allows an attorney representing more than one party the flexibility to indicate which parties are appealing without naming them individually. The test established by the rule for determining whether such designations are sufficient is whether it is objectively clear that a party intended to appeal. A notice of appeal filed by a party proceeding *pro se* is filed on behalf of the party signing the notice and the signer's spouse and minor children, if they are parties, unless the notice clearly indicates a contrary intent.

In class actions, naming each member of a class as an appellant may be extraordinarily burdensome or even impossible. In class actions if class certification has been denied, named plaintiffs may appeal the order denying the class certification on their own behalf and on behalf of putative class members, *United States Parole Comm'n v. Geraghty*, 445 U.S. 388 (1980); or if the named plaintiffs choose not to appeal the order denying the class certification, putative class members may appeal, *United Airlines, Inc. v. McDonald*, 432 U.S. 385 (1977). If no class has been certified, naming each of the putative class members as an appellant would often be impossible. Therefore the amendment provides that in class actions, whether or not the class has been certified, it is sufficient for the notice to name one person qualified to bring the appeal as a representative of the class.

Finally, the rule makes it clear that dismissal of an appeal should not occur when it is otherwise clear from the notice that the party intended to appeal. If a court determines it is objectively clear that a party intended to appeal, there are neither administrative concerns nor fairness concerns that should prevent the appeal from going forward.

Note to subdivision (d). The amendment requires the district court clerk to send to the clerk of the court of appeals a copy of every docket entry in a case after the filing of a notice of appeal. This amendment accompanies the amendment to Rule 4(a)(4), which provides that when one of the posttrial motions enumerated in Rule 4(a)(4) is filed, a notice of appeal filed before the disposition of the motion becomes effective upon disposition of the motion. The court of appeals needs to be advised that the filing of a posttrial motion has suspended a notice of appeal. The court of appeals also needs to know when the district court has ruled on the motion. Sending copies of all docket entries after the filing of a notice of appeal should provide the courts of appeals with the necessary information.

Notes of Advisory Committee on Rules—1994 Amendment

Subdivision (a). The amendment requires a party filing a notice of appeal to provide the court with sufficient copies of the notice for service on all other parties.

Committee Notes on Rules—1998 Amendment

The language and organization of the rule are amended to make the rule more easily understood. In addition to changes made to improve the understanding, the Advisory Committee has changed language to make style and terminology consistent throughout the appellate rules. These changes are generally intended to be stylistic only; in this rule, however, substantive changes are made in subdivisions (a), (b), and (d).

Subdivision (a). The provision in paragraph (a)(3) is transferred from former Rule 3.1(b). The Federal Courts Improvement Act of 1996, Pub. L. No. 104–317, repealed paragraphs (4) and (5) of 28 U.S.C. §636(c). That statutory

Rule 4. Appeal as of Right – When Taken

change made the continued separate existence of Rule 3.1 unnecessary. New paragraph (a)(3) of this rule simply makes it clear that an appeal from a judgment by a magistrate judge is taken in identical fashion to any other appeal from a district-court judgment.

Subdivision (b). A joint appeal is authorized only when two or more persons may appeal from a single judgment or order. A joint appeal is treated as a single appeal and the joint appellants file a single brief. Under existing Rule 3(b) parties decide whether to join their appeals. They may do so by filing a joint notice of appeal or by joining their appeals after filing separate notices of appeal.

In consolidated appeals the separate appeals do not merge into one. The parties do not proceed as a single appellant. Under existing Rule 3(b) it is unclear whether appeals may be consolidated without court order if the parties stipulate to consolidation. The language resolves that ambiguity by requiring court action.

The language also requires court action to join appeals after separate notices of appeal have been filed.

Subdivision (d). Paragraph (d)(2) has been amended to require that when an inmate files a notice of appeal by depositing the notice in the institution's internal mail system, the clerk must note the docketing date—rather than the receipt date—on the notice of appeal before serving copies of it. This change conforms to a change in Rule 4(c). Rule 4(c) is amended to provide that when an inmate files the first notice of appeal in a civil case by depositing the notice in an institution's internal mail system, the time for filing a cross-appeal runs from the date the district court dockets the inmate's notice of appeal. Existing Rule 4(c) says that in such a case the time for filing a cross-appeal runs from the date the district court receives the inmate's notice of appeal. A court may "receive" a paper when its mail is delivered to it even if the mail is not processed for a day or two, making the date of receipt uncertain. "Docketing" is an easily identified event. The change is made to eliminate the uncertainty.

Rule 4. Appeal as of Right – When Taken

(a) Appeal in a Civil Case.
(1) *Time for Filing a Notice of Appeal.*
(A) In a civil case, except as provided in Rules 4(a)(1)(B), 4(a)(4), and 4(c), the notice of appeal required by Rule 3 must be filed with the district clerk within 30 days after entry of the judgment or order appealed from.
(B) The notice of appeal may be filed by any party within 60 days after entry of the judgment or order appealed from if one of the parties is:
(i) the United States;
(ii) a United States agency;
(iii) a United States officer or employee sued in an official capacity; or
(iv) a current or former United States officer or employee sued in an individual capacity for an act or omission occurring in connection with duties performed on the United States' behalf — including all instances in which the United States represents that person when the judgment or order is entered or files the appeal for that person.
(C) An appeal from an order granting or denying an application for a writ of error *coram nobis* is an appeal in a civil case for purposes of Rule 4(a).
(2) *Filing Before Entry of Judgment.* A notice of appeal filed after the court announces a decision or order—but before the entry of the judgment or order—is treated as filed on the date of and after the entry.
(3) *Multiple Appeals.* If one party timely files a notice of appeal, any other party may file a notice of appeal within 14 days after the date when the first notice was filed, or within the time otherwise prescribed by this Rule 4(a), whichever period ends later.
(4) *Effect of a Motion on a Notice of Appeal.*

[The following text of subdivision (A) was effective until December 1, 2016.]

(A) If a party timely files in the district court any of the following motions under the Federal Rules of Civil Procedure, the time to file an appeal runs for all parties from the entry of the order disposing of the last such remaining motion:

Rule 4. Appeal as of Right – When Taken

[The following text of subdivision (A) became effective December 1, 2016.]

(A) If a party files in the district court any of the following motions under the Federal Rules of Civil Procedure—and does so within the time allowed by those rules—the time to file an appeal runs for all parties from the entry of the order disposing of the last such remaining motion:

(i) for judgment under Rule 50(b);
(ii) to amend or make additional factual findings under Rule 52(b), whether or not granting the motion would alter the judgment;
(iii) for attorney's fees under Rule 54 if the district court extends the time to appeal under Rule 58;
(iv) to alter or amend the judgment under Rule 59;
(v) for a new trial under Rule 59; or
(vi) for relief under Rule 60 if the motion is filed no later than 28 days after the judgment is entered.

(B)(i) If a party files a notice of appeal after the court announces or enters a judgment—but before it disposes of any motion listed in Rule 4(a)(4)(A)—the notice becomes effective to appeal a judgment or order, in whole or in part, when the order disposing of the last such remaining motion is entered.

(ii) A party intending to challenge an order disposing of any motion listed in Rule 4(a)(4)(A), or a judgment's alteration or amendment upon such a motion, must file a notice of appeal, or an amended notice of appeal—in compliance with Rule 3(c)—within the time prescribed by this Rule measured from the entry of the order disposing of the last such remaining motion.

(5) *Motion for Extension of Time.*

(A) The district court may extend the time to file a notice of appeal if:

(i) a party so moves no later than 30 days after the time prescribed by this Rule 4(a) expires; and
(ii) regardless of whether its motion is filed before or during the 30 days after the time prescribed by this Rule 4(a) expires, that party shows excusable neglect or good cause.

(B) A motion filed before the expiration of the time prescribed in Rule 4(a)(1) or (3) may be ex parte unless the court requires otherwise. If the motion is filed after the expiration of the prescribed time, notice must be given to the other parties in accordance with local rules.

(C) No extension under this Rule 4(a)(5) may exceed 30 days after the prescribed time or 14 days after the date when the order granting the motion is entered, whichever is later.

(6) *Reopening the Time to File an Appeal.* The district court may reopen the time to file an appeal for a period of 14 days after the date when its order to reopen is entered, but only if all the following conditions are satisfied:

(A) the court finds that the moving party did not receive notice under Federal Rule of Civil Procedure 77 (d) of the entry of the judgment or order sought to be appealed within 21 days after entry;
(B) the motion is filed within 180 days after the judgment or order is entered or within 14 days after the moving party receives notice under Federal Rule of Civil Procedure 77 (d) of the entry, whichever is earlier; and
(C) the court finds that no party would be prejudiced.

(7) *Entry Defined.*

(A) A judgment or order is entered for purposes of this Rule 4(a):

(i) if Federal Rule of Civil Procedure 58 (a) does not require a separate document, when the judgment or order is entered in the civil docket under Federal Rule of Civil Procedure 79 (a); or
(ii) if Federal Rule of Civil Procedure 58 (a) requires a separate document, when the judgment or order is entered in the civil docket under Federal Rule of Civil Procedure 79(a) and when the earlier of these events occurs:

• the judgment or order is set forth on a separate document, or
• 150 days have run from entry of the judgment or order in the civil docket under Federal Rule of Civil Procedure 79 (a).

(B) A failure to set forth a judgment or order on a separate document when required by Federal Rule of Civil Procedure 58 (a) does not affect the validity of an appeal from that judgment or order.

Rule 4. Appeal as of Right – When Taken

(b) Appeal in a Criminal Case.
   (1) *Time for Filing a Notice of Appeal.*
      (A) In a criminal case, a defendant's notice of appeal must be filed in the district court within 14 days after the later of:
         (i) the entry of either the judgment or the order being appealed; or
         (ii) the filing of the government's notice of appeal.
      (B) When the government is entitled to appeal, its notice of appeal must be filed in the district court within 30 days after the later of:
         (i) the entry of the judgment or order being appealed; or
         (ii) the filing of a notice of appeal by any defendant.
   (2) *Filing Before Entry of Judgment.* A notice of appeal filed after the court announces a decision, sentence, or order—but before the entry of the judgment or order—is treated as filed on the date of and after the entry.
   (3) *Effect of a Motion on a Notice of Appeal.*
      (A) If a defendant timely makes any of the following motions under the Federal Rules of Criminal Procedure, the notice of appeal from a judgment of conviction must be filed within 14 days after the entry of the order disposing of the last such remaining motion, or within 14 days after the entry of the judgment of conviction, whichever period ends later. This provision applies to a timely motion:
         (i) for judgment of acquittal under Rule 29;
         (ii) for a new trial under Rule 33, but if based on newly discovered evidence, only if the motion is made no later than 14 days after the entry of the judgment; or
         (iii) for arrest of judgment under Rule 34.
      (B) A notice of appeal filed after the court announces a decision, sentence, or order—but before it disposes of any of the motions referred to in Rule 4(b)(3)(A)—becomes effective upon the later of the following:
         (i) the entry of the order disposing of the last such remaining motion; or
         (ii) the entry of the judgment of conviction.
      (C) A valid notice of appeal is effective—without amendment—to appeal from an order disposing of any of the motions referred to in Rule 4(b)(3)(A).
   (4) *Motion for Extension of Time.* Upon a finding of excusable neglect or good cause, the district court may—before or after the time has expired, with or without motion and notice—extend the time to file a notice of appeal for a period not to exceed 30 days from the expiration of the time otherwise prescribed by this Rule 4(b).
   (5) *Jurisdiction.* The filing of a notice of appeal under this Rule 4(b) does not divest a district court of jurisdiction to correct a sentence under Federal Rule of Criminal Procedure 35(a), nor does the filing of a motion under 35(a) affect the validity of a notice of appeal filed before entry of the order disposing of the motion. The filing of a motion under Federal Rule of Criminal Procedure 35(a) does not suspend the time for filing a notice of appeal from a judgment of conviction.
   (6) *Entry Defined.* A judgment or order is entered for purposes of this Rule 4(b) when it is entered on the criminal docket.

(c) Appeal by an Inmate Confined in an Institution.

[The following text of subdivision (1) was effective until December 1, 2016.]

(1) If an inmate confined in an institution files a notice of appeal in either a civil or a criminal case, the notice is timely if it is deposited in the institution's internal mail system on or before the last day for filing. If an institution has a system designed for legal mail, the inmate must use that system to receive the benefit of this rule. Timely filing may be shown by a declaration in compliance with 28 U.S.C. §1746 or by a notarized statement, either of which must set forth the date of deposit and state that first-class postage has been prepaid.

Rule 4. Appeal as of Right – When Taken

[The following text of subdivision (1) became effective December 1, 2016.]

(1) If an institution has a system designed for legal mail, an inmate confined there must use that system to receive the benefit of this Rule 4(c)(1). If an inmate files a notice of appeal in either a civil or a criminal case, the notice is timely if it is deposited in the institution's internal mail system on or before the last day for filing and:
- (A) it is accompanied by:
    - (i) a declaration in compliance with 28 U.S.C. § 1746—or a notarized statement—setting out the date of deposit and stating that first-class postage is being prepaid; or
    - (ii) evidence (such as a postmark or date stamp) showing that the notice was so deposited and that postage was prepaid; or
- (B) the court of appeals exercises its discretion to permit the later filing of a declaration or notarized statement that satisfies Rule 4(c)(1)(A)(i).

(2) If an inmate files the first notice of appeal in a civil case under this Rule 4(c), the 14-day period provided in Rule 4(a)(3) for another party to file a notice of appeal runs from the date when the district court dockets the first notice.

(3) When a defendant in a criminal case files a notice of appeal under this Rule 4(c), the 30-day period for the government to file its notice of appeal runs from the entry of the judgment or order appealed from or from the district court's docketing of the defendant's notice of appeal, whichever is later.

(d) Mistaken Filing in the Court of Appeals. If a notice of appeal in either a civil or a criminal case is mistakenly filed in the court of appeals, the clerk of that court must note on the notice the date when it was received and send it to the district clerk. The notice is then considered filed in the district court on the date so noted.

(As amended Apr. 30, 1979, eff. Aug. 1, 1979; Pub. L. 100–690, title VII, §7111, Nov. 18, 1988, 102 Stat. 4419; Apr. 30, 1991, eff. Dec. 1, 1991; Apr. 22, 1993, eff. Dec. 1, 1993; Apr. 27, 1995, eff. Dec. 1, 1995; Apr. 24, 1998, eff. Dec. 1, 1998; Apr. 29, 2002, eff. Dec. 1, 2002; Apr. 25, 2005, eff. Dec. 1, 2005; Mar. 26, 2009, eff. Dec. 1, 2009; Apr. 28, 2010, eff. Dec. 1, 2010; Apr. 26, 2011, eff. Dec. 1, 2011; Apr. 28, 2016, eff. Dec. 1, 2016.)

Notes of Advisory Committee on Rules—1967

Subdivision (a). This subdivision is derived from FRCP 73 (a) without any change of substance. The requirement that a request for an extension of time for filing the notice of appeal made after expiration of the time be made by motion and on notice codifies the result reached under the present provisions of FRCP 73 (a) and 6(b). *North Umberland Mining Co. v. Standard Accident Ins. Co.*, 193 F.2d 951 (9th Cir., 1952); *Cohen v. Plateau Natural Gas Co.*, 303 F.2d 273 (10th Cir., 1962); *Plant Economy, Inc. v. Mirror Insulation Co.*, 308 F.2d 275 (3d Cir., 1962).

Since this subdivision governs appeals in all civil cases, it supersedes the provisions of section 25 of the Bankruptcy Act (11 U.S.C. §48). Except in cases to which the United States or an officer or agency thereof is a party, the change is a minor one, since a successful litigant in a bankruptcy proceeding may, under section 25, oblige an aggrieved party to appeal within 30 days after entry of judgment—the time fixed by this subdivision in cases involving private parties only—by serving him with notice of entry on the day thereof, and by the terms of section 25 an aggrieved party must in any event appeal within 40 days after entry of judgment. No reason appears why the time for appeal in bankruptcy should not be the same as that in civil cases generally. Furthermore, section 25 is a potential trap for the uninitiated. The time for appeal which it provides is not applicable to all appeals which may fairly be termed appeals in bankruptcy. Section 25 governs only those cases referred to in section 24 as "proceedings in bankruptcy" and "controversies arising in proceedings in bankruptcy." *Lowenstein v. Reikes*, 54 F.2d 481 (2d Cir., 1931), *cert. den.*, 285 U.S. 539, 52 S.Ct. 311, 76 L.Ed. 932 (1932). The distinction between such cases and other cases which arise out of bankruptcy is often difficult to determine. See 2 Moore's Collier on Bankruptcy 24.12 through 24.36 (1962). As a result it is not always clear whether an appeal is governed by section 25 or by FRCP 73 (a), which is applicable to such appeals in bankruptcy as are not governed by section 25.

In view of the unification of the civil and admiralty procedure accomplished by the amendments of the Federal Rules of Civil Procedure effective July 1, 1966, this subdivision governs appeals in those civil actions which involve admiralty or maritime claims and which prior to that date were known as suits in admiralty.

The only other change possibly effected by this subdivision is in the time for appeal from a decision of a district court

Rule 4. Appeal as of Right – When Taken

on a petition for impeachment of an award of a board of arbitration under the Act of May 20, 1926, c. 347, §9 (44 Stat. 585), 45 U.S.C. §159. The act provides that a notice of appeal from such a decision shall be filed within 10 days of the decision. This singular provision was apparently repealed by the enactment in 1948 of 28 U.S.C. §2107, which fixed 30 days from the date of entry of judgment as the time for appeal in all actions of a civil nature except actions in admiralty or bankruptcy matters or those in which the United States is a party. But it was not expressly repealed, and its status is in doubt. See 7 Moore's Federal Practice 73.09[2] (1966). The doubt should be resolved, and no reason appears why appeals in such cases should not be taken within the time provided for civil cases generally.

Subdivision (b). This subdivision is derived from FRCrP 37 (a)(2) without change of substance.

Notes of Advisory Committee on Rules—1979 Amendment

Subdivision (a)(1). The words "(including a civil action which involves an admiralty or maritime claim and a proceeding in bankruptcy or a controversy arising therein)," which appear in the present rule are struck out as unnecessary and perhaps misleading in suggesting that there may be other categories that are not either civil or criminal within the meaning of Rule 4(a) and (b).

The phrases "within 30 days of such entry" and "within 60 days of such entry" have been changed to read "after" instead of "or." The change is for clarity only, since the word "of" in the present rule appears to be used to mean "after." Since the proposed amended rule deals directly with the premature filing of a notice of appeal, it was thought useful to emphasize the fact that except as provided, the period during which a notice of appeal may be filed is the 30 days, or 60 days as the case may be, following the entry of the judgment or order appealed from. See Notes to Rule 4(a)(2) and (4), below.

Subdivision (a)(2). The proposed amendment to Rule 4(a)(2) would extend to civil cases the provisions of Rule 4(b), dealing with criminal cases, designed to avoid the loss of the right to appeal by filing the notice of appeal prematurely. Despite the absence of such a provision in Rule 4(a) the courts of appeals quite generally have held premature appeals effective. See, e. g., *Matter of Grand Jury Empanelled Jan. 21, 1975*, 541 F.2d 373 (3d Cir. 1976); *Hodge v. Hodge*, 507 F.2d 87 (3d Cir. 1976); *Song Jook Suh v. Rosenberg*, 437 F.2d 1098 (9th Cir. 1971); *Ruby v. Secretary of the Navy*, 365 F.2d 385 (9th Cir. 1966); *Firchau v. Diamond Nat'l Corp.*, 345 F.2d 469 (9th Cir. 1965).

The proposed amended rule would recognize this practice but make an exception in cases in which a post trial motion has destroyed the finality of the judgment. See Note to Rule 4(a)(4) below.

Subdivision (a)(4). The proposed amendment would make it clear that after the filing of the specified post trial motions, a notice of appeal should await disposition of the motion. Since the proposed amendments to Rules 3, 10, and 12 contemplate that immediately upon the filing of the notice of appeal the fees will be paid and the case docketed in the court of appeals, and the steps toward its disposition set in motion, it would be undesirable to proceed with the appeal while the district court has before it a motion the granting of which would vacate or alter the judgment appealed from. See, e. g., *Kieth v. Newcourt*, 530 F.2d 826 (8th Cir. 1976). Under the present rule, since docketing may not take place until the record is transmitted, premature filing is much less likely to involve waste effort. See, e. g., *Stokes v. Peyton's Inc.*, 508 F.2d 1287 (5th Cir. 1975). Further, since a notice of appeal filed before the disposition of a post trial motion, even if it were treated as valid for purposes of jurisdiction, would not embrace objections to the denial of the motion, it is obviously preferable to postpone the notice of appeal until after the motion is disposed of.

The present rule, since it provides for the "termination" of the "running" of the appeal time, is ambiguous in its application to a notice of appeal filed prior to a post trial motion filed within the 10 day limit. The amendment would make it clear that in such circumstances the appellant should not proceed with the appeal during pendency of the motion but should file a new notice of appeal after the motion is disposed of.

Subdivision (a)(5). Under the present rule it is provided that upon a showing of excusable neglect the district court at any time may extend the time for the filing of a notice of appeal for a period not to exceed 30 days from the expiration of the time otherwise prescribed by the rule, but that if the application is made after the original time has run, the order may be made only on motion with such notice as the court deems appropriate.

A literal reading of this provision would require that the extension be ordered and the notice of appeal filed within the 30 day period, but despite the surface clarity of the rule, it has produced considerable confusion. See the discussion by Judge Friendly in *In re Orbitek*, 520 F.2d 358 (2d Cir. 1975). The proposed amendment would make it clear that a motion to extend the time must be filed no later than 30 days after the expiration of the original appeal time, and that if the motion is timely filed the district court may act upon the motion at a later date, and may extend the time not in excess of 10 days measured from the date on which the order granting the motion is entered.

Under the present rule there is a possible implication that prior to the time the initial appeal time has run, the district court may extend the time on the basis of an informal application. The amendment would require that the application must be made by motion, though the motion may be made ex parte. After the expiration of the initial time a motion for the extension of the time must be made in compliance with the F.R.C.P. and local rules of the district court. See Note to

Rule 4. Appeal as of Right – When Taken

proposed amended Rule 1, supra. And see Rules 6(d), 7(b) of the F.R.C.P.

The proposed amended rule expands to some extent the standard for the grant of an extension of time. The present rule requires a "showing of excusable neglect." While this was an appropriate standard in cases in which the motion is made after the time for filing the notice of appeal has run, and remains so, it has never fit exactly the situation in which the appellant seeks an extension before the expiration of the initial time. In such a case "good cause," which is the standard that is applied in the granting of other extensions of time under Rule 26(b) seems to be more appropriate.

Subdivision (a)(6). The proposed amendment would call attention to the requirement of Rule 58 of the F.R.C.P. that the judgment constitute a separate document. See *United States v. Indrelunas*, 411 U.S. 216 (1973). When a notice of appeal is filed, the clerk should ascertain whether any judgment designated therein has been entered in compliance with Rules 58 and 79(a) and if not, so advise all parties and the district judge. While the requirement of Rule 48 is not jurisdictional (see *Bankers Trust Co. v. Mallis*, 431 U.S. 928 (1977)), compliance is important since the time for the filing of a notice of appeal by other parties is measured by the time at which the judgment is properly entered.

Notes of Advisory Committee on Rules—1991 Amendment

The amendment provides a limited opportunity for relief in circumstances where the notice of entry of a judgment or order, required to be mailed by the clerk of the district court pursuant to Rule 77(d) of the Federal Rules of Civil Procedure, is either not received by a party or is received so late as to impair the opportunity to file a timely notice of appeal. The amendment adds a new subdivision (6) allowing a district court to reopen for a brief period the time for appeal upon a finding that notice of entry of a judgment or order was not received from the clerk or a party within 21 days of its entry and that no party would be prejudiced. By "prejudice" the Committee means some adverse consequence other than the cost of having to oppose the appeal and encounter the risk of reversal, consequences that are present in every appeal. Prejudice might arise, for example, if the appellee had taken some action in reliance on the expiration of the normal time period for filing a notice of appeal.

Reopening may be ordered only upon a motion filed within 180 days of the entry of a judgment or order or within 7 days of receipt of notice of such entry, whichever is earlier. This provision establishes an outer time limit of 180 days for a party who fails to receive timely notice of entry of a judgment to seek additional time to appeal and enables any winning party to shorten the 180-day period by sending (and establishing proof of receipt of) its own notice of entry of a judgment, as authorized by Fed. R. Civ. P. 77 (d). Winning parties are encouraged to send their own notice in order to lessen the chance that a judge will accept a claim of non-receipt in the face of evidence that notices were sent by both the clerk and the winning party. Receipt of a winning party's notice will shorten only the time for reopening the time for appeal under this subdivision, leaving the normal time periods for appeal unaffected.

If the motion is granted, the district court may reopen the time for filing a notice of appeal only for a period of 14 days from the date of entry of the order reopening the time for appeal.

Notes of Advisory Committee on Rules—1993 Amendment

Note to Paragraph (a)(1). The amendment is intended to alert readers to the fact that paragraph (a)(4) extends the time for filing an appeal when certain posttrial motions are filed. The Committee hopes that awareness of the provisions of paragraph (a)(4) will prevent the filing of a notice of appeal when a posttrial tolling motion is pending.

Note to Paragraph (a)(2). The amendment treats a notice of appeal filed after the announcement of a decision or order, but before its formal entry, as if the notice had been filed after entry. The amendment deletes the language that made paragraph (a)(2) inapplicable to a notice of appeal filed after announcement of the disposition of a posttrial motion enumerated in paragraph (a)(4) but before the entry of the order, *see Acosta v. Louisiana Dep't of Health & Human Resources*, 478 U.S. 251 (1986) (per curiam); *Alerte v. McGinnis*, 898 F.2d 69 (7th Cir. 1990). Because the amendment of paragraph (a)(4) recognizes all notices of appeal filed after announcement or entry of judgment—even those that are filed while the posttrial motions enumerated in paragraph (a)(4) are pending—the amendment of this paragraph is consistent with the amendment of paragraph (a)(4).

Note to Paragraph (a)(3). The amendment is technical in nature; no substantive change is intended.

Note to Paragraph (a)(4). The 1979 amendment of this paragraph created a trap for an unsuspecting litigant who files a notice of appeal before a posttrial motion, or while a posttrial motion is pending. The 1979 amendment requires a party to file a new notice of appeal after the motion's disposition. Unless a new notice is filed, the court of appeals lacks jurisdiction to hear the appeal. *Griggs v. Provident Consumer Discount Co.*, 459 U.S. 56 (1982). Many litigants, especially pro se litigants, fail to file the second notice of appeal, and several courts have expressed dissatisfaction with the rule. *See, e.g., Averhart v. Arrendondo*, 773 F.2d 919 (7th Cir. 1985); *Harcon Barge Co. v. D & G Boat Rentals, Inc.*, 746 F.2d 278 (5th Cir. 1984), *cert. denied*, 479 U.S. 930 (1986).

The amendment provides that a notice of appeal filed before the disposition of a specified posttrial motion will become

Rule 4. Appeal as of Right – When Taken

effective upon disposition of the motion. A notice filed before the filing of one of the specified motions or after the filing of a motion but before disposition of the motion is, in effect, suspended until the motion is disposed of, whereupon, the previously filed notice effectively places jurisdiction in the court of appeals.

Because a notice of appeal will ripen into an effective appeal upon disposition of a posttrial motion, in some instances there will be an appeal from a judgment that has been altered substantially because the motion was granted in whole or in part. Many such appeals will be dismissed for want of prosecution when the appellant fails to meet the briefing schedule. But, the appellee may also move to strike the appeal. When responding to such a motion, the appellant would have an opportunity to state that, even though some relief sought in a posttrial motion was granted, the appellant still plans to pursue the appeal. Because the appellant's response would provide the appellee with sufficient notice of the appellant's intentions, the Committee does not believe that an additional notice of appeal is needed.

The amendment provides that a notice of appeal filed before the disposition of a posttrial tolling motion is sufficient to bring the underlying case, as well as any orders specified in the original notice, to the court of appeals. If the judgment is altered upon disposition of a posttrial motion, however, and if a party wishes to appeal from the disposition of the motion, the party must amend the notice to so indicate. When a party files an amended notice, no additional fees are required because the notice is an amendment of the original and not a new notice of appeal.

Paragraph (a)(4) is also amended to include, among motions that extend the time for filing a notice of appeal, a Rule 60 motion that is served within 10 days after entry of judgment. This eliminates the difficulty of determining whether a posttrial motion made within 10 days after entry of a judgment is a Rule 59(e) motion, which tolls the time for filing an appeal, or a Rule 60 motion, which historically has not tolled the time. The amendment comports with the practice in several circuits of treating all motions to alter or amend judgments that are made within 10 days after entry of judgment as Rule 59(e) motions for purposes of Rule 4(a)(4). *See, e.g., Finch v. City of Vernon*, 845 F.2d 256 (11th Cir. 1988); *Rados v. Celotex Corp.*, 809 F.2d 170 (2d Cir. 1986); *Skagerberg v. Oklahoma*, 797 F.2d 881 (10th Cir. 1986). To conform to a recent Supreme Court decision, however— *Budinich v. Becton Dickinson and Co.*, 486 U.S. 196 (1988) —the amendment excludes motions for attorney's fees from the class of motions that extend the filing time unless a district court, acting under Rule 58, enters an order extending the time for appeal. This amendment is to be read in conjunction with the amendment of Fed. R. Civ. P. 58.

Note to subdivision (b). The amendment grammatically restructures the portion of this subdivision that lists the types of motions that toll the time for filing an appeal. This restructuring is intended to make the rule easier to read. No substantive change is intended other than to add a motion for judgment of acquittal under Criminal Rule 29 to the list of tolling motions. Such a motion is the equivalent of a Fed. R. Civ. P. 50 (b) motion for judgment notwithstanding the verdict, which tolls the running of time for an appeal in a civil case.

The proposed amendment also eliminates an ambiguity from the third sentence of this subdivision. Prior to this amendment, the third sentence provided that if one of the specified motions was filed, the time for filing an appeal would run from the entry of an order denying the motion. That sentence, like the parallel provision in Rule 4(a)(4), was intended to toll the running of time for appeal if one of the posttrial motions is timely filed. In a criminal case, however, the time for filing the motions runs not from entry of judgment (as it does in civil cases), but from the verdict or finding of guilt. Thus, in a criminal case, a posttrial motion may be disposed of more than 10 days before sentence is imposed, i.e. before the entry of judgment. *United States v. Hashagen*, 816 F.2d 899, 902 n.5 (3d Cir. 1987). To make it clear that a notice of appeal need not be filed before entry of judgment, the amendment states that an appeal may be taken within 10 days after the entry of an order disposing of the motion, or within 10 days after the entry of judgment, whichever is later. The amendment also changes the language in the third sentence providing that an appeal may be taken within 10 days after the entry of an order *denying* the motion; the amendment says instead that an appeal may be taken within 10 days after the entry of an order *disposing of the last such motion outstanding*. (Emphasis added) The change recognizes that there may be multiple posttrial motions filed and that, although one or more motions may be granted in whole or in part, a defendant may still wish to pursue an appeal.

The amendment also states that a notice of appeal filed before the disposition of any of the posttrial tolling motions becomes effective upon disposition of the motions. In most circuits this language simply restates the current practice. *See United States v. Cortes*, 895 F.2d 1245 (9th Cir.), cert. denied, 495 U.S. 939 (1990). Two circuits, however, have questioned that practice in light of the language of the rule, *see United States v. Gargano*, 826 F.2d 610 (7th Cir. 1987), and *United States v. Jones*, 669 F.2d 559 (8th Cir. 1982), and the Committee wishes to clarify the rule. The amendment is consistent with the proposed amendment of Rule 4(a)(4).

Subdivision (b) is further amended in light of new Fed. R. Crim. P. 35 (c), which authorizes a sentencing court to correct any arithmetical, technical, or other clear errors in sentencing within 7 days after imposing the sentence. The Committee believes that a sentencing court should be able to act under Criminal Rule 35(c) even if a notice of appeal has already been filed; and that a notice of appeal should not be affected by the filing of a Rule 35(c) motion or by correction of a sentence under Rule 35(c).

Note to subdivision (c). In *Houston v. Lack*, 487 U.S. 266 (1988), the Supreme Court held that a *pro se* prisoner's notice

Rule 4. Appeal as of Right – When Taken

of appeal is "filed" at the moment of delivery to prison authorities for forwarding to the district court. The amendment reflects that decision. The language of the amendment is similar to that in Supreme Court Rule 29.2.

Permitting an inmate to file a notice of appeal by depositing it in an institutional mail system requires adjustment of the rules governing the filing of cross-appeals. In a civil case, the time for filing a cross-appeal ordinarily runs from the date when the first notice of appeal is filed. If an inmate's notice of appeal is filed by depositing it in an institution's mail system, it is possible that the notice of appeal will not arrive in the district court until several days after the "filing" date and perhaps even after the time for filing a cross-appeal has expired. To avoid that problem, subdivision (c) provides that in a civil case when an institutionalized person files a notice of appeal by depositing it in the institution's mail system, the time for filing a cross-appeal runs from the district court's receipt of the notice. The amendment makes a parallel change regarding the time for the government to appeal in a criminal case.

Notes of Advisory Committee on Rules—1995 Amendment

Subdivision (a). Fed. R. Civ. P. 50, 52, and 59 were previously inconsistent with respect to whether certain postjudgment motions had to be filed or merely served no later than 10 days after entry of judgment. As a consequence Rule 4(a)(4) spoke of making or serving such motions rather than filing them. Civil Rules 50, 52, and 59, are being revised to require filing before the end of the 10-day period. As a consequence, this rule is being amended to provide that "filing" must occur within the 10 day period in order to affect the finality of the judgment and extend the period for filing a notice of appeal.

The Civil Rules require the filing of postjudgment motions "no later than 10 days after entry of judgment"—rather than "within" 10 days—to include postjudgment motions that are filed before actual entry of the judgment by the clerk. This rule is amended, therefore, to use the same terminology.

The rule is further amended to clarify the fact that a party who wants to obtain review of an alteration or amendment of a judgment must file a notice of appeal or amend a previously filed notice to indicate intent to appeal from the altered judgment.

Committee Notes on Rules—1998 Amendment

The language and organization of the rule are amended to make the rule more easily understood. In addition to changes made to improve the understanding, the Advisory Committee has changed language to make style and terminology consistent throughout the appellate rules. These changes are intended to be stylistic only; in this rule, however, substantive changes are made in paragraphs (a)(6) and (b)(4), and in subdivision (c).

Subdivision (a), paragraph (1). Although the Advisory Committee does not intend to make any substantive changes in this paragraph, cross-references to Rules 4(a)(1)(B) and 4(c) have been added to subparagraph (a)(1)(A).

Subdivision (a), paragraph (4). Item (vi) in subparagraph (A) of Rule 4(a)(4) provides that filing a motion for relief under Fed. R. Civ. P. 60 will extend the time for filing a notice of appeal if the Rule 60 motion is filed no later than 10 days after judgment is entered. Again, the Advisory Committee does not intend to make any substantive change in this paragraph. But because Fed. R. Civ. P. 6 (a) and Fed. R. App. P. 26 (a) have different methods for computing time, one might be uncertain whether the 10-day period referred to in Rule 4(a)(4) is computed using Civil Rule 6(a) or Appellate Rule 26(a). Because the Rule 60 motion is filed in the district court, and because Fed. R. App. P. 1 (a)(2) says that when the appellate rules provide for filing a motion in the district court, "the procedure must comply with the practice of the district court," the rule provides that the 10-day period is computed using Fed. R. Civ. P. 6 (a).

Subdivision (a), paragraph (6). Paragraph (6) permits a district court to reopen the time for appeal if a party has not received notice of the entry of judgment and no party would be prejudiced by the reopening. Before reopening the time for appeal, the existing rule requires the district court to find that the moving party was entitled to notice of the entry of judgment and did not receive it "from the clerk or any party within 21 days of its entry." The Advisory Committee makes a substantive change. The finding must be that the movant did not receive notice "from the district court or any party within 21 days after entry." This change broadens the type of notice that can preclude reopening the time for appeal. The existing rule provides that only notice from a party or from the clerk bars reopening. The new language precludes reopening if the movant has received notice from "the court."

Subdivision (b). Two substantive changes are made in what will be paragraph (b)(4). The current rule permits an extension of time to file a notice of appeal if there is a "showing of excusable neglect." First, the rule is amended to permit a court to extend the time for "good cause" as well as for excusable neglect. Rule 4(a) permits extensions for both reasons in civil cases and the Advisory Committee believes that "good cause" should be sufficient in criminal cases as well. The amendment does not limit extensions for good cause to instances in which the motion for extension of time is filed before the original time has expired. The rule gives the district court discretion to grant extensions for good cause whenever the court believes it appropriate to do so provided that the extended period does not exceed 30 days after the expiration of the

Rule 4. Appeal as of Right – When Taken

time otherwise prescribed by Rule 4(b). Second, paragraph (b)(4) is amended to require only a "finding" of excusable neglect or good cause and not a "showing" of them. Because the rule authorizes the court to provide an extension without a motion, a "showing" is obviously not required; a "finding" is sufficient.

Subdivision (c). Substantive amendments are made in this subdivision. The current rule provides that if an inmate confined in an institution files a notice of appeal by depositing it in the institution's internal mail system, the notice is timely filed if deposited on or before the last day for filing. Some institutions have special internal mail systems for handling legal mail; such systems often record the date of deposit of mail by an inmate, the date of delivery of mail to an inmate, etc. The Advisory Committee amends the rule to require an inmate to use the system designed for legal mail, if there is one, in order to receive the benefit of this subdivision.

When an inmate uses the filing method authorized by subdivision (c), the current rule provides that the time for other parties to appeal begins to run from the date the district court "receives" the inmate's notice of appeal. The rule is amended so that the time for other parties begins to run when the district court "dockets" the inmate's appeal. A court may "receive" a paper when its mail is delivered to it even if the mail is not processed for a day or two, making the date of receipt uncertain. "Docketing" is an easily identified event. The change eliminates uncertainty. Paragraph (c)(3) is further amended to make it clear that the time for the government to file its appeal runs from the later of the entry of the judgment or order appealed from or the district court's docketing of a defendant's notice filed under this paragraph (c).

Committee Notes on Rules—2002 Amendment

Subdivision (a)(1)(C). The federal courts of appeals have reached conflicting conclusions about whether an appeal from an order granting or denying an application for a writ of error *coram nobis* is governed by the time limitations of Rule 4(a) (which apply in civil cases) or by the time limitations of Rule 4(b) (which apply in criminal cases). *Compare United States v. Craig,* 907 F.2d 653, 655–57, *amended* 919 F.2d 57 (7th Cir. 1990); *United States v. Cooper,* 876 F.2d 1192, 1193–94 (5th Cir. 1989); and *United States v. Keogh,* 391 F.2d 138, 140 (2d Cir. 1968) (applying the time limitations of Rule 4(a)); *with Yasui v. United States,* 772 F.2d 1496, 1498–99 (9th Cir. 1985); and *United States v. Mills,* 430 F.2d 526, 527–28 (8th Cir. 1970) (applying the time limitations of Rule 4(b)). A new part (C) has been added to Rule 4(a)(1) to resolve this conflict by providing that the time limitations of Rule 4(a) will apply.

Subsequent to the enactment of Fed. R. Civ. P. 60 (b) and 28 U.S.C. §2255, the Supreme Court has recognized the continued availability of a writ of error *coram nobis* in at least one narrow circumstance. In 1954, the Court permitted a litigant who had been convicted of a crime, served his full sentence, and been released from prison, but who was continuing to suffer a legal disability on account of the conviction, to seek a writ of error *coram nobis* to set aside the conviction. *United States v. Morgan,* 346 U.S. 502 (1954). As the Court recognized, in the *Morgan* situation an application for a writ of error *coram nobis* "is of the same general character as [a motion] under 28 U.S.C. §2255." *Id.* at 506 n.4. Thus, it seems appropriate that the time limitations of Rule 4(a), which apply when a district court grants or denies relief under 28 U.S.C. §2255, should also apply when a district court grants or denies a writ of error *coram nobis.* In addition, the strong public interest in the speedy resolution of criminal appeals that is reflected in the shortened deadlines of Rule 4(b) is not present in the *Morgan* situation, as the party seeking the writ of error *coram nobis* has already served his or her full sentence.

Notwithstanding *Morgan,* it is not clear whether the Supreme Court continues to believe that the writ of error *coram nobis* is available in federal court. In civil cases, the writ has been expressly abolished by Fed. R. Civ. P. 60 (b). In criminal cases, the Supreme Court has recently stated that it has become " 'difficult to conceive of a situation' " in which the writ " 'would be necessary or appropriate.' " *Carlisle v. United States,* 517 U.S. 416, 429 (1996) (quoting *United States v. Smith,* 331 U.S. 469, 475 n.4 (1947)). The amendment to Rule 4(a)(1) is not intended to express any view on this issue; rather, it is merely meant to specify time limitations for appeals.

Rule 4(a)(1)(C) applies only to motions that are in substance, and not merely in form, applications for writs of error *coram nobis.* Litigants may bring and label as applications for a writ of error *coram nobis* what are in reality motions for a new trial under Fed. R. Crim. P. 33 or motions for correction or reduction of a sentence under Fed. R. Crim. P. 35. In such cases, the time limitations of Rule 4(b), and not those of Rule 4(a), should be enforced.

Changes Made After Publication and Comments. No changes were made to the text of the proposed amendment or to the Committee Note.

Subdivision (a)(4)(A)(vi). Rule 4(a)(4)(A)(vi) has been amended to remove a parenthetical that directed that the 10-day deadline be "computed using Federal Rule of Civil Procedure 6 (a)." That parenthetical has become superfluous because Rule 26(a)(2) has been amended to require that all deadlines under 11 days be calculated as they are under Fed. R. Civ. P. 6 (a).

Changes Made After Publication and Comments. No changes were made to the text of the proposed amendment or to the Committee Note.

Subdivision (a)(5)(A)(ii). Rule 4(a)(5)(A) permits the district court to extend the time to file a notice of appeal if two

Rule 4. Appeal as of Right – When Taken

conditions are met. First, the party seeking the extension must file its motion no later than 30 days after the expiration of the time originally prescribed by Rule 4(a). Second, the party seeking the extension must show either excusable neglect or good cause. The text of Rule 4(a)(5)(A) does not distinguish between motions filed prior to the expiration of the original deadline and those filed after the expiration of the original deadline. Regardless of whether the motion is filed before or during the 30 days after the original deadline expires, the district court may grant an extension if a party shows either excusable neglect or good cause.

Despite the text of Rule 4(a)(5)(A), most of the courts of appeals have held that the good cause standard applies only to motions brought prior to the expiration of the original deadline and that the excusable neglect standard applies only to motions brought during the 30 days following the expiration of the original deadline. *See Pontarelli v. Stone*, 930 F.2d 104, 109–10 (1st Cir. 1991) (collecting cases from the Second, Fifth, Sixth, Seventh, Eighth, Ninth, and Eleventh Circuits). These courts have relied heavily upon the Advisory Committee Note to the 1979 amendment to Rule 4(a)(5). But the Advisory Committee Note refers to a draft of the 1979 amendment that was ultimately rejected. The rejected draft directed that the good cause standard apply only to motions filed prior to the expiration of the original deadline. Rule 4(a)(5), as actually amended, did not. *See* 16A Charles Alan Wright, et al., Federal Practice and Procedure §3950.3, at 148–49 (2d ed. 1996).

The failure of the courts of appeals to apply Rule 4(a)(5)(A) as written has also created tension between that rule and Rule 4(b)(4). As amended in 1998, Rule 4(b)(4) permits the district court to extend the time for filing a notice of appeal in a *criminal* case for an additional 30 days upon a finding of excusable neglect or good cause. Both Rule 4(b)(4) and the Advisory Committee Note to the 1998 amendment make it clear that an extension can be granted for either excusable neglect or good cause, regardless of whether a motion for an extension is filed before or during the 30 days following the expiration of the original deadline.

Rule 4(a)(5)(A)(ii) has been amended to correct this misunderstanding and to bring the rule in harmony in this respect with Rule 4(b)(4). A motion for an extension filed prior to the expiration of the original deadline may be granted if the movant shows either excusable neglect or good cause. Likewise, a motion for an extension filed during the 30 days following the expiration of the original deadline may be granted if the movant shows either excusable neglect or good cause.

The good cause and excusable neglect standards have "different domains." *Lorenzen v. Employees Retirement Plan*, 896 F.2d 228, 232 (7th Cir. 1990). They are not interchangeable, and one is not inclusive of the other. The excusable neglect standard applies in situations in which there is fault; in such situations, the need for an extension is usually occasioned by something within the control of the movant. The good cause standard applies in situations in which there is no fault—excusable or otherwise. In such situations, the need for an extension is usually occasioned by something that is not within the control of the movant.

Thus, the good cause standard can apply to motions brought during the 30 days following the expiration of the original deadline. If, for example, the Postal Service fails to deliver a notice of appeal, a movant might have good cause to seek a post-expiration extension. It may be unfair to make such a movant prove that its "neglect" was excusable, given that the movant may not have been neglectful at all. Similarly, the excusable neglect standard can apply to motions brought prior to the expiration of the original deadline. For example, a movant may bring a pre-expiration motion for an extension of time when an error committed by the movant makes it unlikely that the movant will be able to meet the original deadline.

Changes Made After Publication and Comments. No changes were made to the text of the proposed amendment. The stylistic changes to the Committee Note suggested by Judge Newman were adopted. In addition, two paragraphs were added at the end of the Committee Note to clarify the difference between the good cause and excusable neglect standards.

Subdivision (a)(7). Several circuit splits have arisen out of uncertainties about how Rule 4(a)(7)'s definition of when a judgment or order is "entered" interacts with the requirement in Fed. R. Civ. P. 58 that, to be "effective," a judgment must be set forth on a separate document. Rule 4(a)(7) and Fed. R. Civ. P. 58 have been amended to resolve those splits.

1. The first circuit split addressed by the amendments to Rule 4(a)(7) and Fed. R. Civ. P. 58 concerns the extent to which orders that dispose of post-judgment motions must be set forth on separate documents. Under Rule 4(a)(4)(A), the filing of certain post-judgment motions tolls the time to appeal the underlying judgment until the "entry" of the order disposing of the last such remaining motion. Courts have disagreed about whether such an order must be set forth on a separate document before it is treated as "entered." This disagreement reflects a broader dispute among courts about whether Rule 4(a)(7) independently imposes a separate document requirement (a requirement that is distinct from the separate document requirement that is imposed by the Federal Rules of Civil Procedure (" FRCP ")) or whether Rule 4(a)(7) instead incorporates the separate document requirement as it exists in the FRCP. Further complicating the matter, courts in the former "camp" disagree among themselves about the scope of the separate document requirement that they interpret Rule 4(a)(7) as imposing, and courts in the latter "camp" disagree among themselves about the scope of the separate document requirement imposed by the FRCP.

Rule 4(a)(7) has been amended to make clear that it simply incorporates the separate document requirement as it exists in Fed. R. Civ. P. 58. If Fed. R. Civ. P. 58 does not require that a judgment or order be set forth on a separate document, then neither does Rule 4(a)(7); the judgment or order will be deemed entered for purposes of Rule 4(a) when it is entered in the civil docket. If Fed. R. Civ. P. 58 requires that a judgment or order be set forth on a separate document, then so does Rule 4(a)(7); the judgment or order will not be deemed entered for purposes of Rule 4(a) until it is so set forth and entered in the civil docket (with one important exception, described below).

In conjunction with the amendment to Rule 4(a)(7), Fed. R. Civ. P. 58 has been amended to provide that orders disposing of the post-judgment motions listed in new Fed. R. Civ. P. 58 (a)(1) (which post-judgment motions include, but are not limited to, the post-judgment motions that can toll the time to appeal under Rule 4(a)(4)(A)) do not have to be set forth on separate documents. *See* Fed. R. Civ. P. 58 (a)(1). Thus, such orders are entered for purposes of Rule 4(a) when they are entered in the civil docket pursuant to Fed. R. Civ. P. 79 (a). *See* Rule 4(a)(7)(A)(1).

2. The second circuit split addressed by the amendments to Rule 4(a)(7) and Fed. R. Civ. P. 58 concerns the following question: When a judgment or order is required to be set forth on a separate document under Fed. R. Civ. P. 58 but is not, does the time to appeal the judgment or order—or the time to bring post-judgment motions, such as a motion for a new trial under Fed. R. Civ. P. 59 —ever begin to run? According to every circuit except the First Circuit, the answer is "no." The First Circuit alone holds that parties will be deemed to have waived their right to have a judgment or order entered on a separate document three months after the judgment or order is entered in the civil docket. *See Fiore v. Washington County Community Mental Health Ctr.*, 960 F.2d 229, 236 (1st Cir. 1992) (en banc). Other circuits have rejected this cap as contrary to the relevant rules. *See, e.g., United States v. Haynes*, 158 F.3d 1327, 1331 (D.C. Cir. 1998); *Hammack v. Baroid Corp.*, 142 F.3d 266, 269–70 (5th Cir. 1998); *Rubin v. Schottenstein, Zox & Dunn*, 110 F.3d 1247, 1253 n.4 (6th Cir. 1997), *vacated on other grounds*, 143 F.3d 263 (6th Cir. 1998) (en banc). However, no court has questioned the wisdom of imposing such a cap as a matter of policy.

Both Rule 4(a)(7)(A) and Fed. R. Civ. P. 58 have been amended to impose such a cap. Under the amendments, a judgment or order is generally treated as entered when it is entered in the civil docket pursuant to Fed. R. Civ. P. 79 (a). There is one exception: When Fed. R. Civ. P. 58 (a)(1) requires the judgment or order to be set forth on a separate document, that judgment or order is not treated as entered until it is set forth on a separate document (in addition to being entered in the civil docket) or until the expiration of 150 days after its entry in the civil docket, whichever occurs first. This cap will ensure that parties will not be given forever to appeal (or to bring a post-judgment motion) when a court fails to set forth a judgment or order on a separate document in violation of Fed. R. Civ. P. 58 (a)(1).

3. The third circuit split—this split addressed only by the amendment to Rule 4(a)(7)—concerns whether the appellant may waive the separate document requirement over the objection of the appellee. In *Bankers Trust Co. v. Mallis*, 435 U.S. 381, 387 (1978) (per curiam), the Supreme Court held that the "parties to an appeal may waive the separate-judgment requirement of Rule 58." Specifically, the Supreme Court held that when a district court enters an order and "clearly evidence[s] its intent that the . . . order . . . represent[s] the final decision in the case," the order is a "final decision" for purposes of 28 U.S.C. §1291, even if the order has not been set forth on a separate document for purposes of Fed. R. Civ. P. 58. *Id.* Thus, the parties can choose to appeal without waiting for the order to be set forth on a separate document.

Courts have disagreed about whether the consent of all parties is necessary to waive the separate document requirement. Some circuits permit appellees to object to attempted *Mallis* waivers and to force appellants to return to the trial court, request that judgment be set forth on a separate document, and appeal a second time. *See, e.g., Selletti v. Carey*, 173 F.3d 104, 109–10 (2d Cir. 1999); *Williams v. Borg*, 139 F.3d 737, 739–40 (9th Cir. 1998); *Silver Star Enters., Inc. v. M/V Saramacca*, 19 F.3d 1008, 1013 (5th Cir. 1994). Other courts disagree and permit *Mallis* waivers even if the appellee objects. *See, e.g., Haynes*, 158 F.3d at 1331; *Miller v. Artistic Cleaners*, 153 F.3d 781, 783–84 (7th Cir. 1998); *Alvord-Polk, Inc. v. F. Schumacher & Co.*, 37 F.3d 996, 1006 n.8 (3d Cir. 1994).

New Rule 4(a)(7)(B) is intended both to codify the Supreme Court's holding in *Mallis* and to make clear that the decision whether to waive the requirement that the judgment or order be set forth on a separate document is the appellant's alone. It is, after all, the appellant who needs a clear signal as to when the time to file a notice of appeal has begun to run. If the appellant chooses to bring an appeal without waiting for the judgment or order to be set forth on a separate document, then there is no reason why the appellee should be able to object. All that would result from honoring the appellee's objection would be delay.

4. The final circuit split addressed by the amendment to Rule 4(a)(7) concerns the question whether an appellant who chooses to waive the separate document requirement must appeal within 30 days (60 days if the government is a party) from the entry in the civil docket of the judgment or order that should have been set forth on a separate document but was not. In *Townsend v. Lucas*, 745 F.2d 933 (5th Cir. 1984), the district court dismissed a 28 U.S.C. §2254 action on May 6, 1983, but failed to set forth the judgment on a separate document. The plaintiff appealed on January 10, 1984. The Fifth Circuit dismissed the appeal, reasoning that, if the plaintiff waived the separate document requirement, then his appeal would be from the May 6 order, and if his appeal was from the May 6 order, then it was untimely under Rule 4(a)(1). The Fifth Circuit stressed that the plaintiff could return to the district court, move that the judgment be set forth on a separate document, and appeal from that judgment within 30 days. *Id.* at 934. Several other cases have embraced the *Townsend* approach. *See, e.g., Armstrong v. Ahitow*, 36 F.3d 574, 575 (7th Cir. 1994) (per curiam); *Hughes v. Halifax*

Rule 4. Appeal as of Right – When Taken

County Sch. Bd., 823 F.2d 832, 835–36 (4th Cir. 1987); *Harris v. McCarthy*, 790 F.2d 753, 756 n.1 (9th Cir. 1986).

Those cases are in the distinct minority. There are numerous cases in which courts have heard appeals that were not filed within 30 days (60 days if the government was a party) from the judgment or order that should have been set forth on a separate document but was not. *See, e.g., Haynes*, 158 F.3d at 1330–31; *Clough v. Rush*, 959 F.2d 182, 186 (10th Cir. 1992); *McCalden v. California Library Ass'n*, 955 F.2d 1214, 1218–19 (9th Cir. 1990). In the view of these courts, the remand in *Townsend* was "precisely the purposeless spinning of wheels abjured by the Court in the [*Mallis*] case." 15B Charles Alan Wright et al., Federal Practice and Procedure §3915, at 259 n.8 (3d ed. 1992).

The Committee agrees with the majority of courts that have rejected the *Townsend* approach. In drafting new Rule 4(a)(7)(B), the Committee has been careful to avoid phrases such as "otherwise timely appeal" that might imply an endorsement of *Townsend*.

Changes Made After Publication and Comments. No changes were made to the text of proposed Rule 4(a)(7)(B) or to the third or fourth numbered sections of the Committee Note, except that, in several places, references to a judgment being "entered" on a separate document were changed to references to a judgment being "set forth" on a separate document. This was to maintain stylistic consistency. The appellate rules and the civil rules consistently refer to "entering" judgments on the civil docket and to "setting forth" judgments on separate documents.

Two major changes were made to the text of proposed Rule 4(a)(7)(A)—one substantive and one stylistic. The substantive change was to increase the "cap" from 60 days to 150 days. The Appellate Rules Committee and the Civil Rules Committee had to balance two concerns that are implicated whenever a court fails to enter its final decision on a separate document. On the one hand, potential appellants need a clear signal that the time to appeal has begun to run, so that they do not unknowingly forfeit their rights. On the other hand, the time to appeal cannot be allowed to run forever. A party who receives no notice whatsoever of a judgment has only 180 days to move to reopen the time to appeal from that judgment. *See* Rule 4(a)(6)(A). It hardly seems fair to give a party who *does* receive notice of a judgment an unlimited amount of time to appeal, merely because that judgment was not set forth on a separate piece of paper. Potential appellees and the judicial system need *some* limit on the time within which appeals can be brought.

The 150-day cap properly balances these two concerns. When an order is not set forth on a separate document, what signals litigants that the order is final and appealable is a lack of further activity from the court. A 60-day period of inactivity is not sufficiently rare to signal to litigants that the court has entered its last order. By contrast, 150 days of inactivity is much less common and thus more clearly signals to litigants that the court is done with their case.

The major stylistic change to Rule 4(a)(7) requires some explanation. In the published draft, proposed Rule 4(a)(7)(A) provided that "[a] judgment or order is entered for purposes of this Rule 4(a) when it is entered for purposes of Rule 58(b) of the Federal Rules of Civil Procedure." In other words, Rule 4(a)(7)(A) told readers to look to FRCP 58 (b) to ascertain when a judgment is entered for purposes of starting the running of time to appeal. Sending appellate lawyers to the civil rules to discover when time began to run for purposes of the appellate rules was itself somewhat awkward, but it was made more confusing by the fact that, when readers went to proposed FRCP 58 (b), they found this introductory clause: "Judgment is entered for purposes of Rules 50, 52, 54(d)(2)(B), 59, 60, and 62 when . . ."

This introductory clause was confusing for both appellate lawyers and trial lawyers. It was confusing for appellate lawyers because Rule 4(a)(7) informed them that FRCP 58 (b) would tell them when the time begins to run for purposes of the *appellate* rules, but when they got to FRCP 58 (b) they found a rule that, by its terms, dictated only when the time begins to run for purposes of certain *civil* rules. The introductory clause was confusing for trial lawyers because FRCP 58 (b) described when judgment is entered for some purposes under the civil rules, but then was completely silent about when judgment is entered for other purposes.

To avoid this confusion, the Civil Rules Committee, on the recommendation of the Appellate Rules Committee, changed the introductory clause in FRCP 58 (b) to read simply: "Judgment is entered for purposes of *these Rules* when . . . ." In addition, Rule 4(a)(7)(A) was redrafted [A redraft of Rule 4(a)(7) was faxed to members of the Appellate Rules Committee two weeks after our meeting in New Orleans. The Committee consented to the redraft without objection.] so that the triggering events for the running of the time to appeal (entry in the civil docket, and being set forth on a separate document or passage of 150 days) were incorporated directly into Rule 4(a)(7), rather than indirectly through a reference to FRCP 58 (b). This eliminates the need for appellate lawyers to examine Rule 58(b) and any chance that Rule 58(b)'s introductory clause (even as modified) might confuse them.

We do not believe that republication of Rule 4(a)(7) or FRCP 58 is necessary. In *substance*, rewritten Rule 4(a)(7)(A) and FRCP 58 (b) operate identically to the published versions, except that the 60-day cap has been replaced with a 150-day cap—a change that was suggested by some of the commentators and that makes the cap more forgiving.

Subdivision (b)(5). Federal Rule of Criminal Procedure 35 (a) permits a district court, acting within 7 days after the imposition of sentence, to correct an erroneous sentence in a criminal case. Some courts have held that the filing of a motion for correction of a sentence suspends the time for filing a notice of appeal from the judgment of conviction. *See, e.g., United States v. Carmouche*, 138 F.3d 1014, 1016 (5th Cir. 1998) (per curiam); *United States v. Morillo*, 8 F.3d 864, 869 (1st Cir. 1993). Those courts establish conflicting timetables for appealing a judgment of conviction after the filing of a

Rule 4. Appeal as of Right – When Taken

motion to correct a sentence. In the First Circuit, the time to appeal is suspended only for the period provided by Fed. R. Crim. P. 35 (a) for the district court to correct a sentence; the time to appeal begins to run again once 7 days have passed after sentencing, even if the motion is still pending. By contrast, in the Fifth Circuit, the time to appeal does not begin to run again until the district court actually issues an order disposing of the motion.

Rule 4(b)(5) has been amended to eliminate the inconsistency concerning the effect of a motion to correct a sentence on the time for filing a notice of appeal. The amended rule makes clear that the time to appeal continues to run, even if a motion to correct a sentence is filed. The amendment is consistent with Rule 4(b)(3)(A), which lists the motions that toll the time to appeal, and notably omits any mention of a Fed. R. Crim. P. 35 (a) motion. The amendment also should promote certainty and minimize the likelihood of confusion concerning the time to appeal a judgment of conviction.

If a district court corrects a sentence pursuant to Fed. R. Crim. P. 35 (a), the time for filing a notice of appeal of the corrected sentence under Rule 4(b)(1) would begin to run when the court enters a new judgment reflecting the corrected sentence.

Changes Made After Publication and Comments. The reference to Federal Rule of Criminal Procedure 35 (c) was changed to Rule 35(a) to reflect the pending amendment of Rule 35. The proposed amendment to Criminal Rule 35, if approved, will take effect at the same time that the proposed amendment to Appellate Rule 4 will take effect, if approved.

Committee Notes on Rules—2005 Amendment

Rule 4(a)(6) has permitted a district court to reopen the time to appeal a judgment or order upon finding that four conditions were satisfied. First, the district court had to find that the appellant did not receive notice of the entry of the judgment or order from the district court or any party within 21 days after the judgment or order was entered. Second, the district court had to find that the appellant moved to reopen the time to appeal within 7 days after the appellant received notice of the entry of the judgment or order. Third, the district court had to find that the appellant moved to reopen the time to appeal within 180 days after the judgment or order was entered. Finally, the district court had to find that no party would be prejudiced by the reopening of the time to appeal.

Rule 4(a)(6) has been amended to specify more clearly what type of "notice" of the entry of a judgment or order precludes a party from later moving to reopen the time to appeal. In addition, Rule 4(a)(6) has been amended to address confusion about what type of "notice" triggers the 7-day period to bring a motion to reopen. Finally, Rule 4(a)(6) has been reorganized to set forth more logically the conditions that must be met before a district court may reopen the time to appeal.

Subdivision (a)(6)(A). Former subdivision (a)(6)(B) has been redesignated as subdivision (a)(6)(A), and one substantive change has been made. As amended, the subdivision will preclude a party from moving to reopen the time to appeal a judgment or order only if the party receives (within 21 days) formal notice of the entry of that judgment or order under Civil Rule 77(d). No other type of notice will preclude a party.

The reasons for this change take some explanation. Prior to 1998, former subdivision (a)(6)(B) permitted a district court to reopen the time to appeal if it found "that a party entitled to notice of the entry of a judgment or order did not receive such notice from the clerk or any party within 21 days of its entry." The rule was clear that the "notice" to which it referred was the notice required under Civil Rule 77(d), which must be served by the clerk pursuant to Civil Rule 5(b) and may also be served by a party pursuant to that same rule. In other words, prior to 1998, former subdivision (a)(6)(B) was clear that, if a party did not receive formal notice of the entry of a judgment or order under Civil Rule 77(d), that party could later move to reopen the time to appeal (assuming that the other requirements of subdivision (a)(6) were met).

In 1998, former subdivision (a)(6)(B) was amended to change the description of the type of notice that would preclude a party from moving to reopen. As a result of the amendment, former subdivision (a)(6)(B) no longer referred to the failure of the moving party to receive "*such* notice"—that is, the notice required by Civil Rule 77(d)—but instead referred to the failure of the moving party to receive "*the* notice." And former subdivision (a)(6)(B) no longer referred to the failure of the moving party to receive notice from "the *clerk* or any party," both of whom are explicitly mentioned in Civil Rule 77(d). Rather, former subdivision (a)(6)(B) referred to the failure of the moving party to receive notice from "the *district court* or any party."

The 1998 amendment meant, then, that the type of notice that precluded a party from moving to reopen the time to appeal was no longer limited to Civil Rule 77(d) notice. Under the 1998 amendment, *some* type of notice, in addition to Civil Rule 77(d) notice, precluded a party. But the text of the amended rule did not make clear what type of notice qualified. This was an invitation for litigation, confusion, and possible circuit splits.

To avoid such problems, former subdivision (a)(6)(B)—new subdivision (a)(6)(A)—has been amended to restore its pre-1998 simplicity. Under new subdivision (a)(6)(A), if the court finds that the moving party was not notified under Civil Rule 77(d) of the entry of the judgment or order that the party seeks to appeal within 21 days after that judgment or order was entered, then the court is authorized to reopen the time to appeal (if all of the other requirements of subdivision (a)(6) are met). Because Civil Rule 77(d) requires that notice of the entry of a judgment or order be formally served under Civil Rule

Rule 4. Appeal as of Right – When Taken

5(b), any notice that is not so served will not operate to preclude the reopening of the time to appeal under new subdivision (a)(6)(A).

Subdivision (a)(6)(B). Former subdivision (a)(6)(A) required a party to move to reopen the time to appeal "within 7 days after the moving party receives notice of the entry [of the judgment or order sought to be appealed]." Former subdivision (a)(6)(A) has been redesignated as subdivision (a)(6)(B), and one important substantive change has been made: The subdivision now makes clear that only formal notice of the entry of a judgment or order under Civil Rule 77(d) will trigger the 7-day period to move to reopen the time to appeal.

The circuits have been split over what type of "notice" is sufficient to trigger the 7-day period. The majority of circuits that addressed the question held that only *written* notice was sufficient, although nothing in the text of the rule suggested such a limitation. *See, e.g., Bass v. United States Dep't of Agric.*, 211 F.3d 959, 963 (5th Cir. 2000). By contrast, the Ninth Circuit held that while former subdivision (a)(6)(A) did not require written notice, "the quality of the communication [had to] rise to the functional equivalent of written notice." *Nguyen v. Southwest Leasing & Rental, Inc.*, 282 F.3d 1061, 1066 (9th Cir. 2002). Other circuits suggested in dicta that former subdivision (a)(6)(A) required only "actual notice," which, presumably, could have included oral notice that was not "the functional equivalent of written notice." *See, e.g., Lowry v. McDonnell Douglas Corp.*, 211 F.3d 457, 464 (8th Cir. 2000). And still other circuits read into former subdivision (a)(6)(A) restrictions that appeared only in former subdivision (a)(6)(B) (such as the requirement that notice be received "from the district court or any party," *see Benavides v. Bureau of Prisons*, 79 F.3d 1211, 1214 (D.C. Cir. 1996)) or that appeared in neither former subdivision (a)(6)(A) nor former subdivision (a)(6)(B) (such as the requirement that notice be served in the manner prescribed by Civil Rule 5, *see Ryan v. First Unum Life Ins. Co.*, 174 F.3d 302, 304–05 (2d Cir. 1999)).

Former subdivision (a)(6)(A)—new subdivision (a)(6)(B)—has been amended to resolve this circuit split by providing that only formal notice of the entry of a judgment or order under Civil Rule 77(d) will trigger the 7-day period. Using Civil Rule 77(d) notice as the trigger has two advantages: First, because Civil Rule 77(d) is clear and familiar, circuit splits are unlikely to develop over its meaning. Second, because Civil Rule 77(d) notice must be served under Civil Rule 5(b), establishing whether and when such notice was provided should generally not be difficult.

Using Civil Rule 77(d) notice to trigger the 7-day period will not unduly delay appellate proceedings. Rule 4(a)(6) applies to only a small number of cases—cases in which a party was not notified of a judgment or order by either the clerk or another party within 21 days after entry. Even with respect to those cases, an appeal cannot be brought more than 180 days after entry, no matter what the circumstances. In addition, Civil Rule 77(d) permits parties to serve notice of the entry of a judgment or order. The winning party can prevent Rule 4(a)(6) from even coming into play simply by serving notice of entry within 21 days. Failing that, the winning party can always trigger the 7-day deadline to move to reopen by serving belated notice.

Changes Made After Publication and Comments. No change was made to the text of subdivision (A)—regarding the type of notice that precludes a party from later moving to reopen the time to appeal—and only minor stylistic changes were made to the Committee Note to subdivision (A).

A substantial change was made to subdivision (B)—regarding the type of notice that triggers the 7-day deadline for moving to reopen the time to appeal. Under the published version of subdivision (B), the 7-day deadline would have been triggered when "the moving party receives or observes written notice of the entry from any source." The Committee was attempting to implement an "eyes/ears" distinction: The 7-day period was triggered when a party learned of the entry of a judgment or order by reading about it (whether on a piece of paper or a computer screen), but was not triggered when a party merely heard about it.

Above all else, subdivision (B) should be clear and easy to apply; it should neither risk opening another circuit split over its meaning nor create the need for a lot of factfinding by district courts. After considering the public comments—and, in particular, the comments of two committees of the California bar—the Committee decided that subdivision (B) could do better on both counts. The published standard—"receives or observes written notice of the entry from any source"—was awkward and, despite the guidance of the Committee Note, was likely to give courts problems. Even if the standard had proved to be sufficiently clear, district courts would still have been left to make factual findings about whether a particular attorney or party "received" or "observed" notice that was written or electronic.

The Committee concluded that the solution suggested by the California bar—using Civil Rule 77(d) notice to trigger the 7-day period—made a lot of sense. The standard is clear; no one doubts what it means to be served with notice of the entry of judgment under Civil Rule 77(d). The standard is also unlikely to give rise to many factual disputes. Civil Rule 77(d) notice must be formally served under Civil Rule 5(b), so establishing the presence or absence of such notice should be relatively easy. And, for the reasons described in the Committee Note, using Civil Rule 77(d) as the trigger will not unduly delay appellate proceedings.

For these reasons, the Committee amended subdivision (B) so that the 7-day deadline will be triggered only by notice of the entry of a judgment or order that is served under Civil Rule 77(d). (Corresponding changes were made to the Committee Note.) The Committee does not believe that the amendment needs to be published again for comment, as the issue of what type of notice should trigger the 7-day deadline has already been addressed by commentators, the revised

Rule 4. Appeal as of Right – When Taken

version of subdivision (B) is far more forgiving than the published version, and it is highly unlikely that the revised version will be found ambiguous in any respect.

Committee Notes on Rules—2009 Amendment

Subdivision (a)(4)(B)(ii). Subdivision (a)(4)(B)(ii) is amended to address problems that stemmed from the adoption—during the 1998 restyling project—of language referring to "a judgment altered or amended upon" a post-trial motion.

Prior to the restyling, subdivision (a)(4) instructed that "[a]ppellate review of an order disposing of any of [the post-trial motions listed in subdivision (a)(4)] requires the party, in compliance with Appellate Rule 3(c), to amend a previously filed notice of appeal. A party intending to challenge an alteration or amendment of the judgment shall file a notice, or amended notice, of appeal within the time prescribed by this Rule 4 measured from the entry of the order disposing of the last such motion outstanding." After the restyling, subdivision (a)(4)(B)(ii) provided: "A party intending to challenge an order disposing of any motion listed in Rule 4(a)(4)(A), or a judgment altered or amended upon such a motion, must file a notice of appeal, or an amended notice of appeal—in compliance with Rule 3(c)—within the time prescribed by this Rule measured from the entry of the order disposing of the last such remaining motion."

One court has explained that the 1998 amendment introduced ambiguity into the Rule: "The new formulation could be read to expand the obligation to file an amended notice to circumstances where the ruling on the post-trial motion alters the prior judgment in an insignificant manner or in a manner favorable to the appellant, even though the appeal is not directed against the alteration of the judgment." *Sorensen v. City of New York*, 413 F.3d 292, 296 n.2 (2d Cir. 2005). The current amendment removes that ambiguous reference to "a judgment altered or amended upon" a post-trial motion, and refers instead to "a judgment's alteration or amendment" upon such a motion. Thus, subdivision (a)(4)(B)(ii) requires a new or amended notice of appeal when an appellant wishes to challenge an order disposing of a motion listed in Rule 4(a)(4)(A) or a judgment's alteration or amendment upon such a motion.

Changes Made After Publication and Comment. No changes were made to the proposal as published. Instead, the Committee has added the commentators' suggestions to its study agenda.

Subdivision (a)(4)(A)(vi). Subdivision (a)(4) provides that certain timely post-trial motions extend the time for filing an appeal. Lawyers sometimes move under Civil Rule 60 for relief that is still available under another rule such as Civil Rule 59. Subdivision (a)(4)(A)(vi) provides for such eventualities by extending the time for filing an appeal so long as the Rule 60 motion is filed within a limited time. Formerly, the time limit under subdivision (a)(4)(A)(vi) was 10 days, reflecting the 10-day limits for making motions under Civil Rules 50(b), 52(b), and 59. Subdivision (a)(4)(A)(vi) now contains a 28-day limit to match the revisions to the time limits in the Civil Rules.

Subdivision (a)(5)(C). The time set in the former rule at 10 days has been revised to 14 days. See the Note to Rule 26.

Subdivision (a)(6)(B). The time set in the former rule at 7 days has been revised to 14 days. Under the time-computation approach set by former Rule 26(a), "7 days" always meant at least 9 days and could mean as many as 11 or even 13 days. Under current Rule 26(a), intermediate weekends and holidays are counted. Changing the period from 7 to 14 days offsets the change in computation approach. See the Note to Rule 26.

Subdivisions (b)(1)(A) and (b)(3)(A). The times set in the former rule at 10 days have been revised to 14 days. See the Note to Rule 26.

Committee Notes on Rules—2010 Amendment

Subdivision (a)(7). Subdivision (a)(7) is amended to reflect the renumbering of Civil Rule 58 as part of the 2007 restyling of the Civil Rules. References to Civil Rule "58(a)(1)" are revised to refer to Civil Rule "58(a)." No substantive change is intended.

The amendments are technical and conforming. In accordance with established Judicial Conference procedures they were not published for public comment.

Committee Notes on Rules—2011 Amendment

Subdivision (a)(1)(B). Rule 4(a)(1)(B) has been amended to make clear that the 60-day appeal period applies in cases in which an officer or employee of the United States is sued in an individual capacity for acts or omissions occurring in connection with duties performed on behalf of the United States. (A concurrent amendment to Rule 40(a)(1) makes clear that the 45-day period to file a petition for panel rehearing also applies in such cases.)

The amendment to Rule 4(a)(1)(B) is consistent with a 2000 amendment to Civil Rule 12(a)(3), which specified an extended
60-day period to respond to complaints when "[a] United States officer or employee [is] sued in an individual capacity for an act or omission occurring in connection with duties performed on the United States' behalf." The Committee Note to the

Rule 4. Appeal as of Right – When Taken

2000 amendment explained: "Time is needed for the United States to determine whether to provide representation to the defendant officer or employee. If the United States provides representation, the need for an extended answer period is the same as in actions against the United States, a United States agency, or a United States officer sued in an official capacity." The same reasons justify providing additional time to the Solicitor General to decide whether to file an appeal.

However, because of the greater need for clarity of application when appeal rights are at stake, the amendment to Rule 4(a)(1)(B), and the corresponding legislative amendment to 28 U.S.C. § 2107 that is simultaneously proposed, include safe harbor provisions that parties can readily apply and rely upon. Under new subdivision 4(a)(1)(B)(iv), a case automatically qualifies for the 60-day appeal period if (1) a legal officer of the United States has appeared in the case, in an official capacity, as counsel for the current or former officer or employee and has not withdrawn the appearance at the time of the entry of the judgment or order appealed from or (2) a legal officer of the United States appears on the notice of appeal as counsel, in an official capacity, for the current or former officer or employee. There will be cases that do not fall within either safe harbor but that qualify for the longer appeal period. An example would be a case in which a federal employee is sued in an individual capacity for an act occurring in connection with federal duties and the United States does not represent the employee either when the judgment is entered or when the appeal is filed but the United States pays for private counsel for the employee.

Changes Made After Publication and Comment

The Committee made two changes to the proposal after publication and comment.

First, the Committee inserted the words "current or former" before "United States officer or employee." This insertion causes the text of the proposed Rule to diverge slightly from that of Civil Rules 4(i)(3) and 12(a)(3), which refer simply to "a United States officer or employee [etc.]." This divergence, though, is only stylistic. The 2000 Committee Notes to Civil Rules 4(i)(3) and 12(a)(3) make clear that those rules are intended to encompass former as well as current officers or employees. It is desirable to make this clarification in the text of Rule 4(a)(1) because that Rule's appeal time periods are jurisdictional.

Second, the Committee added, at the end of Rule 4(a)(1)(B)(iv), the following new language: "– including all instances in which the United States represents that person when the judgment or order is entered or files the appeal for that person." During the public comment period, concerns were raised that a party might rely on the longer appeal period, only to risk the appeal being held untimely by a court that later concluded that the relevant act or omission had not actually occurred in connection with federal duties. The Committee decided to respond to this concern by adding two safe harbor provisions. These provisions make clear that the longer appeal periods apply in any case where the United States either represents the officer or employee at the time of entry of the relevant judgment or files the notice of appeal on the officer or employee's behalf.

References in Text

The Federal Rules of Civil Procedure, referred to in subd. (a)(4), (6), and (7), are set out in this Appendix.

The Federal Rules of Criminal Procedure, referred to in subd. (b)(3), (5), are set out in the Appendix to Title 18, Crimes and Criminal Procedure.

Amendment by Public Law

1988 —Subd. (b). Pub. L. 100–690 inserted "(i)" and "or (ii) a notice of appeal by the Government" in first sentence, and "(i)" and "or (ii) a notice of appeal by any defendant" in fifth sentence.

Committee Notes on Rules – 2016 Amendment

A clarifying amendment is made to subdivision (a)(4). Former Rule 4(a)(4) provided that "[i]f a party timely files in the district court" certain post-judgment motions, "the time to file an appeal runs for all parties from the entry of the order disposing of the last such remaining motion." Responding to a circuit split concerning the meaning of "timely" in this provision, the amendment adopts the majority approach and rejects the approach taken in *National Ecological Foundation v. Alexander*, 496 F.3d 466 (6th Cir. 2007). A motion made after the time allowed by the Civil Rules will not qualify as a motion that, under Rule 4(a)(4)(A), re-starts the appeal time—and that fact is not altered by, for example, a court order that sets a due date that is later than permitted by the Civil Rules, another party's consent or failure to object to the motion's lateness, or the court's disposition of the motion without explicit reliance on untimeliness.

Rule 4(c)(1) is revised to streamline and clarify the operation of the inmate-filing rule.

The Rule requires the inmate to show timely deposit and prepayment of postage. The Rule is amended to specify that a notice is timely if it is accompanied by a declaration or notarized statement stating the date the notice was deposited in the institution's mail system and attesting to the prepayment of first-class postage. The declaration must state that first-class postage "is being prepaid," not (as directed by the former Rule) that first class postage "has been prepaid." This change reflects the fact that inmates may need to rely upon the institution to affix postage after the inmate has deposited the document in the institution's mail system. New Form 7 in the Appendix of Forms sets out a suggested form of the declaration.

The amended rule also provides that a notice is timely without a declaration or notarized statement if other evidence accompanying the notice shows that the notice was deposited on or before the due date and that postage was prepaid. If the notice is not accompanied by evidence that establishes timely deposit and prepayment of postage, then the court of appeals has discretion to accept a declaration or notarized statement at a later date. The Rule uses the phrase "exercises its discretion to permit"—rather than simply "permits"—to help ensure that pro se inmate litigants are aware that a court will not necessarily forgive a failure to provide the declaration initially.

Rule 5. Appeal by Permission

(a) Petition for Permission to Appeal.

(1) To request permission to appeal when an appeal is within the court of appeals' discretion, a party must file a petition for permission to appeal. The petition must be filed with the circuit clerk with proof of service on all other parties to the district-court action.

(2) The petition must be filed within the time specified by the statute or rule authorizing the appeal or, if no such time is specified, within the time provided by Rule 4(a) for filing a notice of appeal.

(3) If a party cannot petition for appeal unless the district court first enters an order granting permission to do so or stating that the necessary conditions are met, the district court may amend its order, either on its own or in response to a party's motion, to include the required permission or statement. In that event, the time to petition runs from entry of the amended order.

(b) Contents of the Petition; Answer or Cross-Petition; Oral Argument.

(1) The petition must include the following:
   (A) the facts necessary to understand the question presented;
   (B) the question itself;
   (C) the relief sought;
   (D) the reasons why the appeal should be allowed and is authorized by a statute or rule; and
   (E) an attached copy of:
      (i) the order, decree, or judgment complained of and any related opinion or memorandum, and
      (ii) any order stating the district court's permission to appeal or finding that the necessary conditions are met.

(2) A party may file an answer in opposition or a cross-petition within 10 days after the petition is served.

(3) The petition and answer will be submitted without oral argument unless the court of appeals orders otherwise.

[The following text of subdivision (c) was effective until December 1, 2016.]

(c) Form of Papers; Number of Copies. All papers must conform to Rule 32(c)(2). Except by the court's permission, a paper must not exceed 20 pages, exclusive of the disclosure statement, the proof of service, and the accompanying documents required by Rule 5(b)(1)(E). An original and 3 copies must be filed unless the court requires a different number by local rule or by order in a particular case.

[The following text of subdivision (c) became effective December 1, 2016.]

(c) Form of Papers; Number of Copies; Length Limits. All papers must conform to Rule 32(c)(2). An original and 3 copies must be filed unless the court requires a different number by local rule or by order in a particular case. Except by the court's permission, and excluding the accompanying documents required by Rule 5(b)(1)(E):

(1) a paper produced using a computer must not exceed 5,200 words; and
(2) a handwritten or typewritten paper must not exceed 20 pages.

Rule 5. Appeal by Permission

(d) Grant of Permission; Fees; Cost Bond; Filing the Record.
(1) Within 14 days after the entry of the order granting permission to appeal, the appellant must:
(A) pay the district clerk all required fees; and
(B) file a cost bond if required under Rule 7.
(2) A notice of appeal need not be filed. The date when the order granting permission to appeal is entered serves as the date of the notice of appeal for calculating time under these rules.
(3) The district clerk must notify the circuit clerk once the petitioner has paid the fees. Upon receiving this notice, the circuit clerk must enter the appeal on the docket. The record must be forwarded and filed in accordance with Rules 11 and 12(c).
(As amended Apr. 30, 1979, eff. Aug. 1, 1979; Apr. 29, 1994, eff. Dec. 1, 1994; Apr. 24, 1998, eff. Dec. 1, 1998; Apr. 29, 2002, eff. Dec. 1, 2002; Mar. 26, 2009, eff. Dec. 1, 2009; Apr. 28, 2016, eff. Dec. 1, 2016.)

Notes of Advisory Committee on Rules—1967

This rule is derived in the main from Third Circuit Rule 11(2), which is similar to the rule governing appeals under 28 U.S.C. §1292(b) in a majority of the circuits. The second sentence of subdivision (a) resolves a conflict over the question of whether the district court can amend an order by supplying the statement required by §1292(b) at any time after entry of the order, with the result that the time fixed by the statute commences to run on the date of entry of the order as amended. Compare *Milbert v. Bison Laboratories*, 260 F.2d 431 (3d Cir., 1958) with *Sperry Rand Corporation v. Bell Telephone Laboratories*, 272 F.2d (2d Cir., 1959), *Hadjipateras v. Pacifica, S.A.*, 290 F.2d 697 (5th Cir., 1961), and *Houston Fearless Corporation v. Teter*, 313 F.2d 91 (10th Cir., 1962). The view taken by the Second, Fifth and Tenth Circuits seems theoretically and practically sound, and the rule adopts it. Although a majority of the circuits now require the filing of a notice of appeal following the grant of permission to appeal, filing of the notice serves no function other than to provide a time from which the time for transmitting the record and docketing the appeal begins to run.

Notes of Advisory Committee on Rules—1979 Amendment

The proposed amendment adapts to the practice in appeals from interlocutory orders under 28 U.S.C. §1292(b) the provisions of proposed Rule 3(e) above, requiring payment of all fees in the district court upon the filing of the notice of appeal. See Note to proposed amended Rule 3(e), supra.

Notes of Advisory Committee on Rules—1994 Amendment

Subdivision (c). The amendment makes it clear that a court may require a different number of copies either by rule or by order in an individual case. The number of copies of any document that a court of appeals needs varies depending upon the way in which the court conducts business. The internal operation of the courts of appeals necessarily varies from circuit to circuit because of differences in the number of judges, the geographic area included within the circuit, and other such factors. Uniformity could be achieved only by setting the number of copies artificially high so that parties in all circuits file enough copies to satisfy the needs of the court requiring the greatest number. Rather than do that, the Committee decided to make it clear that local rules may require a greater or lesser number of copies and that, if the circumstances of a particular case indicate the need for a different number of copies in that case, the court may so order.

Committee Notes on Rules—1998 Amendment

In 1992 Congress added subsection (e) to 28 U.S.C. §1292. Subsection (e) says that the Supreme Court has power to prescribe rules that "provide for an appeal of an interlocutory decision to the courts of appeals that is not otherwise provided for" in section 1292. The amendment of Rule 5 was prompted by the possibility of new rules authorizing additional interlocutory appeals. Rather than add a separate rule governing each such appeal, the Committee believes it is preferable to amend Rule 5 so that is will govern all such appeals.
In addition the Federal Courts Improvement Act of 1996, Pub. L. 104–317, abolished appeals by permission under 28 U.S.C. §636(c)(5), making Rule 5.1 obsolete.
This new Rule 5 is intended to govern all discretionary appeals from district-court orders, judgments, or decrees. At this time that includes interlocutory appeals under 28 U.S.C. §1292(b), (c)(1), and (d)(1) & (2). If additional interlocutory appeals are authorized under §1292(e), the new Rule is intended to govern them if the appeals are discretionary.

Rule 5. Appeal by Permission

Subdivision (a). Paragraph (a)(1) says that when granting an appeal is within a court of appeals' discretion, a party may file a petition for permission to appeal. The time for filing provision states only that the petition must be filed within the time provided in the statute or rule authorizing the appeal or, if no such time is specified, within the time provided by Rule 4(a) for filing a notice of appeal.

Section 1292(b), (c), and (d) provide that the petition must be filed within 10 days after entry of the order containing the statement prescribed in the statute. Existing Rule 5(a) provides that if a district court amends an order to contain the prescribed statement, the petition must be filed within 10 days after entry of the amended order. The new rule similarly says that if a party cannot petition without the district court's permission or statement that necessary circumstances are present, the district court may amend its order to include such a statement and the time to petition runs from the entry of the amended order.

The provision that the Rule 4(a) time for filing a notice of appeal should apply if the statute or rule is silent about the filing time was drawn from existing Rule 5.1.

Subdivision (b). The changes made in the provisions in paragraph (b)(1) are intended only to broaden them sufficiently to make them appropriate for all discretionary appeals.

In paragraph (b)(2) a uniform time—7 days—is established for filing an answer in opposition or cross-petition. Seven days is the time for responding under existing Rule 5 and is an appropriate length of time when dealing with an interlocutory appeal. Although existing Rule 5.1 provides 14 days for responding, the Committee does not believe that the longer response time is necessary.

Subdivision (c). Subdivision (c) is substantively unchanged.

Subdivision (d). Paragraph (d)(2) is amended to state that "the date when the order granting permission to appeal is entered serves as the date of the notice of appeal" for purposes of calculating time under the rules. That language simply clarifies existing practice.

Committee Notes on Rules—2002 Amendment

Subdivision (c). A petition for permission to appeal, a cross-petition for permission to appeal, and an answer to a petition or cross-petition for permission to appeal are all "other papers" for purposes of Rule 32(c)(2), and all of the requirements of Rule 32(a) apply to those papers, except as provided in Rule 32(c)(2). During the 1998 restyling of the Federal Rules of Appellate Procedure, Rule 5(c) was inadvertently changed to suggest that only the requirements of Rule 32(a)(1) apply to such papers. Rule 5(c) has been amended to correct that error.

Rule 5(c) has been further amended to limit the length of papers filed under Rule 5.

Changes Made After Publication and Comments. No changes were made to the text of the proposed amendment or to the Committee Note.

Committee Notes on Rules—2009 Amendment

Subdivision (b)(2). Subdivision (b)(2) is amended in the light of the change in Rule 26(a)'s time computation rules. Subdivision (b)(2) formerly required that an answer in opposition to a petition for permission to appeal, or a cross-petition for permission to appeal, be filed "within 7 days after the petition is served." Under former Rule 26(a), "7 days" always meant at least 9 days and could mean as many as 11 or even 13 days. Under current Rule 26(a), intermediate weekends and holidays are counted. Changing the period from 7 to 10 days offsets the change in computation approach. See the Note to Rule 26.

Subdivision (d)(1). The time set in the former rule at 10 days has been revised to 14 days. See the Note to Rule 26.

Committee Notes on Rules – 2016 Amendment

The page limits previously employed in Rules 5, 21, 27, 35, and 40 have been largely overtaken by changes in technology. For papers produced using a computer, those page limits are now replaced by word limits. The word limits were derived from the current page limits using the assumption that one page is equivalent to 260 words. Papers produced using a computer must include the certificate of compliance required by Rule 32(g); Form 6 in the Appendix of Forms suffices to meet that requirement. Page limits are retained for papers prepared without the aid of a computer (i.e., handwritten or typewritten papers). For both the word limit and the page limit, the calculation excludes the accompanying documents required by Rule 5(b)(1)(E) and any items listed in Rule 32(f).

Rule 6. Appeal in a Bankruptcy Case from a Final Judgment, Order, or Decree of a District Court or Bankruptcy Appellate Panel

(a) Appeal From a Judgment, Order, or Decree of a District Court Exercising Original Jurisdiction in a Bankruptcy Case. An appeal to a court of appeals from a final judgment, order, or decree of a district court exercising jurisdiction under 28 U.S.C. §1334 is taken as any other civil appeal under these rules.

(b) Appeal From a Judgment, Order, or Decree of a District Court or Bankruptcy Appellate Panel Exercising Appellate Jurisdiction in a Bankruptcy Case.

(1) *Applicability of Other Rules.* These rules apply to an appeal to a court of appeals under 28 U.S.C. §158(d) from a final judgment, order, or decree of a district court or bankruptcy appellate panel exercising appellate jurisdiction under 28 U.S.C. §158(a) or (b). But there are 3 exceptions:

(A) Rules 4(a)(4), 4(b), 9, 10, 11, 12(b), 13–20, 22–23, and 24(b) do not apply;

(B) the reference in Rule 3(c) to "Form 1 in the Appendix of Forms" must be read as a reference to Form 5; and

(C) when the appeal is from a bankruptcy appellate panel, the term "district court," as used in any applicable rule, means "appellate panel."

(2) *Additional Rules.* In addition to the rules made applicable by Rule 6(b)(1), the following rules apply:

(A) *Motion for Rehearing.*

(i) If a timely motion for rehearing under Bankruptcy Rule 8015 is filed, the time to appeal for all parties runs from the entry of the order disposing of the motion. A notice of appeal filed after the district court or bankruptcy appellate panel announces or enters a judgment, order, or decree—but before disposition of the motion for rehearing—becomes effective when the order disposing of the motion for rehearing is entered.

(ii) Appellate review of the order disposing of the motion requires the party, in compliance with Rules 3(c) and 6(b)(1)(B), to amend a previously filed notice of appeal. A party intending to challenge an altered or amended judgment, order, or decree must file a notice of appeal or amended notice of appeal within the time prescribed by Rule 4—excluding Rules 4(a)(4) and 4(b)—measured from the entry of the order disposing of the motion.

(iii) No additional fee is required to file an amended notice.

(B) *The record on appeal.*

(i) Within 14 days after filing the notice of appeal, the appellant must file with the clerk possessing the record assembled in accordance with Bankruptcy Rule 8006—and serve on the appellee—a statement of the issues to be presented on appeal and a designation of the record to be certified and sent to the circuit clerk.

(ii) An appellee who believes that other parts of the record are necessary must, within 14 days after being served with the appellant's designation, file with the clerk and serve on the appellant a designation of additional parts to be included.

(iii) The record on appeal consists of:
- the redesignated record as provided above;
- the proceedings in the district court or bankruptcy appellate panel; and
- a certified copy of the docket entries prepared by the clerk under Rule 3(d).

(C) *Forwarding the Record.*

(i) When the record is complete, the district clerk or bankruptcy appellate panel clerk must number the documents constituting the record and send them promptly to the circuit clerk together with a list of the documents correspondingly numbered and reasonably identified. Unless directed to do so by a party or the circuit clerk, the clerk will not send to the court of appeals documents of unusual bulk or weight, physical exhibits other than documents, or other parts of the record designated for omission by local rule of the court of appeals. If the exhibits are unusually bulky or heavy, a party must arrange with the clerks in advance for their transportation and receipt.

(ii) All parties must do whatever else is necessary to enable the clerk to assemble and forward the record. The court of appeals may provide by rule or order that a certified copy of the docket entries be

Rule 6. Appeal in a Bankruptcy Case from a Final Judgment, Order, or Decree of a District Court or Bankruptcy Appellate Panel

sent in place of the redesignated record, but any party may request at any time during the pendency of the appeal that the redesignated record be sent.

(D) *Filing the Record.* Upon receiving the record—or a certified copy of the docket entries sent in place of the redesignated record—the circuit clerk must file it and immediately notify all parties of the filing date.

(As amended Apr. 30, 1979, eff. Aug. 1, 1979; Apr. 25, 1989, eff. Dec. 1, 1989; Apr. 30, 1991, eff. Dec. 1, 1991; Apr. 22, 1993, eff. Dec. 1, 1993; Apr. 24, 1998, eff. Dec. 1, 1998; Mar. 26, 2009, eff. Dec. 1, 2009.)

Notes of Advisory Committee on Rules—1967

This rule is substantially a restatement of present procedure. See D.C. Cir. Rule 34; 6th Cir. Rule 11; 7th Cir. Rule 10(d); 10th Cir. Rule 13.

Present circuit rules commonly provide that the petition for allowance of an appeal shall be filed within the time allowed by Section 25 of the Bankruptcy Act for taking appeals of right. For the reasons explained in the Note accompanying Rule 4, that rule makes the time for appeal in bankruptcy cases the same as that which obtains in other civil cases and thus supersedes Section 25. Thus the present rule simply continues the former practice of making the time for filing the petition in appeals by allowance the same as that provided for filing the notice of appeal in appeals of right.

Notes of Advisory Committee on Rules—1979 Amendment

The proposed amendment adapts to the practice in appeals by allowance in bankruptcy proceedings the provisions of proposed Rule 3(e) above, requiring payment of all fees in the district court at the time of the filing of the notice of appeal. See Note to Rule 3(e), supra.

Notes of Advisory Committee on Rules—1989 Amendment

A new Rule 6 is proposed. The Bankruptcy Reform Act of 1978, Pub. L. No. 95–598, 92 Stat. 2549, the Supreme Court decision in *Northern Pipeline Construction Co. v. Marathon Pipe Line Co.*, 458 U.S. 50 (1982), and the Bankruptcy Amendments and Federal Judgeship Act of 1984, Pub. L. No. 98–353, 98 Stat. 333, have made the existing Rule 6 obsolete.

Subdivision (a). Subdivision (a) provides that when a district court exercises original jurisdiction in a bankruptcy matter, rather than referring it to a bankruptcy judge for a final determination, the appeal should be taken in identical fashion as appeals from district court decisions in other civil actions. A district court exercises original jurisdiction and this subdivision applies when the district court enters a final order or judgment upon consideration of a bankruptcy judge's proposed findings of fact and conclusions of law in a non-core proceeding pursuant to 28 U.S.C. §157(c)(1) or when a district court withdraws a proceeding pursuant to 28 U.S.C. §157(d). This subdivision is included to avoid uncertainty arising from the question of whether a bankruptcy case is a civil case. The rules refer at various points to the procedure "in a civil case", *see*, e.g. Rule 4(a)(1). Subdivision (a) makes it clear that such rules apply to an appeal from a district court bankruptcy decision.

Subdivision (b). Subdivision (b) governs appeals that follow intermediate review of a bankruptcy judge's decision by a district court or a bankruptcy appellate panel.

Subdivision (b)(1). Subdivision (b)(1) provides for the general applicability of the Federal Rules of Appellate Procedure, with specified exceptions, to appeals covered by subdivision (b) and makes necessary word adjustments.

Subdivision (b)(2). Paragraph (i) provides that the time for filing a notice of appeal shall begin to run anew from the entry of an order denying a rehearing or from the entry of a subsequent judgment. The Committee deliberately omitted from the rule any provision governing the validity of a notice of appeal filed prior to the entry of an order denying a rehearing; the Committee intended to leave undisturbed the current state of the law on that issue. Paragraph (ii) calls for a redesignation of the appellate record assembled in the bankruptcy court pursuant to Rule 8006 of the Rules of Bankruptcy Procedure. After an intermediate appeal, a party may well narrow the focus of its efforts on the second appeal and a redesignation of the record may eliminate unnecessary material. The proceedings during the first appeal are included to cover the possibility that independent error in the intermediate appeal, for example failure to follow appropriate procedures, may be assigned in the court of appeals. Paragraph (iii) provides for the transmission of the record and tracks the appropriate subsections of Rule 11. Paragraph (iv) provides for the filing of the record and notices to the parties. Paragraph (ii) and Paragraph (iv) both refer to "a certified copy of the docket entries". The "docket entries" referred to are the docket entries in the district court or the bankruptcy appellate panel, not the entire docket in the bankruptcy court.

Rule 7. Bond for Costs on Appeal in a Civil Case

Notes of Advisory Committee on Rules—1993 Amendment

Note to Subparagraph (b)(2)(i). The amendment accompanies concurrent changes to Rule 4(a)(4). Although Rule 6 never included language such as that being changed in Rule 4(a)(4), language that made a notice of appeal void if it was filed before, or during the pendency of, certain posttrial motions, courts have found that a notice of appeal is premature if it is filed before the court disposes of a motion for rehearing. *See, e.g., In re X-Cel, Inc.*, 823 F.2d 192 (7th Cir. 1987); *In re Shah*, 859 F.2d 1463 (10th Cir. 1988). The Committee wants to achieve the same result here as in Rule 4, the elimination of a procedural trap.

Committee Notes on Rules—1998 Amendment

The language and organization of the rule are amended to make the rule more easily understood. In addition to changes made to improve the understanding, the Advisory Committee has changed language to make style and terminology consistent throughout the appellate rules. These changes are intended to be stylistic only.

Subdivision (b). Language is added to Rule 6(b)(2)(A)(ii) to conform with the corresponding provision in Rule 4(a)(4). The new language is clarifying rather than substantive. The existing rule states that a party intending to challenge an alteration or amendment of a judgment must file an amended notice of appeal. Of course if a party has not previously filed a notice of appeal, the party would simply file a notice of appeal not an amended one. The new language states that the party must file "a notice of appeal or amended notice of appeal."

Committee Notes on Rules—2009 Amendment

Subdivision (b)(2)(B). The times set in the former rule at 10 days have been revised to 14 days. See the Note to Rule 26.

References in Text

The Bankruptcy Rules, referred to in subd. (b)(2)(A)(i), (B)(i), are set out in the Appendix to Title 11, Bankruptcy.

Rule 7. Bond for Costs on Appeal in a Civil Case

In a civil case, the district court may require an appellant to file a bond or provide other security in any form and amount necessary to ensure payment of costs on appeal. Rule 8(b) applies to a surety on a bond given under this rule.

(As amended Apr. 30, 1979, eff. Aug. 1, 1979; Apr. 24, 1998, eff. Dec. 1, 1998.)

Notes of Advisory Committee on Rules—1967

This rule is derived from FRCP 73 (c) without change in substance.

Notes of Advisory Committee on Rules—1979 Amendment

The amendment would eliminate the provision of the present rule that requires the appellant to file a $250 bond for costs on appeal at the time of filing his notice of appeal. The $250 provision was carried forward in the F.R.App.P. from former Rule 73(c) of the F.R.Civ.P., and the $250 figure has remained unchanged since the adoption of that rule in 1937. Today it bears no relationship to actual costs. The amended rule would leave the question of the need for a bond for costs and its amount in the discretion of the court.

Committee Notes on Rules—1998 Amendment

The language of the rule is amended to make the rule more easily understood. In addition to changes made to improve the understanding, the Advisory Committee has changed language to make style and terminology consistent throughout the appellate rules. These changes are intended to be stylistic only.

Rule 8. Stay or Injunction Pending Appeal

(a) Motion for Stay.

(1) *Initial Motion in the District Court.* A party must ordinarily move first in the district court for the following relief:

(A) a stay of the judgment or order of a district court pending appeal;

(B) approval of a supersedeas bond; or

(C) an order suspending, modifying, restoring, or granting an injunction while an appeal is pending.

(2) *Motion in the Court of Appeals; Conditions on Relief.* A motion for the relief mentioned in Rule 8(a)(1) may be made to the court of appeals or to one of its judges.

(A) The motion must:

(i) show that moving first in the district court would be impracticable; or

(ii) state that, a motion having been made, the district court denied the motion or failed to afford the relief requested and state any reasons given by the district court for its action.

(B) The motion must also include:

(i) the reasons for granting the relief requested and the facts relied on;

(ii) originals or copies of affidavits or other sworn statements supporting facts subject to dispute; and

(iii) relevant parts of the record.

(C) The moving party must give reasonable notice of the motion to all parties.

(D) A motion under this Rule 8(a)(2) must be filed with the circuit clerk and normally will be considered by a panel of the court. But in an exceptional case in which time requirements make that procedure impracticable, the motion may be made to and considered by a single judge.

(E) The court may condition relief on a party's filing a bond or other appropriate security in the district court.

(b) Proceeding Against a Surety. If a party gives security in the form of a bond or stipulation or other undertaking with one or more sureties, each surety submits to the jurisdiction of the district court and irrevocably appoints the district clerk as the surety's agent on whom any papers affecting the surety's liability on the bond or undertaking may be served. On motion, a surety's liability may be enforced in the district court without the necessity of an independent action. The motion and any notice that the district court prescribes may be served on the district clerk, who must promptly mail a copy to each surety whose address is known.

(c) Stay in a Criminal Case. Rule 38 of the Federal Rules of Criminal Procedure governs a stay in a criminal case.

(As amended Mar. 10, 1986, eff. July 1, 1986; Apr. 27, 1995, eff. Dec. 1, 1995; Apr. 24, 1998, eff. Dec. 1, 1998.)

Notes of Advisory Committee on Rules—1967

Subdivision (a). While the power of a court of appeals to stay proceedings in the district court during the pendency of an appeal is not explicitly conferred by statute, it exists by virtue of the all writs statute, 28 U.S.C. §1651. *Eastern Greyhound Lines v. Fusco*, 310 F.2d 632 (6th Cir., 1962); *United States v. Lynd*, 301 F.2d 818 (5th Cir., 1962); *Public Utilities Commission of Dist. of Col. v. Capital Transit Co.*, 94 U.S.App.D.C. 140, 214 F.2d 242 (1954). And the Supreme Court has termed the power "inherent" (*In re McKenzie*, 180 U.S. 536, 551, 21 S.Ct. 468, 45 L.Ed. 657 (1901)) and "part of its (the court of appeals) traditional equipment for the administration of justice." (*Scripps-Howard Radio v. F.C.C.*, 316 U.S. 4, 9 –10, 62 S.Ct. 875, 86 L.Ed. 1229 (1942)). The power of a single judge of the court of appeals to grant a stay pending appeal was recognized in *In re McKenzie, supra. Alexander v. United States*, 173 F.2d 865 (9th Cir., 1949) held that a single judge could not stay the judgment of a district court, but it noted the absence of a rule of court authorizing the practice. FRCP 62 (g) adverts to the grant of a stay by a single judge of the appellate court. The requirement that application be first made to the district court is the case law rule. *Cumberland Tel. & Tel. Co. v. Louisiana Public Service Commission*, 260 U.S. 212, 219, 43 S.Ct. 75, 67 L.Ed. 217 (1922); *United States v. El-O-Pathic Pharmacy*, 192 F.2d 62 (9th Cir., 1951); *United States v. Hansell*, 109 F.2d 613 (2d Cir., 1940). The requirement is explicitly stated in FRCrP 38 (c) and in the rules of the First, Third, Fourth and Tenth Circuits. See also Supreme Court Rules 18 and 27.

The statement of the requirement in the proposed rule would work a minor change in present practice. FRCP 73 (e) requires that if a bond for costs on appeal or a supersedeas bond is offered after the appeal is docketed, leave to file the bond must be obtained from the court of appeals. There appears to be no reason why matters relating to supersedeas and cost bonds should not be initially presented to the district court whenever they arise prior to the disposition of the appeal.

Rule 9. Release in a Criminal Case

The requirement of FRCP 73 (e) appears to be a concession to the view that once an appeal is perfected, the district court loses all power over its judgment. See *In re Federal Facilities Trust,* 227 F.2d 651 (7th Cir., 1955) and cases—cited at 654–655. No reason appears why all questions related to supersedeas or the bond for costs on appeal should not be presented in the first instance to the district court in the ordinary case.

Subdivision (b). The provisions respecting a surety upon a bond or other undertaking are based upon FRCP 65.1.

Notes of Advisory Committee on Rules—1986 Amendment

The amendments to Rule 8(b) are technical. No substantive change is intended.

Notes of Advisory Committee on Rules—1995 Amendment

Subdivision (c). The amendment conforms subdivision (c) to previous amendments to Fed. R. Crim. P. 38. This amendment strikes the reference to subdivision (a) of Fed. R. Crim. P. 38 so that Fed. R. App. P. 8 (c) refers instead to all of Criminal Rule 38. When Rule 8(c) was adopted Fed. R. Crim. P. 38 (a) included the procedures for obtaining a stay of execution when the sentence in question was death, imprisonment, a fine, or probation. Criminal Rule 38 was later amended and now addresses those topics in separate subdivisions. Subdivision 38(a) now addresses only stays of death sentences. The proper cross reference is to all of Criminal Rule 38.

Committee Notes on Rules—1998 Amendment

The language and organization of the rule are amended to make the rule more easily understood. In addition to changes made to improve the understanding, the Advisory Committee has changed language to make style and terminology consistent throughout the appellate rules. These changes are intended to be stylistic only.

References in Text

Rule 38 of the Federal Rules of Criminal Procedure, referred to in subd. (c), are set out in the Appendix to Title 18, Crimes and Criminal Procedure.

Rule 9. Release in a Criminal Case

(a) Release Before Judgment of Conviction.
    (1) The district court must state in writing, or orally on the record, the reasons for an order regarding the release or detention of a defendant in a criminal case. A party appealing from the order must file with the court of appeals a copy of the district court's order and the court's statement of reasons as soon as practicable after filing the notice of appeal. An appellant who questions the factual basis for the district court's order must file a transcript of the release proceedings or an explanation of why a transcript was not obtained.
    (2) After reasonable notice to the appellee, the court of appeals must promptly determine the appeal on the basis of the papers, affidavits, and parts of the record that the parties present or the court requires. Unless the court so orders, briefs need not be filed.
    (3) The court of appeals or one of its judges may order the defendant's release pending the disposition of the appeal.
(b) Release After Judgment of Conviction. A party entitled to do so may obtain review of a district-court order regarding release after a judgment of conviction by filing a notice of appeal from that order in the district court, or by filing a motion in the court of appeals if the party has already filed a notice of appeal from the judgment of conviction. Both the order and the review are subject to Rule 9(a). The papers filed by the party seeking review must include a copy of the judgment of conviction.
(c) Criteria for Release. The court must make its decision regarding release in accordance with the applicable provisions of 18 U.S.C. §§3142, 3143, and 3145(c).
(As amended Apr. 24, 1972, eff. Oct. 1, 1972; Pub. L. 98–473, title II, §210, Oct. 12, 1984, 98 Stat. 1987; Apr. 29, 1994, eff. Dec. 1, 1994; Apr. 24, 1998, eff. Dec. 1, 1998.)

Rule 9. Release in a Criminal Case

Notes of Advisory Committee on Rules—1967

Subdivision (a). The appealability of release orders entered prior to a judgment of conviction is determined by the provisions of 18 U.S.C. §3147, as qualified by 18 U.S.C. §3148, and by the rule announced in *Stack v. Boyle*, 342 U.S. 1, 72 S.Ct. 1, 96 L.Ed. 3 (1951), holding certain orders respecting release appealable as final orders under 28 U.S.C. §1291. The language of the rule, "(an)n appeal authorized by law from an order refusing or imposing conditions of release," is intentionally broader than that used in 18 U.S.C. §3147 in describing orders made appealable by that section. The summary procedure ordained by the rule is intended to apply to all appeals from orders respecting release, and it would appear that at least some orders not made appealable by 18 U.S.C. §3147 are nevertheless appealable under the *Stack v. Boyle* rationale. See, for example, *United States v. Foster*, 278 F.2d 567 (2d Cir., 1960), holding appealable an order refusing to extend bail limits. Note also the provisions of 18 U.S.C. §3148, which after withdrawing from persons charged with an offense punishable by death and from those who have been convicted of an offense the right of appeal granted by 18 U.S.C. §3147, expressly preserves "other rights to judicial review of conditions of release or orders of detention."

The purpose of the subdivision is to insure the expeditious determination of appeals respecting release orders, an expedition commanded by 18 U.S.C. §3147 and by the Court in *Stack v. Boyle*, supra. It permits such appeals to be heard on an informal record without the necessity of briefs and on reasonable notice. Equally important to the just and speedy disposition of these appeals is the requirement that the district court state the reasons for its decision. See *Jones v. United States*, 358 F.2d 543 (D.C. Cir., 1966); *Rhodes v. United States*, 275 F.2d 78 (4th Cir., 1960); *United States v. Williams*, 253 F.2d 144 (7th Cir., 1958).

Subdivision (b). This subdivision regulates procedure for review of an order respecting release at a time when the jurisdiction of the court of appeals has already attached by virtue of an appeal from the judgment of conviction. Notwithstanding the fact that jurisdiction has passed to the court of appeals, both 18 U.S.C. §3148 and FRCrP 38 (c) contemplate that the initial determination of whether a convicted defendant is to be released pending the appeal is to be made by the district court. But at this point there is obviously no need for a separate appeal from the order of the district court respecting release. The court of appeals or a judge thereof has power to effect release on motion as an incident to the pending appeal. See FRCrP 38 (c) and 46(a)(2). But the motion is functionally identical with the appeal regulated by subdivision (a) and requires the same speedy determination if relief is to be effective. Hence the similarity of the procedure outlined in the two subdivisions.

Notes of Advisory Committee on Rules—1972 Amendment

Subdivision (c) is intended to bring the rule into conformity with 18 U.S.C. §3148 and to allocate to the defendant the burden of establishing that he will not flee and that he poses no danger to any other person or to the community. The burden is placed upon the defendant in the view that the fact of his conviction justifies retention in custody in situations where doubt exists as to whether he can be safely released pending disposition of his appeal. Release pending appeal may also be denied if "it appears that an appeal is frivolous or taken for delay." 18 U.S.C. §3148. The burden of establishing the existence of these criteria remains with the government.

Notes of Advisory Committee on Rules—1994 Amendment

Rule 9 has been entirely rewritten. The basic structure of the rule has been retained. Subdivision (a) governs appeals from bail decisions made before the judgment of conviction is entered at the time of sentencing. Subdivision (b) governs review of bail decisions made after sentencing and pending appeal.

Subdivision (a). The subdivision applies to appeals from "an order regarding release or detention" of a criminal defendant before judgment of conviction, *i.e.*, before sentencing. See Fed.R.Crim.P. 32. The old rule applied only to a defendant's appeal from an order "refusing or imposing conditions of release." The new broader language is needed because the government is now permitted to appeal bail decisions in certain circumstances. 18 U.S.C. §§3145 and 3731. For the same reason, the rule now requires a district court to state reasons for its decision in all instances, not only when it refuses release or imposes conditions on release.

The rule requires a party appealing from a district court's decision to supply the court of appeals with a copy of the district court's order and its statement of reasons. In addition, an appellant who questions the factual basis for the district court's decision must file a transcript of the release proceedings, if possible. The rule also permits a court to require additional papers. A court must act promptly to decide these appeals; lack of pertinent information can cause delays. The old rule left the determination of what should be filed entirely within the party's discretion; it stated that the court of appeals would hear the appeal "upon such papers, affidavits, and portions of the record as the parties shall present."

Subdivision (b). This subdivision applies to review of a district court's decision regarding release made after judgment of conviction. As in subdivision (a), the language has been changed to accommodate the government's ability to seek

Rule 10. The Record on Appeal

review.

The word "review" is used in this subdivision, rather than "appeal" because review may be obtained, in some instances, upon motion. Review may be obtained by motion if the party has already filed a notice of appeal from the judgment of conviction. If the party desiring review of the release decision has not filed such a notice of appeal, review may be obtained only by filing a notice of appeal from the order regarding release.

The requirements of subdivision (a) apply to both the order and the review. That is, the district court must state its reasons for the order. The party seeking review must supply the court of appeals with the same information required by subdivision (a). In addition, the party seeking review must also supply the court with information about the conviction and the sentence.

Subdivision (c). This subdivision has been amended to include references to the correct statutory provisions.

Committee Notes on Rules—1998 Amendment

The language and organization of the rule are amended to make the rule more easily understood. In addition to changes made to improve the understanding, the Advisory Committee has changed language to make style and terminology consistent throughout the appellate rules. These changes are intended to be stylistic only.

Amendment by Public Law

1984 —Subd. (c). Pub. L. 98–473 substituted "3143" for "3148" and inserted "and that the appeal is not for purpose of delay and raises a substantial question of law or fact likely to result in reversal or in an order for a new trial" after "community".

Rule 10. The Record on Appeal

(a) Composition of the Record on Appeal. The following items constitute the record on appeal:

(1) the original papers and exhibits filed in the district court;

(2) the transcript of proceedings, if any; and

(3) a certified copy of the docket entries prepared by the district clerk.

(b) The Transcript of Proceedings.

(1) *Appellant's Duty to Order.* Within 14 days after filing the notice of appeal or entry of an order disposing of the last timely remaining motion of a type specified in Rule 4(a)(4)(A), whichever is later, the appellant must do either of the following:

(A) order from the reporter a transcript of such parts of the proceedings not already on file as the appellant considers necessary, subject to a local rule of the court of appeals and with the following qualifications:

(i) the order must be in writing;

(ii) if the cost of the transcript is to be paid by the United States under the Criminal Justice Act, the order must so state; and

(iii) the appellant must, within the same period, file a copy of the order with the district clerk; or

(B) file a certificate stating that no transcript will be ordered.

(2) *Unsupported Finding or Conclusion.* If the appellant intends to urge on appeal that a finding or conclusion is unsupported by the evidence or is contrary to the evidence, the appellant must include in the record a transcript of all evidence relevant to that finding or conclusion.

(3) *Partial Transcript.* Unless the entire transcript is ordered:

(A) the appellant must—within the 14 days provided in Rule 10(b)(1)—file a statement of the issues that the appellant intends to present on the appeal and must serve on the appellee a copy of both the order or certificate and the statement;

(B) if the appellee considers it necessary to have a transcript of other parts of the proceedings, the appellee must, within 14 days after the service of the order or certificate and the statement of the issues, file and serve on the appellant a designation of additional parts to be ordered; and

(C) unless within 14 days after service of that designation the appellant has ordered all such parts, and has so notified the appellee, the appellee may within the following 14 days either order the parts or

Rule 10. The Record on Appeal

move in the district court for an order requiring the appellant to do so.

(4) *Payment.* At the time of ordering, a party must make satisfactory arrangements with the reporter for paying the cost of the transcript.

(c) Statement of the Evidence When the Proceedings Were Not Recorded or When a Transcript Is Unavailable. If the transcript of a hearing or trial is unavailable, the appellant may prepare a statement of the evidence or proceedings from the best available means, including the appellant's recollection. The statement must be served on the appellee, who may serve objections or proposed amendments within 14 days after being served. The statement and any objections or proposed amendments must then be submitted to the district court for settlement and approval. As settled and approved, the statement must be included by the district clerk in the record on appeal.

(d) Agreed Statement as the Record on Appeal. In place of the record on appeal as defined in Rule 10(a), the parties may prepare, sign, and submit to the district court a statement of the case showing how the issues presented by the appeal arose and were decided in the district court. The statement must set forth only those facts averred and proved or sought to be proved that are essential to the courts resolution of the issues. If the statement is truthful, it—together with any additions that the district court may consider necessary to a full presentation of the issues on appeal—must be approved by the district court and must then be certified to the court of appeals as the record on appeal. The district clerk must then send it to the circuit clerk within the time provided by Rule 11. A copy of the agreed statement may be filed in place of the appendix required by Rule 30.

(e) Correction or Modification of the Record.

(1) If any difference arises about whether the record truly discloses what occurred in the district court, the difference must be submitted to and settled by that court and the record conformed accordingly.

(2) If anything material to either party is omitted from or misstated in the record by error or accident, the omission or misstatement may be corrected and a supplemental record may be certified and forwarded:

(A) on stipulation of the parties;

(B) by the district court before or after the record has been forwarded; or

(C) by the court of appeals.

(3) All other questions as to the form and content of the record must be presented to the court of appeals.

(As amended Apr. 30, 1979, eff. Aug. 1, 1979; Mar. 10, 1986, eff. July 1, 1986; Apr. 30, 1991, eff. Dec. 1, 1991; Apr. 22, 1993, eff. Dec. 1, 1993; Apr. 27, 1995, eff. Dec. 1, 1995; Apr. 24, 1998, eff. Dec. 1, 1998; Mar. 26, 2009, eff. Dec. 1, 2009.)

Notes of Advisory Committee on Rules—1967

This rule is derived from FRCP 75 (a), (b), (c) and (d) and FRCP 76, without change in substance.

Notes of Advisory Committee on Rules—1979 Amendment

The proposed amendments to Rule 10(b) would require the appellant to place with the reporter a written order for the transcript of proceedings and file a copy with the clerk, and to indicate on the order if the transcript is to be provided under the Criminal Justice Act. If the appellant does not plan to order a transcript of any of the proceedings, he must file a certificate to that effect. These requirements make the appellant's steps in readying the appeal a matter of record and give the district court notice of requests for transcripts at the expense of the United States under the Criminal Justice Act. They are also the third step in giving the court of appeals some control over the production and transmission of the record. See Note to Rules 3(d)(e) above and Rule 11 below.

In the event the appellant orders no transcript, or orders a transcript of less than all the proceedings, the procedure under the proposed amended rule remains substantially as before. The appellant must serve on the appellee a copy of his order or in the event no order is placed, of the certificate to that effect, and a statement of the issues he intends to present on appeal, and the appellee may thereupon designate additional parts of the transcript to be included, and upon appellant's refusal to order the additional parts, may either order them himself or seek an order requiring the appellant to order them. The only change proposed in this procedure is to place a 10 day time limit on motions to require the appellant to order the additional portions.

Rule 10(b) is made subject to local rules of the courts of appeals in recognition of the practice in some circuits in some classes of cases, e. g., appeals by indigents in criminal cases after a short trial, of ordering immediate preparation of a

Rule 11. Forwarding the Record

complete transcript, thus making compliance with the rule unnecessary.

Notes of Advisory Committee on Rules—1986 Amendment

The amendments to Rules 10(b) and (c) are technical. No substantive change is intended.

Notes of Advisory Committee on Rules—1993 Amendment

The amendment is technical and no substantive change is intended.

Notes of Advisory Committee on Rules—1995 Amendment

Subdivision (b)(1). The amendment conforms this rule to amendments made in Rule 4(a)(4) in 1993. The amendments to Rule 4(a)(4) provide that certain postjudgment motions have the effect of suspending a filed notice of appeal until the disposition of the last of such motions. The purpose of this amendment is to suspend the 10-day period for ordering a transcript if a timely postjudgment motion is made and a notice of appeal is suspended under Rule 4(a)(4). The 10-day period set forth in the first sentence of this rule begins to run when the order disposing of the last of such postjudgment motions outstanding is entered.

Committee Notes on Rules—1998 Amendment

The language and organization of the rule are amended to make the rule more easily understood. In addition to changes made to improve the understanding, the Advisory Committee has changed language to make style and terminology consistent throughout the appellate rules. These changes are intended to be stylistic only.

Committee Notes on Rules—2009 Amendment

Subdivisions (b)(1), (b)(3), and (c). The times set in the former rule at 10 days have been revised to 14 days. See the Note to Rule 26.

References in Text

The Criminal Justice Act, referred to in subd. (b)(1)(A)(ii), probably means the Criminal Justice Act of 1964, Pub. L. 88–455, Aug. 20, 1964, 78 Stat. 552, as amended, which enacted section 3006A of Title 18, Crimes and Criminal Procedure, and provisions set out as notes under section 3006A of Title 18. For complete classification of this Act to the Code, see Short Title note set out under section 3006A of Title 18 and Tables.

Rule 11. Forwarding the Record

(a) Appellant's Duty. An appellant filing a notice of appeal must comply with Rule 10(b) and must do whatever else is necessary to enable the clerk to assemble and forward the record. If there are multiple appeals from a judgment or order, the clerk must forward a single record.

(b) Duties of Reporter and District Clerk.

(1) *Reporter's Duty to Prepare and File a Transcript.* The reporter must prepare and file a transcript as follows:

(A) Upon receiving an order for a transcript, the reporter must enter at the foot of the order the date of its receipt and the expected completion date and send a copy, so endorsed, to the circuit clerk.

(B) If the transcript cannot be completed within 30 days of the reporters receipt of the order, the reporter may request the circuit clerk to grant additional time to complete it. The clerk must note on the docket the action taken and notify the parties.

(C) When a transcript is complete, the reporter must file it with the district clerk and notify the circuit clerk of the filing.

(D) If the reporter fails to file the transcript on time, the circuit clerk must notify the district judge and do whatever else the court of appeals directs.

Rule 11. Forwarding the Record

(2) *District Clerk's Duty to Forward.* When the record is complete, the district clerk must number the documents constituting the record and send them promptly to the circuit clerk together with a list of the documents correspondingly numbered and reasonably identified. Unless directed to do so by a party or the circuit clerk, the district clerk will not send to the court of appeals documents of unusual bulk or weight, physical exhibits other than documents, or other parts of the record designated for omission by local rule of the court of appeals. If the exhibits are unusually bulky or heavy, a party must arrange with the clerks in advance for their transportation and receipt.

(c) Retaining the Record Temporarily in the District Court for Use in Preparing the Appeal. The parties may stipulate, or the district court on motion may order, that the district clerk retain the record temporarily for the parties to use in preparing the papers on appeal. In that event the district clerk must certify to the circuit clerk that the record on appeal is complete. Upon receipt of the appellee's brief, or earlier if the court orders or the parties agree, the appellant must request the district clerk to forward the record.

(d) [Abrogated.]

(e) Retaining the Record by Court Order.

(1) The court of appeals may, by order or local rule, provide that a certified copy of the docket entries be forwarded instead of the entire record. But a party may at any time during the appeal request that designated parts of the record be forwarded.

(2) The district court may order the record or some part of it retained if the court needs it while the appeal is pending, subject, however, to call by the court of appeals.

(3) If part or all of the record is ordered retained, the district clerk must send to the court of appeals a copy of the order and the docket entries together with the parts of the original record allowed by the district court and copies of any parts of the record designated by the parties.

(f) Retaining Parts of the Record in the District Court by Stipulation of the Parties. The parties may agree by written stipulation filed in the district court that designated parts of the record be retained in the district court subject to call by the court of appeals or request by a party. The parts of the record so designated remain a part of the record on appeal.

(g) Record for a Preliminary Motion in the Court of Appeals. If, before the record is forwarded, a party makes any of the following motions in the court of appeals:

- for dismissal;
- for release;
- for a stay pending appeal;
- for additional security on the bond on appeal or on a supersedeas bond; or
- for any other intermediate order—

the district clerk must send the court of appeals any parts of the record designated by any party.

(As amended Apr. 30, 1979, eff. Aug. 1, 1979; Mar. 10, 1986, eff. July 1, 1986; Apr. 24, 1998, eff. Dec. 1, 1998.)

Notes of Advisory Committee on Rules—1967

Subdivisions (a) and (b). These subdivisions are derived from FRCP 73 (g) and FRCP 75 (e). FRCP 75 (e) presently directs the clerk of the district court to transmit the record within the time allowed or fixed for its filing, which, under the provisions of FRCP 73 (g) is within 40 days from the date of filing the notice of appeal, unless an extension is obtained from the district court. The precise time at which the record must be transmitted thus depends upon the time required for delivery of the record from the district court to the court of appeals, since, to permit its timely filing, it must reach the court of appeals before expiration of the 40-day period of an extension thereof. Subdivision (a) of this rule provides that the record is to be transmitted within the 40-day period, or any extension thereof; subdivision (b) provides that transmission is effected when the clerk of the district court mails or otherwise forwards the record to the clerk of the court of appeals; Rule 12(b) directs the clerk of the court of appeals to file the record upon its receipt following timely docketing and transmittal. It can thus be determined with certainty precisely when the clerk of the district court must forward the record to the clerk of the court of appeals in order to effect timely filing: the final day of the 40-day period or of any extension thereof.

Subdivision (c). This subdivision is derived from FRCP 75 (e) without change of substance.

Subdivision (d). This subdivision is derived from FRCP 73 (g) and FRCrP 39 (c). Under present rules the district court is empowered to extend the time for filing the record and docketing the appeal. Since under the proposed rule timely transmission now insures timely filing (see note to subdivisions (a) and (b) above) the power of the district court is

Rule 11. Forwarding the Record

expressed in terms of its power to extend the time for transmitting the record. Restriction of that power to a period of 90 days after the filing of the notice of appeal represents a change in the rule with respect to appeals in criminal cases. FRCrP 39 (c) now permits the district court to extend the time for filing and docketing without restriction. No good reason appears for a difference between the civil and criminal rule in this regard, and subdivision (d) limits the power of the district court to extend the time for transmitting the record in all cases to 90 days from the date of filing the notice of appeal, just as its power is now limited with respect to docketing and filing in civil cases. Subdivision (d) makes explicit the power of the court of appeals to permit the record to be filed at any time. See *Pyramid Motor Freight Corporation v. Ispass*, 330, U.S. 695, 67 S.Ct. 954, 91 L.Ed. 1184 (1947).

Subdivisions (e), (f) and (g). These subdivisions are derived from FRCP 75 (f), (a) and (g), respectively, without change of substance.

Notes of Advisory Committee on Rules—1979 Amendment

Under present Rule 11(a) it is provided that the record shall be transmitted to the court of appeals within 40 days after the filing of the notice of appeal. Under present Rule 11(d) the district court, on request made during the initial time or any extension thereof, and cause shown, may extend the time for the transmission of the record to a point not more than 90 days after the filing of the first notice of appeal. If the district court is without authority to grant a request to extend the time, or denies a request for extension, the appellant may make a motion for extension of time in the court of appeals. Thus the duty to see that the record is transmitted is placed on the appellant. Aside from ordering the transcript within the time prescribed the appellant has no control over the time at which the record is transmitted, since all steps beyond this point are in the hands of the reporter and the clerk. The proposed amendments recognize this fact and place the duty directly on the reporter and the clerk. After receiving the written order for the transcript (See Note to Rule 10(b) above), the reporter must acknowledge its receipt, indicate when he expects to have it completed, and mail the order so endorsed to the clerk of the court of appeals. Requests for extensions of time must be made by the reporter to the clerk of the court of appeals and action on such requests is entered on the docket. Thus from the point at which the transcript is ordered the clerk of the court of appeals is made aware of any delays. If the transcript is not filed on time, the clerk of the court of appeals will notify the district judge.

Present Rule 11(b) provides that the record shall be transmitted when it is "complete for the purposes of the appeal." The proposed amended rule continues this requirement. The record is complete for the purposes of the appeal when it contains the original papers on file in the clerk's office, all necessary exhibits, and the transcript, if one is to be included. Cf. present Rule 11(c). The original papers will be in the custody of the clerk of the district court at the time the notice of appeal is filed. See Rule 5(e) of the F.R.C.P. The custody of exhibits is often the subject of local rules. Some of them require that documentary exhibits must be deposited with the clerk. See Local Rule 13 of the Eastern District of Virginia. Others leave exhibits with counsel, subject to order of the court. See Local Rule 33 of the Northern District of Illinois. If under local rules the custody of exhibits is left with counsel, the district court should make adequate provision for their preservation during the time during which an appeal may be taken, the prompt deposit with the clerk of such as under Rule 11(b) are to be transmitted to the court of appeals, and the availability of others in the event that the court of appeals should require their transmission. Cf. Local Rule 11 of the Second Circuit.

Usually the record will be complete with the filing of the transcript. While the proposed amendment requires transmission "forthwith" when the record is complete, it was not designed to preclude a local requirement by the court of appeals that the original papers and exhibits be transmitted when complete without awaiting the filing of the transcript.

The proposed amendments continue the provision in the present rule that documents of unusual bulk or weight and physical exhibits other than documents shall not be transmitted without direction by the parties or by the court of appeals, and the requirement that the parties make special arrangements for transmission and receipt of exhibits of unusual bulk or weight. In addition, they give recognition to local rules that make transmission of other record items subject to order of the court of appeals. See Local Rule 4 of the Seventh Circuit.

Notes of Advisory Committee on Rules—1986 Amendment

The amendments to Rule 11(b) are technical. No substantive change is intended.

Committee Notes on Rules—1998 Amendment

The language and organization of the rule are amended to make the rule more easily understood. In addition to changes made to improve the understanding, the Advisory Committee has changed language to make style and terminology consistent throughout the appellate rules. These changes are intended to be stylistic only.

Rule 12. Docketing the Appeal; Filing a Representation Statement; Filing the Record

(a) Docketing the Appeal. Upon receiving the copy of the notice of appeal and the docket entries from the district clerk under Rule 3(d), the circuit clerk must docket the appeal under the title of the district-court action and must identify the appellant, adding the appellant's name if necessary.

(b) Filing a Representation Statement. Unless the court of appeals designates another time, the attorney who filed the notice of appeal must, within 14 days after filing the notice, file a statement with the circuit clerk naming the parties that the attorney represents on appeal.

(c) Filing the Record, Partial Record, or Certificate. Upon receiving the record, partial record, or district clerk's certificate as provided in Rule 11, the circuit clerk must file it and immediately notify all parties of the filing date.

(As amended Apr. 1, 1979, eff. Aug. 1, 1979; Mar. 10, 1986, eff. July 1, 1986; Apr. 22, 1993, eff. Dec. 1, 1993; Apr. 24, 1998, eff. Dec. 1, 1998; Mar. 26, 2009, eff. Dec. 1, 2009.)

Notes of Advisory Committee on Rules—1967

Subdivision (a). All that is involved in the docketing of an appeal is the payment of the docket fee. In practice, after the clerk of the court of appeals receives the record from the clerk of the district court he notifies the appellant of its receipt and requests payment of the fee. Upon receipt of the fee, the clerk enters the appeal upon the docket and files the record. The appellant is allowed to pay the fee at any time within the time allowed or fixed for transmission of the record and thereby to discharge his responsibility for docketing. The final sentence is added in the interest of facilitating future reference and citation and location of cases in indexes. Compare 3d Cir. Rule 10(2); 4th Cir. Rule 9(8); 6th Cir. Rule 14(1).

Subdivision (c). The rules of the circuits generally permit the appellee to move for dismissal in the event the appellant fails to effect timely filing of the record. See 1st Cir. Rule 21(3); 3d Cir. Rule 21(4); 5th Cir. Rule 16(1); 8th Cir. Rule 7(d).

Notes of Advisory Committee on Rules—1979 Amendment

Subdivision (a). Under present Rule 12(a) the appellant must pay the docket fee within the time fixed for the transmission of the record, and upon timely payment of the fee, the appeal is docketed. The proposed amendment takes the docketing out of the hands of the appellant. The fee is paid at the time the notice of appeal is filed and the appeal is entered on the docket upon receipt of a copy of the notice of appeal and of the docket entries, which are sent to the court of appeals under the provisions of Rule 3(d). This is designed to give the court of appeals control of its docket at the earliest possible time so that within the limits of its facilities and personnel it can screen cases for appropriately different treatment, expedite the proceedings through prehearing conferences or otherwise, and in general plan more effectively for the prompt disposition of cases.

Subdivision (b). The proposed amendment conforms the provision to the changes in Rule 11.

Notes of Advisory Committee on Rules—1986 Amendment

The amendment to Rule 12(a) is technical. No substantive change is intended.

Notes of Advisory Committee on Rules—1993 Amendment

Note to new subdivision (b). This amendment is a companion to the amendment of Rule 3(c). The Rule 3(c) amendment allows an attorney who represents more than one party on appeal to "specify" the appellants by general description rather than by naming them individually. The requirement added here is that whenever an attorney files a notice of appeal, the attorney must soon thereafter file a statement indicating all parties represented on the appeal by that attorney. Although the notice of appeal is the jurisdictional document and it must clearly indicate who is bringing the appeal, the representation statement will be helpful especially to the court of appeals in identifying the individual appellants.

The rule allows a court of appeals to require the filing of the representation statement at some time other than specified in the rule so that if a court of appeals requires a docketing statement or appearance form the representation statement may be combined with it.

Committee Notes on Rules—1998 Amendment

The language of the rule is amended to make the rule more easily understood. In addition to changes made to improve

Rule 12.1 Remand After an Indicative Ruling by the District Court on a Motion for Relief That Is Barred by a Pending Appeal

the understanding, the Advisory Committee has changed language to make style and terminology consistent throughout the appellate rules. These changes are intended to be stylistic only.

Committee Notes on Rules—2009 Amendment

Subdivision (b). The time set in the former rule at 10 days has been revised to 14 days. See the Note to Rule 26.

Rule 12.1 Remand After an Indicative Ruling by the District Court on a Motion for Relief That Is Barred by a Pending Appeal

(a) Notice to the Court of Appeals. If a timely motion is made in the district court for relief that it lacks authority to grant because of an appeal that has been docketed and is pending, the movant must promptly notify the circuit clerk if the district court states either that it would grant the motion or that the motion raises a substantial issue.

(b) Remand After an Indicative Ruling. If the district court states that it would grant the motion or that the motion raises a substantial issue, the court of appeals may remand for further proceedings but retains jurisdiction unless it expressly dismisses the appeal. If the court of appeals remands but retains jurisdiction, the parties must promptly notify the circuit clerk when the district court has decided the motion on remand.

(As added Mar. 26, 2009, eff. Dec. 1, 2009.)

Committee Notes on Rules—2009

This new rule corresponds to Federal Rule of Civil Procedure 62.1, which adopts for any motion that the district court cannot grant because of a pending appeal the practice that most courts follow when a party moves under Civil Rule 60(b) to vacate a judgment that is pending on appeal. After an appeal has been docketed and while it remains pending, the district court cannot grant relief under a rule such as Civil Rule 60(b) without a remand. But it can entertain the motion and deny it, defer consideration, state that it would grant the motion if the court of appeals remands for that purpose, or state that the motion raises a substantial issue. Experienced lawyers often refer to the suggestion for remand as an "indicative ruling." (Appellate Rule 4(a)(4) lists six motions that, if filed within the relevant time limit, suspend the effect of a notice of appeal filed before or after the motion is filed until the last such motion is disposed of. The district court has authority to grant the motion without resorting to the indicative ruling procedure.)

The procedure formalized by Rule 12.1 is helpful when relief is sought from an order that the court cannot reconsider because the order is the subject of a pending appeal. In the criminal context, the Committee anticipates that Rule 12.1 will be used primarily if not exclusively for newly discovered evidence motions under Criminal Rule 33(b)(1) (*see United States v. Cronic*, 466 U.S. 648, 667 n.42 (1984)), reduced sentence motions under Criminal Rule 35(b), and motions under 18 U.S.C. §3582(c).

Rule 12.1 does not attempt to define the circumstances in which an appeal limits or defeats the district court's authority to act in the face of a pending appeal. The rules that govern the relationship between trial courts and appellate courts may be complex, depending in part on the nature of the order and the source of appeal jurisdiction. Appellate Rule 12.1 applies only when those rules deprive the district court of authority to grant relief without appellate permission.

To ensure proper coordination of proceedings in the district court and in the court of appeals, the movant must notify the circuit clerk if the district court states that it would grant the motion or that the motion raises a substantial issue. The "substantial issue" standard may be illustrated by the following hypothetical: The district court grants summary judgment dismissing a case. While the plaintiff's appeal is pending, the plaintiff moves for relief from the judgment, claiming newly discovered evidence and also possible fraud by the defendant during the discovery process. If the district court reviews the motion and indicates that the motion "raises a substantial issue," the court of appeals may well wish to remand rather than proceed to determine the appeal.

If the district court states that it would grant the motion or that the motion raises a substantial issue, the movant may ask the court of appeals to remand so that the district court can make its final ruling on the motion. In accordance with Rule 47(a)(1), a local rule may prescribe the format for the litigants' notifications and the district court's statement.

Remand is in the court of appeals' discretion. The court of appeals may remand all proceedings, terminating the initial appeal. In the context of postjudgment motions, however, that procedure should be followed only when the appellant has stated clearly its intention to abandon the appeal. The danger is that if the initial appeal is terminated and the district court then denies the requested relief, the time for appealing the initial judgment will have run out and a court might rule

Rule 12.1 Remand After an Indicative Ruling by the District Court on a Motion for Relief That Is Barred by a Pending Appeal

that the appellant is limited to appealing the denial of the postjudgment motion. The latter appeal may well not provide the appellant with the opportunity to raise all the challenges that could have been raised on appeal from the underlying judgment. *See, e.g., Browder v. Dir., Dep't of Corrections of Ill.*, 434 U.S. 257, 263 n.7 (1978) ("[A]n appeal from denial of Rule 60(b) relief does not bring up the underlying judgment for review."). The Committee does not endorse the notion that a court of appeals should decide that the initial appeal was abandoned—despite the absence of any clear statement of intent to abandon the appeal—merely because an unlimited remand occurred, but the possibility that a court might take that troubling view underscores the need for caution in delimiting the scope of the remand.

The court of appeals may instead choose to remand for the sole purpose of ruling on the motion while retaining jurisdiction to proceed with the appeal after the district court rules on the motion (if the appeal is not moot at that point and if any party wishes to proceed). This will often be the preferred course in the light of the concerns expressed above. It is also possible that the court of appeals may wish to proceed to hear the appeal even after the district court has granted relief on remand; thus, even when the district court indicates that it would grant relief, the court of appeals may in appropriate circumstances choose a limited rather than unlimited remand.

If the court of appeals remands but retains jurisdiction, subdivision (b) requires the parties to notify the circuit clerk when the district court has decided the motion on remand. This is a joint obligation that is discharged when the required notice is given by any litigant involved in the motion in the district court.

When relief is sought in the district court during the pendency of an appeal, litigants should bear in mind the likelihood that a new or amended notice of appeal will be necessary in order to challenge the district court's disposition of the motion. *See, e.g., Jordan v. Bowen*, 808 F.2d 733, 736–37 (10th Cir. 1987) (viewing district court's response to appellant's motion for indicative ruling as a denial of appellant's request for relief under Rule 60(b), and refusing to review that denial because appellant had failed to take an appeal from the denial); *TAAG Linhas Aereas de Angola v. Transamerica Airlines, Inc.*, 915 F.2d 1351, 1354 (9th Cir. 1990) ("[W]here a 60(b) motion is filed subsequent to the notice of appeal and considered by the district court after a limited remand, an appeal specifically from the ruling on the motion must be taken if the issues raised in that motion are to be considered by the Court of Appeals.").

Changes Made After Publication and Comment. No changes were made to the text of Rule 12.1. The Appellate Rules Committee made two changes to the Note in response to public comments, and made additional changes in consultation with the Civil Rules Committee and in response to some Appellate Rules Committee members' suggestions. The Standing Committee made two further changes to the Note.

As published for comment, the second paragraph of the Note read: "[Appellate Rule 12.1 is not limited to the Civil Rule 62.1 context; Rule 12.1 may also be used, for example, in connection with motions under Criminal Rule 33. *See United States v. Cronic*, 466 U.S. 648, 667 n.42 (1984).] The procedure formalized by Rule 12.1 is helpful whenever relief is sought from an order that the court cannot reconsider because the order is the subject of a pending appeal." The Appellate Rules Committee discussed the Solicitor General's concern that Appellate Rule 12.1 might be misused in the criminal context. In response, the Appellate Rules Committee deleted the second paragraph as published and substituted the following language: "The procedure formalized by Rule 12.1 is helpful when relief is sought from an order that the court cannot reconsider because the order is the subject of a pending appeal. In the criminal context, the Committee anticipates that Rule 12.1's use will be limited to newly discovered evidence motions under Criminal Rule 33(b)(1) (*see United States v. Cronic*, 466 U.S. 648, 667 n.42 (1984)), reduced sentence motions under Criminal Rule 35(b), and motions under 18 U.S.C. §3582(c)." The Standing Committee further revised the latter sentence to read: "In the criminal context, the Committee anticipates that Rule 12.1 will be used primarily if not exclusively for newly discovered evidence motions under Criminal Rule 33(b)(1) (*see United States v. Cronic*, 466 U.S. 648, 667 n.42 (1984)), reduced sentence motions under Criminal Rule 35(b), and motions under 18 U.S.C. §3582(c)."

As published for comment, the first sentence of the Note's last paragraph read: "When relief is sought in the district court during the pendency of an appeal, litigants should bear in mind the likelihood that a separate notice of appeal will be necessary in order to challenge the district court's disposition of the motion." In response to a suggestion by Public Citizen, the Appellate Rules Committee revised this sentence to refer to a "new or amended" notice of appeal rather than a "separate" notice of appeal.

The Appellate Rules Committee, in consultation with the Civil Rules Committee, added the following parenthetical at the end of the Note's first paragraph: "(The effect of a notice of appeal on district-court authority is addressed by Appellate Rule 4(a)(4), which lists six motions that, if filed within the relevant time limit, suspend the effect of a notice of appeal filed before or after the motion is filed until the last such motion is disposed of. The district court has authority to grant the motion without resorting to the indicative ruling procedure.)" This parenthetical is designed to forestall confusion concerning the effect of tolling motions on a district court's power to act. The Standing Committee approved a change to the first sentence of the parenthetical; it now reads: "Appellate Rule 4(a)(4) lists six motions that, if filed within the relevant time limit, suspend the effect of a notice of appeal filed before or after the motion is filed until the last such motion is disposed of."

Rule 13. Review of a Decision of the Tax Court

The Appellate Rules Committee, acting at the suggestion of the Civil Rules Committee, altered the wording of one sentence in the first paragraph and one sentence in the fifth paragraph of the Note. The changes are designed to remove references to remands of "the action," since those references would be in tension with the Note's advice concerning the advisability of limited remands. Thus, in the Note's first paragraph "if the action is remanded" became "if the court of appeals remands for that purpose," and in the Note's fifth paragraph "may ask the court of appeals to remand the action" became "may ask the court of appeals to remand."

The Appellate Rules Committee also made stylistic changes to the Note's first and third paragraphs. "Experienced appeal lawyers" became "Experienced lawyers," and "act in face of a pending appeal" became "act in the face of a pending appeal."

TITLE III. REVIEW OF A DECISION OF THE UNITED STATES TAX COURT

Rule 13. Review of a Decision of the Tax Court

(a) Appeal as of Right.

(1) *How Obtained; Time for Filing Notice of Appeal.*

(A) An appeal as of right from the United States Tax Court is commenced by filing a notice of appeal with the Tax Court clerk within 90 days after the entry of the Tax Court's decision. At the time of filing, the appellant must furnish the clerk with enough copies of the notice to enable the clerk to comply with Rule 3(d). If one party files a timely notice of appeal, any other party may file a notice of appeal within 120 days after the Tax Court's decision is entered.

(B) If, under Tax Court rules, a party makes a timely motion to vacate or revise the Tax Court's decision, the time to file a notice of appeal runs from the entry of the order disposing of the motion or from the entry of a new decision, whichever is later.

(2) *Notice of Appeal; How Filed.* The notice of appeal may be filed either at the Tax Court clerk's office in the District of Columbia or by mail addressed to the clerk. If sent by mail the notice is considered filed on the postmark date, subject to §7502 of the Internal Revenue Code, as amended, and the applicable regulations.

(3) *Contents of the Notice of Appeal; Service; Effect of Filing and Service.* Rule 3 prescribes the contents of a notice of appeal, the manner of service, and the effect of its filing and service. Form 2 in the Appendix of Forms is a suggested form of a notice of appeal.

(4) *The Record on Appeal; Forwarding; Filing.*

(A) Except as otherwise provided under Tax Court rules for the transcript of proceedings, the appeal is governed by the parts of Rules 10, 11, and 12 regarding the record on appeal from a district court, the time and manner of forwarding and filing, and the docketing in the court of appeals.

(B) If an appeal is taken to more than one court of appeals, the original record must be sent to the court named in the first notice of appeal filed. In an appeal to any other court of appeals, the appellant must apply to that other court to make provision for the record.

(b) Appeal by Permission. An appeal by permission is governed by Rule 5.

(As amended Apr. 1, 1979, eff. Aug. 1, 1979; Apr. 29, 1994, eff. Dec. 1, 1994; Apr. 24, 1998, eff. Dec. 1, 1998; Apr. 16, 2013, eff. Dec. 1, 2013.)

Notes of Advisory Committee on Rules—1967

Subdivision (a). This subdivision effects two changes in practice respecting review of Tax Court decisions: (1) Section 7483 of the Internal Revenue Code, 68A Stat. 891, 26 U.S.C. §7483, provides that review of a Tax Court decision may be obtained by filing a petition for review. The subdivision provides for review by the filing of the simple and familiar notice of appeal used to obtain review of district court judgments; (2) Section 7483, *supra*, requires that a petition for review be filed within 3 months after a decision is rendered, and provides that if a petition is so filed by one party, any other party may file a petition for review within 4 months after the decision is rendered. In the interest of fixing the time for review with precision, the proposed rule substitutes "90 days" and "120 days" for the statutory "3 months" and "4 months", respectively. The power of the Court to regulate these details of practice is clear. Title 28 U.S.C. §2072, as amended by the Act of November 6, 1966, 80 Stat. 1323 (1 U.S. Code Cong. & Ad. News, p. 1546 (1966)), authorizes the Court to regulate ".

Rule 14. Applicability of Other Rules to the Review of a Tax Court Decision

. . practice and procedure in proceedings for the review by the courts of appeals of decisions of the Tax Court of the United States. . . ."

The second paragraph states the settled teaching of the case law. See *Robert Louis Stevenson Apartments, Inc. v. C.I.R.*, 337 F.2d 681, 10 A.L.R.3d 112 (8th Cir., 1964); *Denholm & McKay Co. v. C.I.R.*, 132 F.2d 243 (1st Cir., 1942); *Helvering v. Continental Oil Co.*, 63 App.D.C. 5, 68 F.2d 750 (1934); *Burnet v. Lexington Ice & Coal Co.*, 62 F.2d 906 (4th Cir., 1933); *Griffiths v. C.I.R.*, 50 F.2d 782 (7th Cir., 1931).

Subdivision (b). The subdivision incorporates the statutory provision (Title 26, U.S.C. §7502) that timely mailing is to be treated as timely filing. The statute contains special provisions respecting other than ordinary mailing. If the notice of appeal is sent by registered mail, registration is deemed prima facie evidence that the notice was delivered to the clerk of the Tax Court, and the date of registration is deemed the postmark date. If the notice of appeal is sent by certified mail, the effect of certification with respect to prima facie evidence of delivery and the postmark date depends upon regulations of the Secretary of the Treasury. The effect of a postmark made other than by the United States Post Office likewise depends upon regulations of the Secretary. Current regulations are found in 26 CFR §301.7502–1.

Notes of Advisory Committee on Rules—1979 Amendment

The proposed amendment reflects the change in the title of the Tax Court to "United States Tax Court." See 26 U.S.C. §7441.

Notes of Advisory Committee on Rules—1994 Amendment

Subdivision (a). The amendment requires a party filing a notice of appeal to provide the court with sufficient copies of the notice for service on all other parties.

Committee Notes on Rules—1998 Amendment

The language and organization of the rule are amended to make the rule more easily understood. In addition to changes made to improve the understanding, the Advisory Committee has changed language to make style and terminology consistent throughout the appellate rules. These changes are intended to be stylistic only.

Committee Notes on Rules—2013 Amendment

Rules 13 and 14 are amended to address the treatment of permissive interlocutory appeals from the Tax Court under 26 U.S.C. §7482(a)(2). Rules 13 and 14 do not currently address such appeals; instead, those Rules address only appeals as of right from the Tax Court. The existing Rule 13—governing appeals as of right—is revised and becomes Rule 13(a). New subdivision (b) provides that Rule 5 governs appeals by permission. The definition of district court and district clerk in current subdivision (d)(1) is deleted; definition are now addressed in Rule 14. The caption of Title III is amended to reflect the broadened application of this Title.

Changes Made After Publication and Comment. No changes were made after publication and comment.

References in Text

Section 7502 of the Internal Revenue Code, referred to in subd. (b), is classified to section 112 of Title 26, Internal Revenue Code.

Rule 14. Applicability of Other Rules to the Review of a Tax Court Decision

All provisions of these rules, except Rules 4, 6-9, 15–20, and 22–23, apply to appeals from the Tax Court. References in any applicable rule (other than Rule 24(a)) to the district court and district clerk are to be read as referring to the Tax Court and its clerk.
(As amended Apr. 24, 1998, eff. Dec. 1, 1998; Apr. 16, 2013, eff. Dec. 1, 2013.)

Notes of Advisory Committee on Rules—1967

The proposed rule continues the present uniform practice of the circuits of regulating review of decisions of the Tax

Rule 15. Review or Enforcement of an Agency Order

Court by the general rules applicable to appeals from judgments of the district courts.

Committee Notes on Rules—1998 Amendment

The language of the rule is amended to make the rule more easily understood. In addition to changes made to improve the understanding, the Advisory Committee has changed language to make style and terminology consistent throughout the appellate rules. These changes are intended to be stylistic only.

Committee Notes on Rules—2013 Amendment

Rule 13 currently addresses appeals as of right from the Tax Court, and Rule 14 currently addresses the applicability of the Appellate Rules to such appeals. Rule 13 is amended to add a new subdivision (b) treating permissive interlocutory appeals from the Tax Court under 26 U.S.C. § 7482(a)(2). Rule 14 is amended to address the applicability of the Appellate Rules to both appeals as of right and appeals by permission. Because the latter are governed by Rule 5, that rule is deleted from Rule 14's list of inapplicable provisions. Rule 14 is amended to define the terms "district court" and "district clerk" in applicable rules (excluding Rule 24(a)) to include the Tax Court and its clerk. Rule 24(a) is excluded from this definition because motions to appeal from the Tax Court in forma pauperis are governed by Rule 24(b), not Rule 24(a).

Changes Made After Publication and Comment. No changes were made after publication and comment.

TITLE IV. REVIEW OR ENFORCEMENT OF AN ORDER OF AN ADMINISTRATIVE AGENCY, BOARD, COMMISSION, OR OFFICER

Rule 15. Review or Enforcement of an Agency Order

(a) Petition for Review; Joint Petition.

(1) Review of an agency order is commenced by filing, within the time prescribed by law, a petition for review with the clerk of a court of appeals authorized to review the agency order. If their interests make joinder practicable, two or more persons may join in a petition to the same court to review the same order.

(2) The petition must:

(A) name each party seeking review either in the caption or the body of the petition—using such terms as "et al.," "petitioners," or "respondents" does not effectively name the parties;

(B) name the agency as a respondent (even though not named in the petition, the United States is a respondent if required by statute); and

(C) specify the order or part thereof to be reviewed.

(3) Form 3 in the Appendix of Forms is a suggested form of a petition for review.

(4) In this rule "agency" includes an agency, board, commission, or officer; "petition for review" includes a petition to enjoin, suspend, modify, or otherwise review, or a notice of appeal, whichever form is indicated by the applicable statute.

(b) Application or Cross-Application to Enforce an Order; Answer; Default.

(1) An application to enforce an agency order must be filed with the clerk of a court of appeals authorized to enforce the order. If a petition is filed to review an agency order that the court may enforce, a party opposing the petition may file a cross-application for enforcement.

(2) Within 21 days after the application for enforcement is filed, the respondent must serve on the applicant an answer to the application and file it with the clerk. If the respondent fails to answer in time, the court will enter judgment for the relief requested.

(3) The application must contain a concise statement of the proceedings in which the order was entered, the facts upon which venue is based, and the relief requested.

(c) Service of the Petition or Application. The circuit clerk must serve a copy of the petition for review, or an application or cross-application to enforce an agency order, on each respondent as prescribed by Rule 3(d), unless a different manner of service is prescribed by statute. At the time of filing, the petitioner must:

(1) serve, or have served, a copy on each party admitted to participate in the agency proceedings, except for the respondents;

(2) file with the clerk a list of those so served; and

Rule 15. Review or Enforcement of an Agency Order

(3) give the clerk enough copies of the petition or application to serve each respondent.

(d) Intervention. Unless a statute provides another method, a person who wants to intervene in a proceeding under this rule must file a motion for leave to intervene with the circuit clerk and serve a copy on all parties. The motion—or other notice of intervention authorized by statute—must be filed within 30 days after the petition for review is filed and must contain a concise statement of the interest of the moving party and the grounds for intervention.

(e) Payment of Fees. When filing any separate or joint petition for review in a court of appeals, the petitioner must pay the circuit clerk all required fees.

(As amended Apr. 22, 1993, eff. Dec. 1, 1993; Apr. 24, 1998, eff. Dec. 1, 1998; Mar. 26, 2009, eff. Dec. 1, 2009.)

Notes of Advisory Committee on Rules—1967

General Note. The power of the Supreme Court to prescribe rules of practice and procedure for the judicial review or enforcement of orders of administrative agencies, boards, commissions, and officers is conferred by 28 U.S.C. §2072, as amended by the Act of November 6, 1966, §1, 80 Stat. 1323 (1 U.S. Code Cong. & Ad. News, p. 1546 (1966)). Section 11 of the Hobbs Administrative Orders Review Act of 1950, 64 Stat. 1132, reenacted as 28 U.S.C. §2352 (28 U.S.C.A. §2352 (Suppl. 1966)), repealed by the Act of November 6, 1966, §4, *supra*, directed the courts of appeals to adopt and promulgate, subject to approval by the Judicial Conference rules governing practice and procedure in proceedings to review the orders of boards, commissions and officers whose orders were made reviewable in the courts of appeals by the Act. Thereafter, the Judicial Conference approved a uniform rule, and that rule, with minor variations, is now in effect in all circuits. Third Circuit Rule 18 is a typical circuit rule, and for convenience it is referred to as the uniform rule in the notes which accompany rules under this Title.

Subdivision (a). The uniform rule (see General Note above) requires that the petition for review contain "a concise statement, in barest outline, of the nature of the proceedings as to which relief is sought, the facts upon which venue is based, the grounds upon which relief is sought, and the relief prayed." That language is derived from Section 4 of the Hobbs Administrative Orders Review Act of 1950, 64 Stat. 1130, reenacted as 28 U.S.C. §2344 (28 U.S.C.A. §2344 (Suppl. 1966)). A few other statutes also prescribe the content of the petition, but the great majority are silent on the point. The proposed rule supersedes 28 U.S.C. §2344 and other statutory provisions prescribing the form of the petition for review and permits review to be initiated by the filing of a simple petition similar in form to the notice of appeal used in appeals from judgments of district courts. The more elaborate form of petition for review now required is rarely useful either to the litigants or to the courts. There is no effective, reasonable way of obliging petitioners to come to the real issues before those issues are formulated in the briefs. Other provisions of this subdivision are derived from sections 1 and 2 of the uniform rule.

Subdivision (b). This subdivision is derived from sections 3, 4 and 5 of the uniform rule.

Subdivision (c). This subdivision is derived from section 1 of the uniform rule.

Subdivision (d). This subdivision is based upon section 6 of the uniform rule. Statutes occasionally permit intervention by the filing of a notice of intention to intervene. The uniform rule does not fix a time limit for intervention, and the only time limits fixed by statute are the 30–day periods found in the Communications Act Amendments, 1952, §402(e), 66 Stat. 719, 47 U.S.C. §402(e), and the Sugar Act of 1948, §205(d), 61 Stat. 927, 7 U.S.C. §1115(d).

Notes of Advisory Committee on Rules—1993 Amendment

Subdivision (a). The amendment is a companion to the amendment of Rule 3(c). Both Rule 3(c) and Rule 15(a) state that a notice of appeal or petition for review must name the parties seeking appellate review. Rule 3(c), however, provides an attorney who represents more than one party on appeal the flexibility to describe the parties in general terms rather than naming them individually. Rule 15(a) does not allow that flexibility; each petitioner must be named. A petition for review of an agency decision is the first filing in any court and, therefore, is analogous to a complaint in which all parties must be named.

Subdivision (e). The amendment adds subdivision (e). Subdivision (e) parallels Rule 3(e) that requires the payment of fees when filing a notice of appeal. The omission of such a requirement from Rule 15 is an apparent oversight. Five circuits have local rules requiring the payment of such fees, *see, e.g.*, Fifth Cir. Loc. R. 15.1, and Fed. Cir. Loc. R. 15(a)(2).

Committee Notes on Rules—1998 Amendment

The language and organization of the rule are amended to make the rule more easily understood. In addition to changes made to improve the understanding, the Advisory Committee has changed language to make style and

Rule 15.1 Briefs and Oral Argument in a National Labor Relations Board Proceeding

terminology consistent throughout the appellate rules. These changes are intended to be stylistic only.

Committee Notes on Rules—2009 Amendment

Subdivision (b)(2). The time set in the former rule at 20 days has been revised to 21 days. See the Note to Rule 26.

Rule 15.1 Briefs and Oral Argument in a National Labor Relations Board Proceeding

In either an enforcement or a review proceeding, a party adverse to the National Labor Relations Board proceeds first on briefing and at oral argument, unless the court orders otherwise.
(As added Mar. 10, 1986, eff. July 1, 1986; amended Apr. 24, 1998, eff. Dec. 1, 1998.)

Notes of Advisory Committee on Rules—1986

This rule simply confirms the existing practice in most circuits.

Committee Notes on Rules—1998 Amendment

The language of the rule is amended to make the rule more easily understood. In addition to changes made to improve the understanding, the Advisory Committee has changed language to make style and terminology consistent throughout the appellate rules. These changes are intended to be stylistic only.

Rule 16. The Record on Review or Enforcement

(a) Composition of the Record. The record on review or enforcement of an agency order consists of:
    (1) the order involved;
    (2) any findings or report on which it is based; and
    (3) the pleadings, evidence, and other parts of the proceedings before the agency.

(b) Omissions From or Misstatements in the Record. The parties may at any time, by stipulation, supply any omission from the record or correct a misstatement, or the court may so direct. If necessary, the court may direct that a supplemental record be prepared and filed.
(As amended Apr. 24, 1998, eff. Dec. 1, 1998.)

Notes of Advisory Committee on Rules—1967

Subdivision (a) is based upon 28 U.S.C. §2112(b). There is no distinction between the record compiled in the agency proceeding and the record on review; they are one and the same. The record in agency cases is thus the same as that in appeals from the district court—the original papers, transcripts and exhibits in the proceeding below. Subdivision (b) is based upon section 8 of the uniform rule (see General Note following Rule 15).

Committee Notes on Rules—1998 Amendment

The language and organization of the rule are amended to make the rule more easily understood. In addition to changes made to improve the understanding, the Advisory Committee has changed language to make style and terminology consistent throughout the appellate rules. These changes are intended to be stylistic only.

Rule 17. Filing the Record

(a) Agency to File; Time for Filing; Notice of Filing. The agency must file the record with the circuit clerk within 40 days after being served with a petition for review, unless the statute authorizing review provides otherwise, or within 40 days after it files an application for enforcement unless the respondent fails to answer or the court orders otherwise. The court may shorten or extend the time to file the record. The clerk must notify all parties of the date when the record is filed.
(b) Filing—What Constitutes.
    (1) The agency must file:

Rule 18. Stay Pending Review

(A) the original or a certified copy of the entire record or parts designated by the parties; or

(B) a certified list adequately describing all documents, transcripts of testimony, exhibits, and other material constituting the record, or describing those parts designated by the parties.

(2) The parties may stipulate in writing that no record or certified list be filed. The date when the stipulation is filed with the circuit clerk is treated as the date when the record is filed.

(3) The agency must retain any portion of the record not filed with the clerk. All parts of the record retained by the agency are a part of the record on review for all purposes and, if the court or a party so requests, must be sent to the court regardless of any prior stipulation.

(As amended Apr. 24, 1998, eff. Dec. 1, 1998.)

Notes of Advisory Committee on Rules—1967

Subdivision (a). This subdivision is based upon section 7 of the uniform rule (see General Note following Rule 15). That rule does not prescribe a time for filing the record in enforcement cases. Forty days are allowed in order to avoid useless preparation of the record or certified list in cases where the application for enforcement is not contested.

Subdivision (b). This subdivision is based upon 28 U.S.C. §2112 and section 7 of the uniform rule. It permits the agency to file either the record itself or a certified list of its contents. It also permits the parties to stipulate against transmission of designated parts of the record without the fear that an inadvertent stipulation may "diminish" the record. Finally, the parties may, in cases where consultation of the record is unnecessary, stipulate that neither the record nor a certified list of its contents be filed.

Committee Notes on Rules—1998 Amendment

The language and organization of the rule are amended to make the rule more easily understood. In addition to changes made to improve the understanding, the Advisory Committee has changed language to make style and terminology consistent throughout the appellate rules. These changes are intended to be stylistic only; a substantive change is made, however, in subdivision (b).

Subdivision (b). The current rule provides that when a court of appeals is asked to review or enforce an agency order, the agency must file either "the entire record or such parts thereof as the parties may designate by stipulation filed with the agency" or a certified list describing the documents, transcripts, exhibits, and other material constituting the record. If the agency is not filing a certified list, the current rule requires the agency to file the entire record unless the parties file a "stipulation" designating only parts of the record. Such a "stipulation" presumably requires agreement of the parties as to the parts to be filed. The amended language in subparagraph (b)(1)(A) permits the agency to file the entire record or "parts designated by the parties." The new language permits the filing of less than the entire record even when the parties do not agree as to which parts should be filed. Each party can designate the parts that it wants filed; the agency can then forward the parts designated by each party. In contrast, paragraph (b)(2) continues to require stipulation, that is agreement of the parties, that the agency need not file either the record or a certified list.

Rule 18. Stay Pending Review

(a) Motion for a Stay.

(1) *Initial Motion Before the Agency.* A petitioner must ordinarily move first before the agency for a stay pending review of its decision or order.

(2) *Motion in the Court of Appeals.* A motion for a stay may be made to the court of appeals or one of its judges.

(A) The motion must:

(i) show that moving first before the agency would be impracticable; or

(ii) state that, a motion having been made, the agency denied the motion or failed to afford the relief requested and state any reasons given by the agency for its action.

(B) The motion must also include:

(i) the reasons for granting the relief requested and the facts relied on;

(ii) originals or copies of affidavits or other sworn statements supporting facts subject to dispute; and

(iii) relevant parts of the record.

(C) The moving party must give reasonable notice of the motion to all parties.

Rule 19. Settlement of a Judgment Enforcing an Agency Order in Part

(D) The motion must be filed with the circuit clerk and normally will be considered by a panel of the court. But in an exceptional case in which time requirements make that procedure impracticable, the motion may be made to and considered by a single judge.

(b) Bond. The court may condition relief on the filing of a bond or other appropriate security.

(As amended Apr. 24, 1998, eff. Dec. 1, 1998.)

Notes of Advisory Committee on Rules—1967

While this rule has no counterpart in present rules regulating review of agency proceedings, it merely assimilates the procedure for obtaining stays in agency proceedings with that for obtaining stays in appeals from the district courts. The same considerations which justify the requirement of an initial application to the district court for a stay pending appeal support the requirement of an initial application to the agency pending review. See Note accompanying Rule 8. Title 5, U.S.C. §705 (5 U.S.C.A. §705 (1966 Pamphlet)) confers general authority on both agencies and reviewing courts to stay agency action pending review. Many of the statutes authorizing review of agency action by the courts of appeals deal with the question of stays, and at least one, the Act of June 15, 1936, 49 Stat. 1499 (7 U.S.C. §10a), prohibits a stay pending review. The proposed rule in nowise affects such statutory provisions respecting stays. By its terms, it simply indicates the procedure to be followed when a stay is sought.

Committee Notes on Rules—1998 Amendment

The language and organization of the rule are amended to make the rule more easily understood. In addition to changes made to improve the understanding, the Advisory Committee has changed language to make style and terminology consistent throughout the appellate rules. These changes are intended to be stylistic only.

Rule 19. Settlement of a Judgment Enforcing an Agency Order in Part

When the court files an opinion directing entry of judgment enforcing the agency's order in part, the agency must within 14 days file with the clerk and serve on each other party a proposed judgment conforming to the opinion. A party who disagrees with the agency's proposed judgment must within 10 days file with the clerk and serve the agency with a proposed judgment that the party believes conforms to the opinion. The court will settle the judgment and direct entry without further hearing or argument.

(As amended Mar. 10, 1986, eff. July 1, 1986; Apr. 24, 1998, eff. Dec. 1, 1998; Mar. 26, 2009, eff. Dec. 1, 2009.)

Notes of Advisory Committee on Rules—1967

This is section 12 of the uniform rule (see General Note following Rule 15) with changes in phraseology.

Notes of Advisory Committee on Rules—1986 Amendment

The deletion of the words "in whole or" is designed to eliminate delay in the issuance of a judgment when the court of appeals has either enforced completely the order of an agency or denied completely such enforcement. In such a clear-cut situation, it serves no useful purpose to delay the issuance of the judgment until a proposed judgment is submitted by the agency and reviewed by the respondent. This change conforms the Rule to the existing practice in most circuits. Other amendments are technical and no substantive change is intended.

Committee Notes on Rules—1998 Amendment

The language of the rule is amended to make the rule more easily understood. In addition to changes made to improve the understanding, the Advisory Committee has changed language to make style and terminology consistent throughout the appellate rules. These changes are intended to be stylistic only.

Committee Notes on Rules—2009 Amendment

Rule 19 formerly required a party who disagreed with the agency's proposed judgment to file a proposed judgment "within 7 days." Under former Rule 26(a), "7 days" always meant at least 9 days and could mean as many as 11 or even 13 days. Under current Rule 26(a), intermediate weekends and holidays are counted. Changing the period from 7 to 10 days offsets the change in computation approach. See the Note to Rule 26.

Rule 20. Applicability of Rules to the Review or Enforcement of an Agency Order

All provisions of these rules, except Rules 3–14 and 22–23, apply to the review or enforcement of an agency order. In these rules, "appellant" includes a petitioner or applicant, and "appellee" includes a respondent.
(As amended Apr. 24, 1998, eff. Dec. 1, 1998.)

Notes of Advisory Committee on Rules—1967

The proposed rule continues the present uniform practice of the circuits of regulating agency review or enforcement proceedings by the general rules applicable to appeals from judgments of the district courts.

Committee Notes on Rules—1998 Amendment

The language of the rule is amended to make the rule more easily understood. In addition to changes made to improve the understanding, the Advisory Committee has changed language to make style and terminology consistent throughout the appellate rules. These changes are intended to be stylistic only.

TITLE V. EXTRAORDINARY WRITS

Rule 21. Writs of Mandamus and Prohibition, and Other Extraordinary Writs

(a) Mandamus or Prohibition to a Court: Petition, Filing, Service, and Docketing.
(1) A party petitioning for a writ of mandamus or prohibition directed to a court must file a petition with the circuit clerk with proof of service on all parties to the proceeding in the trial court. The party must also provide a copy to the trial-court judge. All parties to the proceeding in the trial court other than the petitioner are respondents for all purposes.
(2)(A) The petition must be titled "In re [name of petitioner]."
  (B) The petition must state:
    (i) the relief sought;
    (ii) the issues presented;
    (iii) the facts necessary to understand the issue presented by the petition; and
    (iv) the reasons why the writ should issue.
  (C) The petition must include a copy of any order or opinion or parts of the record that may be essential to understand the matters set forth in the petition.
(3) Upon receiving the prescribed docket fee, the clerk must docket the petition and submit it to the court.
(b) Denial; Order Directing Answer; Briefs; Precedence.
(1) The court may deny the petition without an answer. Otherwise, it must order the respondent, if any, to answer within a fixed time.
(2) The clerk must serve the order to respond on all persons directed to respond.
(3) Two or more respondents may answer jointly.
(4) The court of appeals may invite or order the trial-court judge to address the petition or may invite an amicus curiae to do so. The trial-court judge may request permission to address the petition but may not do so unless invited or ordered to do so by the court of appeals.
(5) If briefing or oral argument is required, the clerk must advise the parties, and when appropriate, the trial-court judge or amicus curiae.
(6) The proceeding must be given preference over ordinary civil cases.
(7) The circuit clerk must send a copy of the final disposition to the trial-court judge.
(c) Other Extraordinary Writs. An application for an extraordinary writ other than one provided for in Rule 21(a) must be made by filing a petition with the circuit clerk with proof of service on the respondents.

Rule 21. Writs of Mandamus and Prohibition, and Other Extraordinary Writs

Proceedings on the application must conform, so far as is practicable, to the procedures prescribed in Rule 21(a) and (b).

[The following text of subdivision (d) was effective until December 1, 2016.]

(d) Form of Papers; Number of Copies. All papers must conform to Rule 32(c)(2). Except by the court's permission, a paper must not exceed 30 pages, exclusive of the disclosure statement, the proof of service, and the accompanying documents required by Rule 21(a)(2)(C). An original and 3 copies must be filed unless the court requires the filing of a different number by local rule or by order in a particular case.

[The following text of subdivision (d) became effective December 1, 2016.]

(d) Form of Papers; Number of Copies; Length Limits. All papers must conform to Rule 32(c)(2). An original and 3 copies must be filed unless the court requires the filing of a different number by local rule or by order in a particular case. Except by the court's permission, and excluding the accompanying documents required by Rule 21(a)(2)(C):

(1) a paper produced using a computer must not exceed 7,800 words; and

(2) a handwritten or typewritten paper must not exceed 30 pages.

(As amended Apr. 29, 1994, eff. Dec. 1, 1994; Apr. 23, 1996, eff. Dec. 1, 1996; Apr. 24, 1998, eff. Dec. 1, 1998; Apr. 29, 2002, eff. Dec. 1, 2002; Apr. 28, 2016, eff. Dec. 1, 2016.)

Notes of Advisory Committee on Rules—1967

The authority of courts of appeals to issue extraordinary writs is derived from 28 U.S.C. §1651. Subdivisions (a) and (b) regulate in detail the procedure surrounding the writs most commonly sought—mandamus or prohibition directed to a judge or judges. Those subdivisions are based upon Supreme Court Rule 31, with certain changes which reflect the uniform practice among the circuits (Seventh Circuit Rule 19 is a typical circuit rule). Subdivision (c) sets out a very general procedure to be followed in applications for the variety of other writs which may be issued under the authority of 28 U.S.C. §1651.

Notes of Advisory Committee on Rules—1994 Amendment

Subdivision (d). The amendment makes it clear that a court may require a different number of copies either by rule or by order in an individual case. The number of copies of any document that a court of appeals needs varies depending upon the way in which the court conducts business. The internal operation of the courts of appeals necessarily varies from circuit to circuit because of differences in the number of judges, the geographic area included within the circuit, and other such factors. Uniformity could be achieved only by setting the number of copies artificially high so that parties in all circuits file enough copies to satisfy the needs of the court requiring the greatest number. Rather than do that, the Committee decided to make it clear that local rules may require a greater or lesser number of copies and that, if the circumstances of a particular case indicate the need for a different number of copies in that case, the court may so order.

Notes of Advisory Committee on Rules—1996 Amendment

In most instances, a writ of mandamus or prohibition is not actually directed to a judge in any more personal way than is an order reversing a court's judgment. Most often a petition for a writ of mandamus seeks review of the intrinsic merits of a judge's action and is in reality an adversary proceeding between the parties. See, *e.g., Walker v. Columbia Broadcasting System, Inc.*, 443 F.2d 33 (7th Cir. 1971). In order to change the tone of the rule and of mandamus proceedings generally, the rule is amended so that the judge is not treated as a respondent. The caption and subdivision (a) are amended by deleting the reference to the writs as being "directed to a judge or judges."

Subdivision (a). Subdivision (a) applies to writs of mandamus or prohibition directed to a court, but it is amended so that a petition for a writ of mandamus or prohibition does not bear the name of the judge. The amendments to subdivision (a) speak, however, about mandamus or prohibition "directed to a court." This language is inserted to distinguish subdivision (a) from subdivision (c). Subdivision (c) governs all other extraordinary writs, including a writ of mandamus or prohibition directed to an administrative agency rather than to a court and a writ of habeas corpus.

The amendments require the petitioner to provide a copy of the petition to the trial court judge. This will alert the judge to the filing of the petition. This is necessary because the trial court judge is not treated as a respondent and, as a result, is not served. A companion amendment is made in subdivision (b). It requires the circuit clerk to send a copy of the disposition of the petition to the trial court judge.

Subdivision (b). The amendment provides that even if relief is requested of a particular judge, although the judge may request permission to respond, the judge may not do so unless the court invites or orders a response.

The court of appeals ordinarily will be adequately informed not only by the opinions or statements made by the trial court judge contemporaneously with the entry of the challenged order but also by the arguments made on behalf of the party opposing the relief. The latter does not create an attorney-client relationship between the party's attorney and the judge whose action is challenged, nor does it give rise to any right to compensation from the judge.

If the court of appeals desires to hear from the trial court judge, however, the court may invite or order the judge to respond. In some instances, especially those involving court administration or the failure of a judge to act, it may be that no one other than the judge can provide a thorough explanation of the matters at issue. Because it is ordinarily undesirable to place the trial court judge, even temporarily, in an adversarial posture with a litigant, the rule permits a court of appeals to invite an *amicus curiae* to provide a response to the petition. In those instances in which the respondent does not oppose issuance of the writ or does not have sufficient perspective on the issue to provide an adequate response, participation of an *amicus* may avoid the need for the trial judge to participate.

Subdivision (c). The changes are stylistic only. No substantive changes are intended.

Committee Notes on Rules—1998 Amendment

The language and organization of the rule are amended to make the rule more easily understood. In addition to changes made to improve the understanding, the Advisory Committee has changed language to make style and terminology consistent throughout the appellate rules. These changes are intended to be stylistic only.

Committee Notes on Rules—2002 Amendment

Subdivision (d). A petition for a writ of mandamus or prohibition, an application for another extraordinary writ, and an answer to such a petition or application are all "other papers" for purposes of Rule 32(c)(2), and all of the requirements of Rule 32(a) apply to those papers, except as provided in Rule 32(c)(2). During the 1998 restyling of the Federal Rules of Appellate Procedure, Rule 21(d) was inadvertently changed to suggest that only the requirements of Rule 32(a)(1) apply to such papers. Rule 21(d) has been amended to correct that error.

Rule 21(d) has been further amended to limit the length of papers filed under Rule 21.

Changes Made After Publication and Comments. No changes were made to the text of the proposed amendment or to the Committee Note, except that the page limit was increased from 20 pages to 30 pages. The Committee was persuaded by some commentators that petitions for extraordinary writs closely resemble principal briefs on the merits and should be allotted more than 20 pages.

Committee Notes on Rules – 2016 Amendment

The page limits previously employed in Rules 5, 21, 27, 35, and 40 have been largely overtaken by changes in technology. For papers produced using a computer, those page limits are now replaced by word limits. The word limits were derived from the current page limits using the assumption that one page is equivalent to 260 words. Papers produced using a computer must include the certificate of compliance required by Rule 32(g); Form 6 in the Appendix of Forms suffices to meet that requirement. Page limits are retained for papers prepared without the aid of a computer (i.e., handwritten or typewritten papers). For both the word limit and the page limit, the calculation excludes the accompanying documents required by Rule 21(a)(2)(C) and any items listed in Rule 32(f).

TITLE VI. HABEAS CORPUS; PROCEEDINGS IN FORMA PAUPERIS

Rule 22. Habeas Corpus and Section 2255 Proceedings

(a) Application for the Original Writ. An application for a writ of habeas corpus must be made to the appropriate district court. If made to a circuit judge, the application must be transferred to the appropriate district court. If a district court denies an application made or transferred to it, renewal of the application before a circuit judge is not permitted. The applicant may, under 28 U.S.C. §2253, appeal to the court of

Rule 22. Habeas Corpus and Section 2255 Proceedings

appeals from the district court's order denying the application.

(b) Certificate of Appealability.

(1) In a habeas corpus proceeding in which the detention complained of arises from process issued by a state court, or in a 28 U.S.C. §2255 proceeding, the applicant cannot take an appeal unless a circuit justice or a circuit or district judge issues a certificate of appealability under 28 U.S.C. §2253(c). If an applicant files a notice of appeal, the district clerk must send to the court of appeals the certificate (if any) and the statement described in Rule 11(a) of the Rules Governing Proceedings Under 28 U.S.C. §2254 or §2255 (if any), along with the notice of appeal and the file of the district-court proceedings. If the district judge has denied the certificate, the applicant may request a circuit judge to issue it.

(2) A request addressed to the court of appeals may be considered by a circuit judge or judges, as the court prescribes. If no express request for a certificate is filed, the notice of appeal constitutes a request addressed to the judges of the court of appeals.

(3) A certificate of appealability is not required when a state or its representative or the United States or its representative appeals.

(As amended Pub. L. 104–132, title I, §103, Apr. 24, 1996, 110 Stat. 1218; Apr. 24, 1998, eff. Dec. 1, 1998; Mar. 26, 2009, eff. Dec. 1, 2009.)

Notes of Advisory Committee on Rules—1967

Subdivision (a). Title 28 U.S.C. §2241(a) authorizes circuit judges to issue the writ of habeas corpus. Section 2241(b), however, authorizes a circuit judge to decline to entertain an application and to transfer it to the appropriate district court, and this is the usual practice. The first two sentences merely make present practice explicit. Title 28 U.S.C. §2253 seems clearly to contemplate that once an application is presented to a district judge and is denied by him, the remedy is an appeal from the order of denial. But the language of 28 U.S.C. §2241 seems to authorize a second original application to a circuit judge following a denial by a district judge. *In re Gersing,* 79 U.S.App.D.C. 245, 145 F.2d 481 (D.C. Cir., 1944) and *Chapman v. Teets,* 241 F.2d 186 (9th Cir., 1957) acknowledge the availability of such a procedure. But the procedure is ordinarily a waste of time for all involved, and the final sentence attempts to discourage it.

A court of appeals has no jurisdiction as a court to grant an original writ of habeas corpus, and courts of appeals have dismissed applications addressed to them. *Loum v. Alvis,* 263 F.2d 836 (6th Cir., 1959); *In re Berry,* 221 F.2d 798 (9th Cir., 1955); *Posey v. Dowd,* 134 F.2d 613 (7th Cir., 1943). The fairer and more expeditious practice is for the court of appeals to regard an application addressed to it as being addressed to one of its members, and to transfer the application to the appropriate district court in accordance with the provisions of this rule. Perhaps such a disposition is required by the rationale of *In re Burwell,* 350 U.S. 521, 76 S.Ct. 539, 100 L.Ed. 666 (1956).

Subdivision (b). Title 28 U.S.C. §2253 provides that an appeal may not be taken in a habeas corpus proceeding where confinement is under a judgment of a state court unless the judge who rendered the order in the habeas corpus proceeding, or a circuit justice or judge, issues a certificate of probable cause. In the interest of insuring that the matter of the certificate will not be overlooked and that, if the certificate is denied, the reasons for denial in the first instance will be available on any subsequent application, the proposed rule requires the district judge to issue the certificate or to state reasons for its denial.

While 28 U.S.C. §2253 does not authorize the court of appeals as a court to grant a certificate of probable cause, *In re Burwell,* 350 U.S. 521, 76 S.Ct. 539, 100 L.Ed. 666 (1956) makes it clear that a court of appeals may not decline to consider a request for the certificate addressed to it as a court but must regard the request as made to the judges thereof. The fourth sentence incorporates the Burwell rule.

Although 28 U.S.C. §2253 appears to require a certificate of probable cause even when an appeal is taken by a state or its representative, the legislative history strongly suggests that the intention of Congress was to require a certificate only in the case in which an appeal is taken by an applicant for the writ. See *United States ex rel. Tillery v. Cavell,* 294 F.2d 12 (3d Cir., 1960). Four of the five circuits which have ruled on the point have so interpreted section 2253. *United States ex rel. Tillery v. Cavell,* supra; *Buder v. Bell,* 306 F.2d 71 (6th Cir., 1962); *United States ex rel. Calhoun v. Pate,* 341 F.2d 885 (7th Cir., 1965); *State of Texas v. Graves,* 352 F.2d 514 (5th Cir., 1965). Cf. *United States ex rel. Carrol v. LaVallee,* 342 F.2d 641 (2d Cir., 1965). The final sentence makes it clear that a certificate of probable cause is not required of a state or its representative.

Committee Notes on Rules—1998 Amendment

The language and organization of the rule are amended to make the rule more easily understood. In addition to

Rule 22. Habeas Corpus and Section 2255 Proceedings

changes made to improve the understanding, the Advisory Committee has changed language to make style and terminology consistent throughout the appellate rules. These changes are intended to be stylistic only; in this rule, however, substantive changes are made in paragraphs (b)(1) and (b)(3).

Subdivision (b), paragraph (1). Two substantive changes are made in this paragraph. First, the paragraph is made applicable to 28 U.S.C. §2255 proceedings. This brings the rule into conformity with 28 U.S.C. §2253 as amended by the Anti-Terrorism and Effective Death Penalty Act of 1996, Pub. L. No. 104–132. Second, the rule states that a certificate of appealability may be issued by "a circuit justice or a circuit or district judge." That language adds a reference to the circuit justice which also brings the rule into conformity with section 2253. The language continues to state that in addition to the circuit justice, both a circuit and a district judge may issue a certificate of appealability. The language of section 2253 is ambiguous; it states that a certificate of appealability may be issued by "a circuit justice or judge." Since the enactment of the Anti-Terrorism and Effective Death Penalty Act, three circuits have held that both district and circuit judges, as well as the circuit justice, may issue a certificate of appealability. *Else v. Johnson*, 104 F.3d 82 (5th Cir. 1997); *Lyons v. Ohio Adult Parole Authority*, 105 F.3d 1063 (6th Cir. 1997); and *Hunter v. United States*, 101 F.3d 1565 (11th Cir. 1996). The approach taken by the rule is consistent with those decisions.

Subdivision (b), paragraph (3). The Anti-Terrorism and Effective Death Penalty Act of 1996, Pub. L. No. 104–132, amended 28 U.S.C. §2253 to make it applicable to §2255 proceedings. Accordingly, paragraph (3) is amended to provide that when the United States or its representative appeals, a certificate of appealability is not required.

Committee Notes on Rules—2009 Amendment

Subdivision (b)(1). The requirement that the district judge who rendered the judgment either issue a certificate of appealability or state why a certificate should not issue has been deleted from subdivision (b)(1). Rule 11(a) of the Rules Governing Proceedings under 28 U.S.C. §2254 or §2255 now delineates the relevant requirement. When an applicant has filed a notice of appeal, the district clerk must transmit the record to the court of appeals; if the district judge has issued a certificate of appealability, the district clerk must include in this transmission the certificate and the statement of reasons for grant of the certificate.

Changes Made After Publication and Comment. The Appellate Rules Committee approved the proposed amendment to Appellate Rule 22(b) with the style changes (described below) [omitted] which were suggested by Professor Kimble. As detailed in the report of the Criminal Rules Committee, a number of changes were made to the proposals concerning Rule 11 of the habeas and Section 2255 rules in response to public comment.

At the Standing Committee's direction, the language proposed for Appellate Rule 22(b) was circulated to the circuit clerks for their comment. Pursuant to comments received from the circuit clerks, the second sentence of Rule 22(b) was revised to make clear that the Rule requires the transmission of the record by the district court when an appeal is filed, regardless of whether the certificate of appealability was granted or denied by the district judge; a conforming change was made to the last sentence of the Committee Note.

Amendment by Public Law

1996—Pub. L. 104–132 inserted "and section 2255" after "corpus" in catchline and amended text generally. Prior to amendment, text read as follows:

"(a) *Application for the original writ.*—An application for a writ of habeas corpus shall be made to the appropriate district court. If application is made to a circuit judge, the application will ordinarily be transferred to the appropriate district court. If an application is made to or transferred to the district court and denied, renewal of the application before a circuit judge is not favored; the proper remedy is by appeal to the court of appeals from the order of the district court denying the writ.

"(b) *Necessity of certificate of probable cause for appeal.*—In a habeas corpus proceeding in which the detention complained of arises out of process issued by a state court, an appeal by the applicant for the writ may not proceed unless a district or a circuit judge issues a certificate of probable cause. If an appeal is taken by the applicant, the district judge who rendered the judgment shall either issue a certificate of probable cause or state the reasons why such a certificate should not issue. The certificate or the statement shall be forwarded to the court of appeals with the notice of appeal and the file of the proceedings in the district court. If the district judge has denied the certificate, the applicant for the writ may then request issuance of the certificate by a circuit judge. If such a request is addressed to the court of appeals, it shall be deemed addressed to the judges thereof and shall be considered by a circuit judge or judges as the court deems appropriate. If no express request for a certificate is filed, the notice of appeal shall be deemed to constitute a request addressed to the judges of the court of appeals. If an appeal is taken by a state or its representative, a certificate of probable cause is not required."

Rule 23. Custody or Release of a Prisoner in a Habeas Corpus Proceeding

(a) Transfer of Custody Pending Review. Pending review of a decision in a habeas corpus proceeding commenced before a court, justice, or judge of the United States for the release of a prisoner, the person having custody of the prisoner must not transfer custody to another unless a transfer is directed in accordance with this rule. When, upon application, a custodian shows the need for a transfer, the court, justice, or judge rendering the decision under review may authorize the transfer and substitute the successor custodian as a party.

(b) Detention or Release Pending Review of Decision Not to Release. While a decision not to release a prisoner is under review, the court or judge rendering the decision, or the court of appeals, or the Supreme Court, or a judge or justice of either court, may order that the prisoner be:

(1) detained in the custody from which release is sought;

(2) detained in other appropriate custody; or

(3) released on personal recognizance, with or without surety.

(c) Release Pending Review of Decision Ordering Release. While a decision ordering the release of a prisoner is under review, the prisoner must—unless the court or judge rendering the decision, or the court of appeals, or the Supreme Court, or a judge or justice of either court orders otherwise—be released on personal recognizance, with or without surety.

(d) Modification of the Initial Order on Custody. An initial order governing the prisoner's custody or release, including any recognizance or surety, continues in effect pending review unless for special reasons shown to the court of appeals or the Supreme Court, or to a judge or justice of either court, the order is modified or an independent order regarding custody, release, or surety is issued.

(As amended Mar. 10, 1986, eff. July 1, 1986; Apr. 24, 1998, eff. Dec. 1, 1998.)

Notes of Advisory Committee on Rules—1967

The rule is the same as Supreme Court Rule 49, as amended on June 12, 1967, effective October 2, 1967.

Notes of Advisory Committee on Rules—1986 Amendment

The amendments to Rules 23(b) and (c) are technical. No substantive change is intended.

Committee Notes on Rules—1998 Amendment

The language and organization of the rule are amended to make the rule more easily understood. In addition to changes made to improve the understanding, the Advisory Committee has changed language to make style and terminology consistent throughout the appellate rules. These changes are intended to be stylistic only.

Subdivison (d). The current rule states that the initial order governing custody or release "shall govern review" in the court of appeals. The amended language says that the initial order generally "continues in effect" pending review.

When Rule 23 was adopted it used the same language as Supreme Court Rule 49, which then governed custody of prisoners in habeas corpus proceedings. The "shall govern review" language was drawn from the Supreme Court Rule. The Supreme Court has since amended its rule, now Rule 36, to say that the initial order "shall continue in effect" unless for reasons shown it is modified or a new order is entered. Rule 23 is amended to similarly state that the initial order "continues in effect." The new language is clearer. It removes the possible implication that the initial order created law of the case, a strange notion to attach to an order regarding custody or release.

Rule 24. Proceeding in Forma Pauperis

(a) Leave to Proceed in Forma Pauperis.

(1) *Motion in the District Court.* Except as stated in Rule 24(a)(3), a party to a district-court action who desires to appeal in forma pauperis must file a motion in the district court. The party must attach an affidavit that:

(A) shows in the detail prescribed by Form 4 of the Appendix of Forms the party's inability to pay or to give security for fees and costs;

Rule 24. Proceeding in Forma Pauperis

(B) claims an entitlement to redress; and

(C) states the issues that the party intends to present on appeal.

(2) *Action on the Motion.* If the district court grants the motion, the party may proceed on appeal without prepaying or giving security for fees and costs, unless a statute provides otherwise. If the district court denies the motion, it must state its reasons in writing.

(3) *Prior Approval.* A party who was permitted to proceed in forma pauperis in the district-court action, or who was determined to be financially unable to obtain an adequate defense in a criminal case, may proceed on appeal in forma pauperis without further authorization, unless:

(A) the district court—before or after the notice of appeal is filed—certifies that the appeal is not taken in good faith or finds that the party is not otherwise entitled to proceed in forma pauperis and states in writing its reasons for the certification or finding; or

(B) a statute provides otherwise.

(4) *Notice of District Court's Denial.* The district clerk must immediately notify the parties and the court of appeals when the district court does any of the following:

(A) denies a motion to proceed on appeal in forma pauperis;

(B) certifies that the appeal is not taken in good faith; or

(C) finds that the party is not otherwise entitled to proceed in forma pauperis.

(5) *Motion in the Court of Appeals.* A party may file a motion to proceed on appeal in forma pauperis in the court of appeals within 30 days after service of the notice prescribed in Rule 24(a)(4). The motion must include a copy of the affidavit filed in the district court and the district court's statement of reasons for its action. If no affidavit was filed in the district court, the party must include the affidavit prescribed by Rule 24(a)(1).

(b) Leave to Proceed in Forma Pauperis on Appeal from the United States Tax Court or on Appeal or Review of an Administrative-Agency Proceeding. A party may file in the court of appeals a motion for leave to proceed on appeal in forma pauperis with an affidavit prescribed by Rule 24(a)(1):

(1) in an appeal from the United States Tax Court; and

(2) when an appeal or review of a proceeding before an administrative agency, board, commission, or officer proceeds directly in the court of appeals.

(c) Leave to Use Original Record. A party allowed to proceed on appeal in forma pauperis may request that the appeal be heard on the original record without reproducing any part.

(As amended Apr. 1, 1979, eff. Aug. 1, 1979; Mar. 10, 1986, eff. July 1, 1986; Apr. 24, 1998, eff. Dec. 1, 1998; Apr. 29, 2002, eff. Dec. 1, 2002; Apr. 16, 2013, eff. Dec. 1, 2013.)

Notes of Advisory Committee on Rules—1967

Subdivision (a). Authority to allow prosecution of an appeal in forma pauperis is vested in "[a]ny court of the United States" by 28 U.S.C. §1915(a). The second paragraph of section 1915(a) seems to contemplate initial application to the district court for permission to proceed in forma pauperis, and although the circuit rules are generally silent on the question, the case law requires initial application to the district court. *Hayes v. United States,* 258 F.2d 400 (5th Cir., 1958), *cert. den.* 358 U.S. 856, 79 S.Ct. 87, 3 L.Ed.2d 89 (1958); *Elkins v. United States,* 250 F.2d 145 (9th Cir., 1957) see 364 U.S. 206, 80 S.Ct. 1437, 4 L.Ed.2d 1669 (1960); *United States v. Farley,* 238 F.2d 575 (2d Cir., 1956) see 354 U.S. 521, 77 S.Ct. 1371, 1 L.Ed.2d 1529 (1957). D.C. Cir. Rule 41(a) requires initial application to the district court. The content of the affidavit follows the language of the statute; the requirement of a statement of the issues comprehends the statutory requirement of a statement of "the nature of the . . . appeal. . . ." The second sentence is in accord with the decision in *McGann v. United States,* 362 U.S. 309, 80 S.Ct. 725, 4 L.Ed.2d 734 (1960). The requirement contained in the third sentence has no counterpart in present circuit rules, but it has been imposed by decision in at least two circuits. *Ragan v. Cox,* 305 F.2d 58 (10th Cir., 1962); *United States ex rel. Breedlove v. Dowd,* 269 F.2d 693 (7th Cir., 1959).

The second paragraph permits one whose indigency has been previously determined by the district court to proceed on appeal in forma pauperis without the necessity of a redetermination of indigency, while reserving to the district court its statutory authority to certify that the appeal is not taken in good faith, 28 U.S.C. §1915(a), and permitting an inquiry into whether the circumstances of the party who was originally entitled to proceed in forma pauperis have changed during the course of the litigation. Cf. Sixth Circuit Rule 26.

The final paragraph establishes a subsequent motion in the court of appeals, rather than an appeal from the order of

Rule 24. Proceeding in Forma Pauperis

denial or from the certification of lack of good faith, as the proper procedure for calling in question the correctness of the action of the district court. The simple and expeditious motion procedure seems clearly preferable to an appeal. This paragraph applies only to applications for leave to appeal in forma pauperis. The order of a district court refusing leave to initiate an action in the district court in forma pauperis is reviewable on appeal. See *Roberts v. United States District Court*, 339 U.S. 844, 70 S.Ct. 954, 94 L.Ed. 1326 (1950).

Subdivision (b). Authority to allow prosecution in forma pauperis is vested only in a "court of the United States" (see Note to subdivision (a), above). Thus in proceedings brought directly in a court of appeals to review decisions of agencies or of the Tax Court, authority to proceed in forma pauperis should be sought in the court of appeals. If initial review of agency action is had in a district court, an application to appeal to a court of appeals in forma pauperis from the judgment of the district court is governed by the provisions of subdivision (a).

Notes of Advisory Committee on Rules—1979 Amendment

The proposed amendment reflects the change in the title of the Tax Court to "United States Tax Court." See 26 U.S.C. §7441.

Notes of Advisory Committee on Rules—1986 Amendment

The amendments to Rule 24(a) are technical. No substantive change is intended.

Committee Notes on Rules—1998 Amendment

The language and organization of the rule are amended to make the rule more easily understood. In addition to changes made to improve the understanding, the Advisory Committee has changed language to make style and terminology consistent throughout the appellate rules. These changes are intended to be stylistic only. The Advisory Committee deletes the language in subdivision (c) authorizing a party proceeding in forma pauperis to file papers in typewritten form because the authorization is unnecessary. The rules permit all parties to file typewritten documents.

Committee Notes on Rules—2002 Amendment

Subdivision (a)(2). Section 804 of the Prison Litigation Reform Act of 1995 ("PLRA") amended 28 U.S.C. §1915 to require that prisoners who bring civil actions or appeals from civil actions must "pay the full amount of a filing fee." 28 U.S.C. §1915(b)(1). Prisoners who are unable to pay the full amount of the filing fee at the time that their actions or appeals are filed are generally required to pay part of the fee and then to pay the remainder of the fee in installments. 28 U.S.C. §1915(b). By contrast, Rule 24(a)(2) has provided that, after the district court grants a litigant's motion to proceed on appeal in forma pauperis, the litigant may proceed "without prepaying or giving security for fees and costs." Thus, the PLRA and Rule 24(a)(2) appear to be in conflict.

Rule 24(a)(2) has been amended to resolve this conflict. Recognizing that future legislation regarding prisoner litigation is likely, the Committee has not attempted to incorporate into Rule 24 all of the requirements of the current version of 28 U.S.C. §1915. Rather, the Committee has amended Rule 24(a)(2) to clarify that the rule is not meant to conflict with anything required by the PLRA or any other statute.

Subdivision (a)(3). Rule 24(a)(3) has also been amended to eliminate an apparent conflict with the PLRA. Rule 24(a)(3) has provided that a party who was permitted to proceed in forma pauperis in the district court may continue to proceed in forma pauperis in the court of appeals without further authorization, subject to certain conditions. The PLRA, by contrast, provides that a prisoner who was permitted to proceed in forma pauperis in the district court and who wishes to continue to proceed in forma pauperis on appeal may not do so "automatically," but must seek permission. *See, e.g., Morgan v. Haro*, 112 F.3d 788, 789 (5th Cir. 1997) ("A prisoner who seeks to proceed IFP on appeal must obtain leave to so proceed despite proceeding IFP in the district court.").

Rule 24(a)(3) has been amended to resolve this conflict. Again, recognizing that future legislation regarding prisoner litigation is likely, the Committee has not attempted to incorporate into Rule 24 all of the requirements of the current version of 28 U.S.C. §1915. Rather, the Committee has amended Rule 24(a)(3) to clarify that the rule is not meant to conflict with anything required by the PLRA or any other statute.

Changes Made After Publication and Comments. No changes were made to the text of the proposed amendment or to the Committee Note, except that "a statute provides otherwise" was substituted in place of "the law requires otherwise" in the text of the rule and conforming changes (as well as a couple of minor stylistic changes) were made to the Committee Note.

Rule 25. Filing and Service

Committee Notes on Rules—2013 Amendment

Rule 24(b) currently refers to review of proceedings "before an administrative agency, board, commission, or officer (including for the purpose of this rule the United States Tax Court)." Experience suggests that Rule 24(b) contributes to confusion by fostering the impression that the Tax Court is an executive branch agency rather than a court. (As a general example of that confusion, appellate courts have returned Tax Court records to the Internal Revenue Service, believing the Tax Court to be part of that agency.) To remove this possible source of confusion, the quoted parenthetical is deleted from subdivision (b) and appeals from the Tax Court are separately listed in subdivision (b)'s heading and in new subdivision (b)(1).

Changes Made After Publication and Comment. No changes were made after publication and comment.

TITLE VII. GENERAL PROVISIONS

Rule 25. Filing and Service
(a) Filing.
(1) *Filing with the Clerk.* A paper required or permitted to be filed in a court of appeals must be filed with the clerk.
(2) *Filing: Method and Timeliness.*
  (A) *In General.* Filing may be accomplished by mail addressed to the clerk, but filing is not timely unless the clerk receives the papers within the time fixed for filing.
  (B) *A brief or appendix.* A brief or appendix is timely filed, however, if on or before the last day for filing, it is:
   (i) mailed to the clerk by First-Class Mail, or other class of mail that is at least as expeditious, postage prepaid; or
   (ii) dispatched to a third-party commercial carrier for delivery to the clerk within 3 days.

[The following text of subdivision (C) was effective until December 1, 2016.]

(C) *Inmate Filing.* A paper filed by an inmate confined in an institution is timely if deposited in the institution's internal mailing system on or before the last day for filing. If an institution has a system designed for legal mail, the inmate must use that system to receive the benefit of this rule. Timely filing may be shown by a declaration in compliance with 28 U.S.C. §1746 or by a notarized statement, either of which must set forth the date of deposit and state that first-class postage has been prepaid.

[The following text of subdivision (C) became effective December 1, 2016.]

(C) Inmate Filing. If an institution has a system designed for legal mail, an inmate
confined there must use that system to receive the benefit of this Rule 25(a)(2)(C). A paper filed by an inmate is timely if it is deposited in the institution's internal mail system on or before the last day for filing and:
  (i) it is accompanied by:
   • a declaration in compliance with 28 U.S.C. § 1746—or a notarized statement—setting out the date of deposit and stating that first-class postage is being prepaid; or
   • evidence (such as a postmark or date stamp) showing that the paper was so deposited and that postage was prepaid; or
  (ii) the court of appeals exercises its discretion to permit the later filing of a declaration or notarized statement that satisfies Rule 25(a)(2)(C)(i).

(D) *Electronic Filing.* A court of appeals may by local rule permit or require papers to be filed, signed, or verified by electronic means that are consistent with technical standards, if any, that the Judicial Conference of the United States establishes. A local rule may require filing by electronic means only if

Rule 25. Filing and Service

reasonable exceptions are allowed. A paper filed by electronic means in compliance with a local rule constitutes a written paper for the purpose of applying these rules.

(3) *Filing a Motion with a Judge.* If a motion requests relief that may be granted by a single judge, the judge may permit the motion to be filed with the judge; the judge must note the filing date on the motion and give it to the clerk.

(4) *Clerk's Refusal of Documents.* The clerk must not refuse to accept for filing any paper presented for that purpose solely because it is not presented in proper form as required by these rules or by any local rule or practice.

(5) *Privacy Protection.* An appeal in a case whose privacy protection was governed by Federal Rule of Bankruptcy Procedure 9037, Federal Rule of Civil Procedure 5.2, or Federal Rule of Criminal Procedure 49.1 is governed by the same rule on appeal. In all other proceedings, privacy protection is governed by Federal Rule of Civil Procedure 5.2, except that Federal Rule of Criminal Procedure 49.1 governs when an extraordinary writ is sought in a criminal case.

(b) Service of All Papers Required. Unless a rule requires service by the clerk, a party must, at or before the time of filing a paper, serve a copy on the other parties to the appeal or review. Service on a party represented by counsel must be made on the party's counsel.

(c) Manner of Service.

(1) Service may be any of the following:

(A) personal, including delivery to a responsible person at the office of counsel;

(B) by mail;

(C) by third-party commercial carrier for delivery within 3 days; or

(D) by electronic means, if the party being served consents in writing.

(2) If authorized by local rule, a party may use the court's transmission equipment to make electronic service under Rule 25(c)(1)(D).

(3) When reasonable considering such factors as the immediacy of the relief sought, distance, and cost, service on a party must be by a manner at least as expeditious as the manner used to file the paper with the court.

(4) Service by mail or by commercial carrier is complete on mailing or delivery to the carrier. Service by electronic means is complete on transmission, unless the party making service is notified that the paper was not received by the party served.

(d) Proof of Service.

(1) A paper presented for filing must contain either of the following:

(A) an acknowledgment of service by the person served; or

(B) proof of service consisting of a statement by the person who made service certifying:

(i) the date and manner of service;

(ii) the names of the persons served; and

(iii) their mail or electronic addresses, facsimile numbers, or the addresses of the places of delivery, as appropriate for the manner of service.

(2) When a brief or appendix is filed by mailing or dispatch in accordance with Rule 25(a)(2)(B), the proof of service must also state the date and manner by which the document was mailed or dispatched to the clerk.

(3) Proof of service may appear on or be affixed to the papers filed.

(e) Number of Copies. When these rules require the filing or furnishing of a number of copies, a court may require a different number by local rule or by order in a particular case.

(As amended Mar. 10, 1986, eff. July 1, 1986; Apr. 30, 1991, eff. Dec. 1, 1991; Apr. 22, 1993, eff. Dec. 1, 1993; Apr. 29, 1994, eff. Dec. 1, 1994; Apr. 23, 1996, eff. Dec. 1, 1996; Apr. 24, 1998, eff. Dec. 1, 1998; Apr. 29, 2002, eff. Dec. 1, 2002; Apr. 12, 2006, eff. Dec. 1, 2006; Apr. 30, 2007, eff. Dec. 1, 2007; Mar. 26, 2009, eff. Dec. 1, 2009; Apr. 28, 2016, eff. Dec. 1, 2016.)

Notes of Advisory Committee on Rules—1967

The rule that filing is not timely unless the papers filed are received within the time allowed is the familiar one. *Ward v. Atlantic Coast Line R.R. Co.*, 265 F.2d 75 (5th Cir., 1959), rev'd on other grounds 362 U.S. 396, 80 S.Ct. 789, 4 L.Ed.2d 820 (1960); *Kahler-Ellis Co. v. Ohio Turnpike Commission*, 225 F.2d 922 (6th Cir., 1955). An exception is made in the case

Rule 25. Filing and Service

of briefs and appendices in order to afford the parties the maximum time for their preparation. By the terms of the exception, air mail delivery must be used whenever it is the most expeditious manner of delivery.

A majority of the circuits now require service of all papers filed with the clerk. The usual provision in present rules is for service on "adverse" parties. In view of the extreme simplicity of service by mail, there seems to be no reason why a party who files a paper should not be required to serve all parties to the proceeding in the court of appeals, whether or not they may be deemed adverse. The common requirement of proof of service is retained, but the rule permits it to be made by simple certification, which may be endorsed on the copy which is filed.

Notes of Advisory Committee on Rules—1986 Amendment

The amendments to Rules 25(a) and (b) are technical. No substantive change is intended.

Notes of Advisory Committee on Rules—1991 Amendment

Subdivision (a). The amendment permits, but does not require, courts of appeals to adopt local rules that allow filing of papers by electronic means. However, courts of appeals cannot adopt such local rules until the Judicial Conference of the United States authorizes filing by facsimile or other electronic means.

Notes of Advisory Committee on Rules—1993 Amendment

The amendment accompanies new subdivision (c) of Rule 4 and extends the holding in *Houston v. Lack*, 487 U.S. 266 (1988), to all papers filed in the courts of appeals by persons confined in institutions.

Notes of Advisory Committee on Rules—1994 Amendment

Subdivision (a). Several circuits have local rules that authorize the office of the clerk to refuse to accept for filing papers that are not in the form required by these rules or by local rules. This is not a suitable role for the office of the clerk and the practice exposes litigants to the hazards of time bars; for these reasons, such rules are proscribed by this rule. This provision is similar to Fed.R.Civ.P. 5 (e) and Fed.R.Bankr.P. 5005.

The Committee wishes to make it clear that the provision prohibiting a clerk from refusing a document does not mean that a clerk's office may no longer screen documents to determine whether they comply with the rules. A court may delegate to the clerk authority to inform a party about any noncompliance with the rules and, if the party is willing to correct the document, to determine a date by which the corrected document must be resubmitted. If a party refuses to take the steps recommended by the clerk or if in the clerk's judgment the party fails to correct the noncompliance, the clerk must refer the matter to the court for a ruling.

Subdivision (d). Two changes have been made in this subdivision. Subdivision (d) provides that a paper presented for filing must contain proof of service.

The last sentence of subdivision (d) has been deleted as unnecessary. That sentence stated that a clerk could permit papers to be filed without acknowledgment or proof of service but must require that it be filed promptly thereafter. In light of the change made in subdivision (a) which states that a clerk may not refuse to accept for filing a document because it is not in the proper form, there is no further need for a provision stating that a clerk may accept a paper lacking a proof of service. The clerk must accept such a paper. That portion of the deleted sentence stating that the clerk must require that proof of service be filed promptly after the filing of the document if the proof is not filed concurrently with the document is also unnecessary.

The second amendment requires that the certificate of service must state the addresses to which the papers were mailed or at which they were delivered. The Federal Circuit has a similar local rule, Fed.Cir.R. 25.

Subdivision (e). Subdivision (e) is a new subdivision. It makes it clear that whenever these rules require a party to file or furnish a number of copies a court may require a different number of copies either by rule or by order in an individual case. The number of copies of any document that a court of appeals needs varies depending upon the way in which the court conducts business. The internal operation of the courts of appeals necessarily varies from circuit to circuit because of differences in the number of judges, the geographic area included within the circuit, and other such factors. Uniformity could be achieved only by setting the number of copies artificially high so that parties in all circuits file enough copies to satisfy the needs of the court requiring the greatest number. Rather than do that, the Committee decided to make it clear that local rules may require a greater or lesser number of copies and that, if the circumstances of a particular case indicate the need for a different number of copies in that case, the court may so order.

A party must consult local rules to determine whether the court requires a different number than that specified in these national rules. The Committee believes it would be helpful if each circuit either: 1) included a chart at the beginning

Rule 25. Filing and Service

of its local rules showing the number of copies of each document required to be filed with the court along with citation to the controlling rule; or 2) made available such a chart to each party upon commencement of an appeal; or both. If a party fails to file the required number of copies, the failure does not create a jurisdictional defect. Rule 3(a) states: "Failure of an appellant to take any step other than the timely filing of a notice of appeal does not affect the validity of the appeal, but is ground only for such action as the court of appeals deems appropriate. . . ."

Notes of Advisory Committee on Rules—1996 Amendment

Subdivision (a). The amendment deletes the language requiring a party to use "the most expeditious form of delivery by mail, except special delivery" in order to file a brief using the mailbox rule. That language was adopted before the Postal Service offered Express Mail and other expedited delivery services. The amendment makes it clear that it is sufficient to use First-Class Mail. Other equally or more expeditious classes of mail service, such as Express Mail, also may be used. In addition, the amendment permits the use of commercial carriers. The use of private, overnight courier services has become commonplace in law practice. Expedited services offered by commercial carriers often provide faster delivery than First-Class Mail; therefore, there should be no objection to the use of commercial carriers as long as they are reliable. In order to make use of the mailbox rule when using a commercial carrier, the amendment requires that the filer employ a carrier who undertakes to deliver the document in no more than three calendar days. The three-calendar-day period coordinates with the three-day extension provided by Rule 26(c).

Subdivision (c). The amendment permits service by commercial carrier if the carrier is to deliver the paper to the party being served within three days of the carrier's receipt of the paper. The amendment also expresses a desire that when reasonable, service on a party be accomplished by a manner as expeditious as the manner used to file the paper with the court. When a brief or motion is filed with the court by hand delivering the paper to the clerk's office, or by overnight courier, the copies should be served on the other parties by an equally expeditious manner—meaning either by personal service, if distance permits, or by overnight courier, if mail delivery to the party is not ordinarily accomplished overnight. The reasonableness standard is included so that if a paper is hand delivered to the clerk's office for filing but the other parties must be served in a different city, state, or region, personal service on them ordinarily will not be expected. If use of an equally expeditious manner of service is not reasonable, use of the next most expeditious manner may be. For example, if the paper is filed by hand delivery to the clerk's office but the other parties reside in distant cities, service on them need not be personal but in most instances should be by overnight courier. Even that may not be required, however, if the number of parties that must be served would make the use of overnight service too costly. A factor that bears upon the reasonableness of serving parties expeditiously is the immediacy of the relief requested.

Subdivision (d). The amendment adds a requirement that when a brief or appendix is filed by mail or commercial carrier, the certificate of service state the date and manner by which the document was mailed or dispatched to the clerk. Including that information in the certificate of service avoids the necessity for a separate certificate concerning the date and manner of filing.

Committee Notes on Rules—1998 Amendment

The language and organization of the rule are amended to make the rule more easily understood. In addition to changes made to improve the understanding, the Advisory Committee has changed language to make style and terminology consistent throughout the appellate rules. These changes are intended to be stylistic only; a substantive amendment is made, however, in subdivision (a).

Subdivision (a). The substantive amendment in this subdivision is in subparagraph (a)(2)(C) and is a companion to an amendment in Rule 4(c). Currently Rule 25(a)(2)(C) provides that if an inmate confined in an institution files a document by depositing it in the institution's internal mail system, the document is timely filed if deposited on or before the last day for filing. Some institutions have special internal mail systems for handling legal mail; such systems often record the date of deposit of mail by an inmate, the date of delivery of mail to an inmate, etc. The Advisory Committee amends the rule to require an inmate to use the system designed for legal mail, if there is one, in order to receive the benefit of this subparagraph.

Committee Notes on Rules—2002 Amendment

Rule 25(a)(2)(D) presently authorizes the courts of appeals to permit papers to be *filed* by electronic means. Rule 25 has been amended in several respects to permit papers also to be *served* electronically. In addition, Rule 25(c) has been reorganized and subdivided to make it easier to understand.

Subdivision (c)(1)(D). New subdivision (c)(1)(D) has been added to permit service to be made electronically, such as by e-mail or fax. No party may be served electronically, either by the clerk or by another party, unless the party has consented in writing to such service.

A court of appeals may not, by local rule, forbid the use of electronic service on a party that has consented to its use. At the same time, courts have considerable discretion to use local rules to regulate electronic service. Difficult and presently unforeseeable questions are likely to arise as electronic service becomes more common. Courts have the flexibility to use their local rules to address those questions. For example, courts may use local rules to set forth specific procedures that a party must follow before the party will be deemed to have given written consent to electronic service.

Parties also have the flexibility to define the terms of their consent; a party's consent to electronic service does not have to be "all-or-nothing." For example, a party may consent to service by facsimile transmission, but not by electronic mail; or a party may consent to electronic service only if "courtesy" copies of all transmissions are mailed within 24 hours; or a party may consent to electronic service of only documents that were created with Corel WordPerfect.

Subdivision (c)(2). The courts of appeals are authorized under Rule 25(a)(2)(D) to permit papers to be filed electronically. Technological advances may someday make it possible for a court to forward an electronically filed paper to all parties automatically or semi-automatically. When such court-facilitated service becomes possible, courts may decide to permit parties to use the courts' transmission facilities to serve electronically filed papers on other parties who have consented to such service. Court personnel would use the court's computer system to forward the papers, but the papers would be considered served by the filing parties, just as papers that are carried from one address to another by the United States Postal Service are considered served by the sending parties. New subdivision (c)(2) has been added so that the courts of appeals may use local rules to authorize such use of their transmission facilities, as well as to address the many questions that court-facilitated electronic service is likely to raise.

Subdivision (c)(4). The second sentence of new subdivision (c)(4) has been added to provide that electronic service is complete upon transmission. Transmission occurs when the sender performs the last act that he or she must perform to transmit a paper electronically; typically, it occurs when the sender hits the "send" or "transmit" button on an electronic mail program. There is one exception to the rule that electronic service is complete upon transmission: If the sender is notified—by the sender's e-mail program or otherwise—that the paper was not received, service is not complete, and the sender must take additional steps to effect service. A paper has been "received" by the party on which it has been served as long as the party has the ability to retrieve it. A party cannot defeat service by choosing not to access electronic mail on its server.

Changes Made After Publication and Comments. No changes were made to the text of the proposed amendment. A paragraph was added to the Committee Note to clarify that consent to electronic service is not an "all-or-nothing" matter.

Subdivision (d)(1)(B)(iii). Subdivision (d)(1)(B)(iii) has been amended to require that, when a paper is served electronically, the proof of service of that paper must include the electronic address or facsimile number to which the paper was transmitted.

Changes Made After Publication and Comments. The text of the proposed amendment was changed to refer to "electronic" addresses (instead of to "e-mail" addresses), to include "facsimile numbers," and to add the concluding phrase "as appropriate for the manner of service." Conforming changes were made to the Committee Note.

Committee Notes on Rules—2006 Amendment

Subdivision (a)(2)(D). Amended Rule 25(a)(2)(D) acknowledges that many courts have required electronic filing by means of a standing order, procedures manual, or local rule. These local practices reflect the advantages that courts and most litigants realize from electronic filing. Courts that mandate electronic filing recognize the need to make exceptions when requiring electronic filing imposes a hardship on a party. Under Rule 25(a)(2)(D), a local rule that requires electronic filing must include reasonable exceptions, but Rule 25(a)(2)(D) does not define the scope of those exceptions. Experience with the local rules that have been adopted and that will emerge will aid in drafting new local rules and will facilitate gradual convergence on uniform exceptions, whether in local rules or in an amended Rule 25(a)(2)(D).

A local rule may require that both electronic and "hard" copies of a paper be filed. Nothing in the last sentence of Rule 25(a)(2)(D) is meant to imply otherwise.

Changes Made After Publication and Comment. Rule 25(a)(2)(D) has been changed in one significant respect: It now authorizes the courts of appeals to require electronic filing only "if reasonable exceptions are allowed." 1 The published version of Rule 25(a)(2)(D) did not require "reasonable exceptions." The change was made in response to the argument of many commentators that the national rule should require that the local rules include exceptions for those for whom mandatory electronic filing would pose a hardship.

Although Rule 25(a)(2)(D) requires that hardship exceptions be included in any local rules that mandate electronic filing, it does not attempt to define the scope of those exceptions. Commentators were largely in agreement that the local rules should include hardship exceptions of some type. But commentators did not agree about the perimeters of those exceptions. The Advisory Committee believes that, at this point, it does not have enough experience with mandatory electronic filing to impose specific hardship exceptions on the circuits. Rather, the Advisory Committee believes that the

Rule 25. Filing and Service

circuits should be free for the time being to experiment with different formulations.

The Committee Note has been changed to reflect the addition of the "reasonable exceptions" clause to the text of the rule. The Committee Note has also been changed to add the final two sentences. Those sentences were added at the request of Judge Sandra L. Lynch, a member of CACM [the Court Administration and Case Management Committee]. Judge Lynch believes that there will be few appellate judges who will want to receive only electronic copies of briefs, but there will be many who will want to receive electronic copies in addition to hard copies. Thus, the local rules of most circuits are likely to require a "written" copy or "paper" copy, in addition to an electronic copy. The problem is that the last sentence of Rule 25(a)(2)(D) provides that "[a] paper filed by electronic means in compliance with a local rule constitutes a written paper for the purpose of applying these rules." Judge Lynch's concern is that this sentence may leave attorneys confused as to whether a local rule requiring a "written" or "paper" copy of a brief requires anything in addition to the electronic copy. The final two sentences of the Committee Note are intended to clarify the matter.

Committee Notes on Rules—2007 Amendment

Subdivision (a)(5). Section 205(c)(3)(A)(i) of the E-Government Act of 2002 (Public Law 107–347, as amended by Public Law 108–281) requires that the rules of practice and procedure be amended "to protect privacy and security concerns relating to electronic filing of documents and the public availability . . . of documents filed electronically." In response to that directive, the Federal Rules of Bankruptcy, Civil, and Criminal Procedure have been amended, not merely to address the privacy and security concerns raised by documents that are filed electronically, but also to address similar concerns raised by documents that are filed in paper form. *See* Fed. R. Bankr. P. 9037; Fed. R. Civ. P. 5.2; and Fed. R. Crim. P. 49.1.

Appellate Rule 25(a)(5) requires that, in cases that arise on appeal from a district court, bankruptcy appellate panel, or bankruptcy court, the privacy rule that applied to the case below will continue to apply to the case on appeal. With one exception, all other cases—such as cases involving the review or enforcement of an agency order, the review of a decision of the tax court, or the consideration of a petition for an extraordinary writ—will be governed by Civil Rule 5.2. The only exception is when an extraordinary writ is sought in a criminal case—that is, a case in which the related trial-court proceeding is governed by Criminal Rule 49.1. In such a case, Criminal Rule 49.1 will govern in the court of appeals as well.

Changes Made After Publication and Comment. The rule is a modified version of the provision as published. The changes from the published proposal implement suggestions by the Style Subcommittee of the Standing Committee on Rules of Practice and Procedure.

Committee Notes on Rules—2009 Amendment

Under former Rule 26(a), short periods that span weekends or holidays were computed without counting those weekends or holidays. To specify that a period should be calculated by counting all intermediate days, including weekends or holidays, the Rules used the term "calendar days." Rule 26(a) now takes a "days-are-days" approach under which all intermediate days are counted, no matter how short the period. Accordingly, "3 calendar days" in subdivisions (a)(2)(B)(ii) and (c)(1)(C) is amended to read simply "3 days."

1 At its June 15–16, 2005, meeting, the Standing Rules Committee with the concurrence of the advisory committee chair agreed to set out the "reasonable exception" clause as a separate sentence in the rule, consistent with drafting conventions of the Style Project.

Committee Notes on Rules – 2016 Amendment

Rule 25(a)(2)(C) is revised to streamline and clarify the operation of the inmate-filing rule.

The Rule requires the inmate to show timely deposit and prepayment of postage. The Rule is amended to specify that a paper is timely if it is accompanied by a declaration or notarized statement stating the date the paper was deposited in the institution's mail system and attesting to the prepayment of first-class postage. The declaration must state that first-class postage "is being prepaid," not (as directed by the former Rule) that first-class postage "has been prepaid." This change reflects the fact that inmates may need to rely upon the institution to affix postage after the inmate has deposited the document in the institution's mail system. New Form 7 in the Appendix of Forms sets out a suggested form of the declaration.

The amended rule also provides that a paper is timely without a declaration or notarized statement if other evidence accompanying the paper shows that the paper was deposited on or before the due date and that postage was prepaid. If the paper is not accompanied by evidence that establishes timely deposit and prepayment of postage, then the court of appeals has discretion to accept a declaration or notarized statement at a later date. The Rule uses the phrase "exercises

Rule 26. Computing and Extending Time

its discretion to permit"—rather than simply "permits"—to help ensure that pro se inmate litigants are aware that a court will not necessarily forgive a failure to provide the declaration initially.

Rule 26. Computing and Extending Time

(a) Computing Time. The following rules apply in computing any time period specified in these rules, in any local rule or court order, or in any statute that does not specify a method of computing time.

(1) *Period Stated in Days or a Longer Unit.* When the period is stated in days or a longer unit of time:
   (A) exclude the day of the event that triggers the period;
   (B) count every day, including intermediate Saturdays, Sundays, and legal holidays; and
   (C) include the last day of the period, but if the last day is a Saturday, Sunday, or legal holiday, the period continues to run until the end of the next day that is not a Saturday, Sunday, or legal holiday.

(2) *Period Stated in Hours.* When the period is stated in hours:
   (A) begin counting immediately on the occurrence of the event that triggers the period;
   (B) count every hour, including hours during intermediate Saturdays, Sundays, and legal holidays; and
   (C) if the period would end on a Saturday, Sunday, or legal holiday, the period continues to run until the same time on the next day that is not a Saturday, Sunday, or legal holiday.

(3) *Inaccessibility of the Clerk's Office.* Unless the court orders otherwise, if the clerk's office is inaccessible:
   (A) on the last day for filing under Rule 26(a)(1), then the time for filing is extended to the first accessible day that is not a Saturday, Sunday, or legal holiday; or
   (B) during the last hour for filing under Rule 26(a)(2), then the time for filing is extended to the same time on the first accessible day that is not a Saturday, Sunday, or legal holiday.

[The following text of subdivision (4) was effective until December 1, 2016.]

(4) *"Last Day" Defined.* Unless a different time is set by a statute, local rule, or court order, the last day ends:
   (A) for electronic filing in the district court, at midnight in the court's time zone;
   (B) for electronic filing in the court of appeals, at midnight in the time zone of the circuit clerk's principal office;
   (C) for filing under Rules 4(c)(1), 25(a)(2)(B), and 25(a)(2)(C)—and filing by mail under Rule 13(b)—at the latest time for the method chosen for delivery to the post office, third-party commercial carrier, or prison mailing system; and
   (D) for filing by other means, when the clerk's office is scheduled to close.

[The following text of subdivision (4) became effective December 1, 2016.]

(4) "Last Day" Defined. Unless a different time is set by a statute, local rule, or court order, the last day ends:
   (A) for electronic filing in the district court, at midnight in the court's time zone;
   (B) for electronic filing in the court of appeals, at midnight in the time zone of the circuit clerk's principal office;
   (C) for filing under Rules 4(c)(1), 25(a)(2)(B), and 25(a)(2)(C)—and filing by mail under Rule 13(a)(2)—at the latest time for the method chosen for delivery to the post office, third-party commercial carrier, or prison mailing system; and
   (D) for filing by other means, when the clerk's office is scheduled to close.

(5) *"Next Day" Defined.* The "next day" is determined by continuing to count forward when the period is measured after an event and backward when measured before an event.

(6) *"Legal Holiday" Defined.* "Legal holiday" means:
   (A) the day set aside by statute for observing New Year's Day, Martin Luther King Jr.'s Birthday,

Rule 26. Computing and Extending Time

Washington's Birthday, Memorial Day, Independence Day, Labor Day, Columbus Day, Veterans' Day, Thanksgiving Day, or Christmas Day;

(B) any day declared a holiday by the President or Congress; and

(C) for periods that are measured after an event, any other day declared a holiday by the state where either of the following is located: the district court that rendered the challenged judgment or order, or the circuit clerk's principal office.

(b) Extending Time. For good cause, the court may extend the time prescribed by these rules or by its order to perform any act, or may permit an act to be done after that time expires. But the court may not extend the time to file:

(1) a notice of appeal (except as authorized in Rule 4) or a petition for permission to appeal; or

(2) a notice of appeal from or a petition to enjoin, set aside, suspend, modify, enforce, or otherwise review an order of an administrative agency, board, commission, or officer of the United States, unless specifically authorized by law.

[The following text of subdivision (c) was effective until December 1, 2016.]

(c) Additional Time after Service. When a party may or must act within a specified time after service, 3 days are added after the period would otherwise expire under Rule 26(a), unless the paper is delivered on the date of service stated in the proof of service. For purposes of this Rule 26(c), a paper that is served electronically is not treated as delivered on the date of service stated in the proof of service.

[The following text of subdivision (c) became effective December 1, 2016.]

(c) Additional Time after Certain Kinds of Service. When a party may or must act within a specified time after being served, 3 days are added after the period would otherwise expire under Rule 26(a), unless the paper is delivered on the date of service stated in the proof of service. For purposes of this Rule 26(c), a paper that is served electronically is treated as delivered on the date of service stated in the proof of service.

(As amended Mar. 1, 1971, eff. July 1, 1971; Mar. 10, 1986, eff. July 1, 1986; Apr. 25, 1989, eff. Dec. 1, 1989; Apr. 30, 1991, eff. Dec. 1, 1991; Apr. 23, 1996, eff. Dec. 1, 1996; Apr. 24, 1998, eff. Dec. 1, 1998; Apr. 29, 2002, eff. Dec. 1, 2002; Apr. 25, 2005, eff. Dec. 1, 2005; Mar. 26, 2009, eff. Dec. 1, 2009; Apr. 28, 2016, eff. Dec. 1, 2016.)

Notes of Advisory Committee on Rules—1967

The provisions of this rule are based upon FRCP 6 (a), (b) and (e). See also Supreme Court Rule 34 and FRCrP 45. Unlike FRCP 6 (b), this rule, read with Rule 27, requires that every request for enlargement of time be made by motion, with proof of service on all parties. This is the simplest, most convenient way of keeping all parties advised of developments. By the terms of Rule 27(b) a motion for enlargement of time under Rule 26(b) may be entertained and acted upon immediately, subject to the right of any party to seek reconsideration. Thus the requirement of motion and notice will not delay the granting of relief of a kind which a court is inclined to grant as of course. Specifically, if a court is of the view that an extension of time sought before expiration of the period originally prescribed or as extended by a previous order ought to be granted in effect ex parte, as FRCP 6 (b) permits, it may grant motions seeking such relief without delay.

Notes of Advisory Committee on Rules—1971 Amendment

The amendment adds Columbus Day to the list of legal holidays to conform the subdivision to the Act of June 28, 1968, 82 Stat. 250, which constituted Columbus Day a legal holiday effective after January 1, 1971.

The Act, which amended Title 5, U.S.C. §6103(a), changes the day on which certain holidays are to be observed. Washington's Birthday, Memorial Day and Veterans Day are to be observed on the third Monday in February, the last Monday in May and the fourth Monday in October, respectively, rather than, as heretofore, on February 22, May 30, and November 11, respectively. Columbus Day is to be observed on the second Monday in October. New Year's Day, Independence Day, Thanksgiving Day and Christmas continue to be observed on the traditional days.

Rule 26. Computing and Extending Time

Notes of Advisory Committee on Rules—1986 Amendment

The Birthday of Martin Luther King, Jr., is added to the list of national holidays in Rule 26(a). The amendment to Rule 26(c) is technical. No substantive change is intended.

Notes of Advisory Committee on Rules—1989 Amendment

The proposed amendment brings Rule 26(a) into conformity with the provisions of Rule 6(a) of the Rules of Civil Procedure, Rule 45(a) of the Rules of Criminal Procedure, and Rule 9006(a) of the Rules of Bankruptcy Procedure which allow additional time for filing whenever a clerk's office is inaccessible on the last day for filing due to weather or other conditions.

Notes of Advisory Committee on Rules—1996 Amendment

The amendment is a companion to the proposed amendments to Rule 25 that permit service on a party by commercial carrier. The amendments to subdivision (c) of this rule make the three-day extension applicable not only when service is accomplished by mail, but whenever delivery to the party being served occurs later than the date of service stated in the proof of service. When service is by mail or commercial carrier, the proof of service recites the date of mailing or delivery to the commercial carrier. If the party being served receives the paper on a later date, the three-day extension applies. If the party being served receives the paper on the same date as the date of service recited in the proof of service, the three-day extension is not available.

The amendment also states that the three-day extension is three calendar days. Rule 26(a) states that when a period prescribed or allowed by the rules is less than seven days, intermediate Saturdays, Sundays, and legal holidays do not count. Whether the three-day extension in Rule 26(c) is such a period, meaning that three-days could actually be five or even six days, is unclear. The D.C. Circuit recently held that the parallel three-day extension provided in the Civil Rules is not such a period and that weekends and legal holidays do count. *CNPq v. Inter-Trade, 50 F.3d 56 (D.C. Cir. 1995)*. The Committee believes that is the right result and that the issue should be resolved. Providing that the extension is three calendar days means that if a period would otherwise end on Thursday but the three-day extension applies, the paper must be filed on Monday. Friday, Saturday, and Sunday are the extension days. Because the last day of the period as extended is Sunday, the paper must be filed the next day, Monday.

Committee Notes on Rules—1998 Amendment

The language and organization of the rule are amended to make the rule more easily understood. In addition to changes made to improve the understanding, the Advisory Committee has changed language to make style and terminology consistent throughout the appellate rules. These changes are intended to be stylistic only; two substantive changes are made, however, in subdivision (a).

Subdivision (a). First, the amendments make the computation method prescribed in this rule applicable to any time period imposed by a local rule. This means that if a local rule establishing a time limit is permitted, the national rule will govern the computation of that period.

Second, paragraph (a)(2) includes language clarifying that whenever the rules establish a time period in "calendar days," weekends and legal holidays are counted.

Committee Notes on Rules—2002 Amendment

Subdivision (a)(2). The Federal Rules of Civil Procedure and the Federal Rules of Criminal Procedure compute time differently than the Federal Rules of Appellate Procedure. Fed. R. Civ. P. 6 (a) and Fed. R. Crim. P. 45 (a) provide that, in computing any period of time, "[w]hen the period of time prescribed or allowed is less than 11 days, intermediate Saturdays, Sundays, and legal holidays shall be excluded in the computation." By contrast, Rule 26(a)(2) provides that, in computing any period of time, a litigant should "[e]xclude intermediate Saturdays, Sundays, and legal holidays when the period is less than 7 days, unless stated in calendar days." Thus, deadlines of 7, 8, 9, and 10 days are calculated differently under the rules of civil and criminal procedure than they are under the rules of appellate procedure. This creates a trap for unwary litigants. No good reason for this discrepancy is apparent, and thus Rule 26(a)(2) has been amended so that, under all three sets of rules, intermediate Saturdays, Sundays, and legal holidays will be excluded when computing deadlines under 11 days but will be counted when computing deadlines of 11 days and over.

Changes Made After Publication and Comments. No changes were made to the text of the proposed amendment or to the Committee Note.

Rule 26. Computing and Extending Time

Subdivision (c). Rule 26(c) has been amended to provide that when a paper is served on a party by electronic means, and that party is required or permitted to respond to that paper within a prescribed period, 3 calendar days are added to the prescribed period. Electronic service is usually instantaneous, but sometimes it is not, because of technical problems. Also, if a paper is electronically transmitted to a party on a Friday evening, the party may not realize that he or she has been served until two or three days later. Finally, extending the "3-day rule" to electronic service will encourage parties to consent to such service under Rule 25(c).

Changes Made After Publication and Comments. No changes were made to the text of the proposed amendment or to the Committee Note.

Committee Notes on Rules—2005 Amendment

Subdivision (a)(4). Rule 26(a)(4) has been amended to refer to the third Monday in February as "Washington's Birthday." A federal statute officially designates the holiday as "Washington's Birthday," reflecting the desire of Congress specially to honor the first president of the United States. *See* 5 U.S.C. §6103(a). During the 1998 restyling of the Federal Rules of Appellate Procedure, references to "Washington's Birthday" were mistakenly changed to "Presidents' Day." The amendment corrects that error.

Changes Made After Publication and Comments. No changes were made to the text of the proposed amendment or to the Committee Note.

Committee Notes on Rules—2009 Amendment

Subdivision (a). Subdivision (a) has been amended to simplify and clarify the provisions that describe how deadlines are computed. Subdivision (a) governs the computation of any time period found in a statute that does not specify a method of computing time, a Federal Rule of Appellate Procedure, a local rule, or a court order. In accordance with Rule 47(a)(1), a local rule may not direct that a deadline be computed in a manner inconsistent with subdivision (a).

The time-computation provisions of subdivision (a) apply only when a time period must be computed. They do not apply when a fixed time to act is set. The amendments thus carry forward the approach taken in *Violette v. P.A. Days, Inc.*, 427 F.3d 1015, 1016 (6th Cir. 2005) (holding that Civil Rule 6(a) "does not apply to situations where the court has established a specific calendar day as a deadline"), and reject the contrary holding of *In re American Healthcare Management, Inc.*, 900 F.2d 827, 832 (5th Cir. 1990) (holding that Bankruptcy Rule 9006(a) governs treatment of date-certain deadline set by court order). If, for example, the date for filing is "no later than November 1, 2007," subdivision (a) does not govern. But if a filing is required to be made "within 10 days" or "within 72 hours," subdivision (a) describes how that deadline is computed.

Subdivision (a) does not apply when computing a time period set by a statute if the statute specifies a method of computing time. *See, e.g.*, 20 U.S.C. §7711(b)(1) (requiring certain petitions for review by a local educational agency or a state to be filed "within 30 working days (as determined by the local educational agency or State) after receiving notice of' federal agency decision).

Subdivision (a)(1). New subdivision (a)(1) addresses the computation of time periods that are stated in days. It also applies to time periods that are stated in weeks, months, or years; though no such time period currently appears in the Federal Rules of Appellate Procedure, such periods may be set by other covered provisions such as a local rule. *See, e.g.*, Third Circuit Local Appellate Rule 46.3(c)(1). Subdivision (a)(1)(B)'s directive to "count every day" is relevant only if the period is stated in days (not weeks, months or years).

Under former Rule 26(a), a period of 11 days or more was computed differently than a period of less than 11 days. Intermediate Saturdays, Sundays, and legal holidays were included in computing the longer periods, but excluded in computing the shorter periods. Former Rule 26(a) thus made computing deadlines unnecessarily complicated and led to counterintuitive results. For example, a 10-day period and a 14-day period that started on the same day usually ended on the same day—and the 10-day period not infrequently ended later than the 14-day period. *See Miltimore Sales, Inc. v. Int'l Rectifier, Inc.*, 412 F.3d 685, 686 (6th Cir. 2005).

Under new subdivision (a)(1), all deadlines stated in days (no matter the length) are computed in the same way. The day of the event that triggers the deadline is not counted. All other days—including intermediate Saturdays, Sundays, and legal holidays—are counted, with only one exception: If the period ends on a Saturday, Sunday, or legal holiday, then the deadline falls on the next day that is not a Saturday, Sunday, or legal holiday. An illustration is provided below in the discussion of subdivision (a)(5). Subdivision (a)(3) addresses filing deadlines that expire on a day when the clerk's office is inaccessible.

Where subdivision (a) formerly referred to the "act, event, or default" that triggers the deadline, new subdivision (a) refers simply to the "event" that triggers the deadline; this change in terminology is adopted for brevity and simplicity, and is not intended to change meaning.

Rule 26. Computing and Extending Time

Periods previously expressed as less than 11 days will be shortened as a practical matter by the decision to count intermediate Saturdays, Sundays, and legal holidays in computing all periods. Many of those periods have been lengthened to compensate for the change. *See, e.g.*, Rules 5(b)(2), 5(d)(1), 28.1(f), & 31(a).

Most of the 10-day periods were adjusted to meet the change in computation method by setting 14 days as the new period. A 14-day period corresponds to the most frequent result of a 10-day period under the former computation method—two Saturdays and two Sundays were excluded, giving 14 days in all. A 14-day period has an additional advantage. The final day falls on the same day of the week as the event that triggered the period—the 14th day after a Monday, for example, is a Monday. This advantage of using week-long periods led to adopting 7-day periods to replace some of the periods set at less than 10 days, and 21-day periods to replace 20-day periods. Thirty-day and longer periods, however, were retained without change.

Subdivision (a)(2). New subdivision (a)(2) addresses the computation of time periods that are stated in hours. No such deadline currently appears in the Federal Rules of Appellate Procedure. But some statutes contain deadlines stated in hours, as do some court orders issued in expedited proceedings.

Under subdivision (a)(2), a deadline stated in hours starts to run immediately on the occurrence of the event that triggers the deadline. The deadline generally ends when the time expires. If, however, the time period expires at a specific time (say, 2:17 p.m.) on a Saturday, Sunday, or legal holiday, then the deadline is extended to the same time (2:17 p.m.) on the next day that is not a Saturday, Sunday, or legal holiday. Periods stated in hours are not to be "rounded up" to the next whole hour. Subdivision (a)(3) addresses situations when the clerk's office is inaccessible during the last hour before a filing deadline expires.

Subdivision (a)(2)(B) directs that every hour be counted. Thus, for example, a 72-hour period that commences at 10:00 a.m. on Friday, November 2, 2007, will run until 9:00 a.m. on Monday, November 5; the discrepancy in start and end times in this example results from the intervening shift from daylight saving time to standard time.

Subdivision (a)(3). When determining the last day of a filing period stated in days or a longer unit of time, a day on which the clerk's office is not accessible because of the weather or another reason is treated like a Saturday, Sunday, or legal holiday. When determining the end of a filing period stated in hours, if the clerk's office is inaccessible during the last hour of the filing period computed under subdivision (a)(2) then the period is extended to the same time on the next day that is not a weekend, holiday or day when the clerk's office is inaccessible.

Subdivision (a)(3)'s extensions apply "[u]nless the court orders otherwise." In some circumstances, the court might not wish a period of inaccessibility to trigger a full 24-hour extension; in those instances, the court can specify a briefer extension.

The text of the rule no longer refers to "weather or other conditions" as the reason for the inaccessibility of the clerk's office. The reference to "weather" was deleted from the text to underscore that inaccessibility can occur for reasons unrelated to weather, such as an outage of the electronic filing system. Weather can still be a reason for inaccessibility of the clerk's office. The rule does not attempt to define inaccessibility. Rather, the concept will continue to develop through caselaw, *see, e.g., Tchakmakjian v. Department of Defense*, 57 Fed. Appx. 438, 441 (Fed. Cir. 2003) (unpublished per curiam opinion) (inaccessibility "due to anthrax concerns"); *cf.* William G. Phelps, *When Is Office of Clerk of Court Inaccessible Due to Weather or Other Conditions for Purpose of Computing Time Period for Filing Papers under Rule 6(a) of Federal Rules of Civil Procedure*, 135 A.L.R. Fed. 259 (1996) (collecting cases). In addition, local provisions may address inaccessibility for purposes of electronic filing.

Subdivision (a)(4). New subdivision (a)(4) defines the end of the last day of a period for purposes of subdivision (a)(1). Subdivision (a)(4) does not apply in computing periods stated in hours under subdivision (a)(2), and does not apply if a different time is set by a statute, local rule, or order in the case. A local rule may, for example, address the problems that might arise under subdivision (a)(4)(A) if a single district has clerk's offices in different time zones, or provide that papers filed in a drop box after the normal hours of the clerk's office are filed as of the day that is date-stamped on the papers by a device in the drop box.

28 U.S.C. §452 provides that "[a]ll courts of the United States shall be deemed always open for the purpose of filing proper papers, issuing and returning process, and making motions and orders." A corresponding provision exists in Rule 45(a)(2). Some courts have held that these provisions permit an after-hours filing by handing the papers to an appropriate official. *See, e.g., Casalduc v. Diaz*, 117 F.2d 915, 917 (1st Cir. 1941). Subdivision (a)(4) does not address the effect of the statute on the question of after-hours filing; instead, the rule is designed to deal with filings in the ordinary course without regard to Section 452.

Subdivision (a)(4)(A) addresses electronic filings in the district court. For example, subdivision (a)(4)(A) would apply to an electronically-filed notice of appeal. Subdivision (a)(4)(B) addresses electronic filings in the court of appeals.

Subdivision (a)(4)(C) addresses filings by mail under Rules 25(a)(2)(B)(i) and 13(b), filings by third-party commercial carrier under Rule 25(a)(2)(B)(ii), and inmate filings under Rules 4(c)(1) and 25(a)(2)(C). For such filings, subdivision (a)(4)(C) provides that the "last day" ends at the latest time (prior to midnight in the filer's time zone) that the filer can properly submit the filing to the post office, third-party commercial carrier, or prison mail system (as applicable) using the

Rule 26. Computing and Extending Time

filer's chosen method of submission. For example, if a correctional institution's legal mail system's rules of operation provide that items may only be placed in the mail system between 9:00 a.m. and 5:00 p.m., then the "last day" for filings under Rules 4(c)(1) and 25(a)(2)(C) by inmates in that institution ends at 5:00 p.m. As another example, if a filer uses a drop box maintained by a third-party commercial carrier, the "last day" ends at the time of that drop box's last scheduled pickup. Filings by mail under Rule 13(b) continue to be subject to §7502 of the Internal Revenue Code, as amended, and the applicable regulations.

Subdivision (a)(4)(D) addresses all other non-electronic filings; for such filings, the last day ends under (a)(4)(D) when the clerk's office in which the filing is made is scheduled to close.

Subdivision (a)(5). New subdivision (a)(5) defines the "next" day for purposes of subdivisions (a)(1)(C) and (a)(2)(C). The Federal Rules of Appellate Procedure contain both forward-looking time periods and backward-looking time periods. A forward-looking time period requires something to be done within a period of time *after* an event. *See, e.g.*, Rule 4(a)(1)(A) (subject to certain exceptions, notice of appeal in a civil case must be filed "within 30 days after the judgment or order appealed from is entered"). A backward-looking time period requires something to be done within a period of time *before* an event. *See, e.g.*, Rule 31(a)(1) ("[A] reply brief must be filed at least 7 days before argument, unless the court, for good cause, allows a later filing."). In determining what is the "next" day for purposes of subdivisions (a)(1)(C) and (a)(2)(C), one should continue counting in the same direction—that is, forward when computing a forward-looking period and backward when computing a backward-looking period. If, for example, a filing is due within 10 days *after* an event, and the tenth day falls on Saturday, September 1, 2007, then the filing is due on Tuesday, September 4, 2007 (Monday, September 3, is Labor Day). But if a filing is due 10 days *before* an event, and the tenth day falls on Saturday, September 1, then the filing is due on Friday, August 31. If the clerk's office is inaccessible on August 31, then subdivision (a)(3) extends the filing deadline forward to the next accessible day that is not a Saturday, Sunday or legal holiday—no earlier than Tuesday, September 4.

Subdivision (a)(6). New subdivision (a)(6) defines "legal holiday" for purposes of the Federal Rules of Appellate Procedure, including the time-computation provisions of subdivision (a). Subdivision (a)(6) continues to include within the definition of "legal holiday" days that are declared a holiday by the President or Congress.

For forward-counted periods—i.e., periods that are measured after an event—subdivision (a)(6)(C) includes certain state holidays within the definition of legal holidays. However, state legal holidays are not recognized in computing backward-counted periods. For both forward- and backward-counted periods, the rule thus protects those who may be unsure of the effect of state holidays. For forward-counted deadlines, treating state holidays the same as federal holidays extends the deadline. Thus, someone who thought that the federal courts might be closed on a state holiday would be safeguarded against an inadvertent late filing. In contrast, for backward-counted deadlines, not giving state holidays the treatment of federal holidays allows filing on the state holiday itself rather than the day before. Take, for example, Monday, April 21, 2008 (Patriot's Day, a legal holiday in the relevant state). If a filing is due 14 days after an event, and the fourteenth day is April 21, then the filing is due on Tuesday, April 22 because Monday, April 21 counts as a legal holiday. But if a filing is due 14 days before an event, and the fourteenth day is April 21, the filing is due on Monday, April 21; the fact that April 21 is a state holiday does not make April 21 a legal holiday for purposes of computing this backward-counted deadline. But note that if the clerk's office is inaccessible on Monday, April 21, then subdivision (a)(3) extends the April 21 filing deadline forward to the next accessible day that is not a Saturday, Sunday or legal holiday—no earlier than Tuesday, April 22.

Subdivision (c). To specify that a period should be calculated by counting all intermediate days, including weekends or holidays, the Rules formerly used the term "calendar days." Because new subdivision (a) takes a "days-are-days" approach under which all intermediate days are counted, no matter how short the period, "3 calendar days" in subdivision (c) is amended to read simply "3 days."

Rule 26(c) has been amended to eliminate uncertainty about application of the 3-day rule. Civil Rule 6(e) was amended in 2004 to eliminate similar uncertainty in the Civil Rules.

Under the amendment, a party that is required or permitted to act within a prescribed period should first calculate that period, without reference to the 3-day rule provided by Rule 26(c), but with reference to the other time computation provisions of the Appellate Rules. After the party has identified the date on which the prescribed period would expire but for the operation of Rule 26(c), the party should add 3 calendar days. The party must act by the third day of the extension, unless that day is a Saturday, Sunday, or legal holiday, in which case the party must act by the next day that is not a Saturday, Sunday, or legal holiday.

To illustrate: A paper is served by mail on Thursday, November 1, 2007. The prescribed time to respond is 30 days. The prescribed period ends on Monday, December 3 (because the 30th day falls on a Saturday, the prescribed period extends to the following Monday). Under Rule 26(c), three calendar days are added—Tuesday, Wednesday, and Thursday—and thus the response is due on Thursday, December 6.

Changes Made After Publication and Comment. No changes were made after publication and comment, except for the style changes (described below) [omitted] which were suggested by Professor Kimble.

Committee Notes on Rules – 2016 Amendment

Subdivision (a)(4)(C). The reference to Rule 13(b) is revised to refer to Rule 13(a)(2) in light of a 2013 amendment to Rule 13. The amendment to subdivision (a)(4)(C) is technical and no substantive change is intended.

Rule 26(c) is amended to remove service by electronic means under Rule 25(c)(1)(D) from the modes of service that allow 3 added days to act after being served.

Rule 25(c) was amended in 2002 to provide for service by electronic means. Although electronic transmission seemed virtually instantaneous even then, electronic service was included in the modes of service that allow 3 added days to act after being served. There were concerns that the transmission might be delayed for some time, and particular concerns that incompatible systems might make it difficult or impossible to open attachments. Those concerns have been substantially alleviated by advances in technology and widespread skill in using electronic transmission.

A parallel reason for allowing the 3 added days was that electronic service was authorized only with the consent of the person to be served. Concerns about the reliability of electronic transmission might have led to refusals of consent; the 3 added days were calculated to alleviate these concerns.

Diminution of the concerns that prompted the decision to allow the 3 added days for electronic transmission is not the only reason for discarding this indulgence. Many rules have been changed to ease the task of computing time by adopting 7-, 14-, 21-, and 28- day periods that allow "day of- the-week" counting. Adding 3 days at the end complicated the counting, and increased the occasions for further complication by invoking the provisions that apply when the last day is a Saturday, Sunday, or legal holiday.

Electronic service after business hours, or just before or during a weekend or holiday, may result in a practical reduction in the time available to respond. Extensions of time may be warranted to prevent prejudice.

Rule 26(c) has also been amended to refer to instances when a party "may or must act . . . after being served" rather than to instances when a party "may or must act . . . after service." If, in future, an Appellate Rule sets a deadline for a party to act after that party itself effects service on another person, this change in language will clarify that Rule 26(c)'s three added days are not accorded to the party who effected service.

Rule 26.1 Corporate Disclosure Statement

(a) Who Must File. Any nongovernmental corporate party to a proceeding in a court of appeals must file a statement that identifies any parent corporation and any publicly held corporation that owns 10% or more of its stock or states that there is no such corporation.

(b) Time for Filing; Supplemental Filing. A party must file the Rule 26.1(a) statement with the principal brief or upon filing a motion, response, petition, or answer in the court of appeals, whichever occurs first, unless a local rule requires earlier filing. Even if the statement has already been filed, the party's principal brief must include the statement before the table of contents. A party must supplement its statement whenever the information that must be disclosed under Rule 26.1(a) changes.

(c) Number of Copies. If the Rule 26.1(a) statement is filed before the principal brief, or if a supplemental statement is filed, the party must file an original and 3 copies unless the court requires a different number by local rule or by order in a particular case.

(As added Apr. 25, 1989, eff. Dec. 1, 1989; amended Apr. 30, 1991, eff. Dec. 1, 1991; Apr. 29, 1994, eff. Dec. 1, 1994; Apr. 24, 1998, eff. Dec. 1, 1998; Apr. 29, 2002, eff. Dec. 1, 2002.)

Notes of Advisory Committee on Rules—1989

The purpose of this rule is to assist judges in making a determination of whether they have any interests in any of a party's related corporate entities that would disqualify the judges from hearing the appeal. The committee believes that this rule represents minimum disclosure requirements. If a Court of Appeals wishes to require additional information, a court is free to do so by local rule. However, the committee requests the courts to consider the desirability of uniformity and the burden that varying circuit rules creates on attorneys who practice in many circuits.

Notes of Advisory Committee on Rules—1994 Amendment

The amendment requires a party to file three copies of the disclosure statement whenever the statement is filed before the party's principal brief. Because the statement is included in each copy of the party's brief, there is no need to require the filing of additional copies at that time. A court of appeals may require the filing of a different number of copies by local

Rule 26.1 Corporate Disclosure Statement

rule or by order in a particular case.

Committee Notes on Rules—1998 Amendment

The language and organization of the rule are amended to make the rule more easily understood. In addition to changes made to improve the understanding, the Advisory Committee has changed language to make style and terminology consistent throughout the appellate rules. These changes are intended to be stylistic only; a substantive change is made, however, in subdivision (a).

Subdivison [sic] (a). The amendment deletes the requirement that a corporate party identify subsidiaries and affiliates that have issued shares to the public. Although several circuit rules require identification of such entities, the Committee believes that such disclosure is unnecessary.

A disclosure statement assists a judge in ascertaining whether or not the judge has an interest that should cause the judge to recuse himself or herself from the case. Given that purpose, disclosure of entities that would not be adversely affected by a decision in the case is unnecessary.

Disclosure of a party's parent corporation is necessary because a judgment against a subsidiary can negatively impact the parent. A judge who owns stock in the parent corporation, therefore, has an interest in litigation involving the subsidiary. The rule requires disclosure of all of a party's parent corporations meaning grandparent and great grandparent corporations as well. For example, if a party is a closely held corporation, the majority shareholder of which is a corporation formed by a publicly traded corporation for the purpose of acquiring and holding the shares of the party, the publicly traded grandparent corporation should be disclosed. Conversely, disclosure of a party's subsidiaries or affiliated corporations is ordinarily unnecessary. For example, if a party is a part owner of a corporation in which a judge owns stock, the possibility is quite remote that the judge might be biased by the fact that the judge and the litigant are co-owners of a corporation.

The amendment, however, adds a requirement that the party lists all its stockholders that are publicly held companies owning 10% or more of the stock of the party. A judgment against a corporate party can adversely affect the value of the company's stock and, therefore, persons owning stock in the party have an interest in the outcome of the litigation. A judge owning stock in a corporate party ordinarily recuses himself or herself. The new requirement takes the analysis one step further and assumes that if a judge owns stock in a publicly held corporation which in turn owns 10% or more of the stock in the party, the judge may have sufficient interest in the litigation to require recusal. The 10% threshold ensures that the corporation in which the judge may own stock is itself sufficiently invested in the party that a judgment adverse to the party could have an adverse impact upon the investing corporation in which the judge may own stock. This requirement is modeled on the Seventh Circuit's disclosure requirement.

Subdivision (b). The language requiring inclusion of the disclosure statement in a party's principal brief is moved to this subdivision because it deals with the time for filing the statement.

Committee Notes on Rules—2002 Amendment

a. Alternative One [At its June 7–8, 2001, meeting, the Committee on Rules of Practice and Procedure voted to reject Alternative One.]

Subdivision (a). Rule 26.1(a) presently requires nongovernmental corporate parties to file a "corporate disclosure statement." In that statement, a nongovernmental corporate party is required to identify all of its parent corporations and all publicly held corporations that own 10% or more of its stock. The corporate disclosure statement is intended to assist judges in determining whether they must recuse themselves by reason of "a financial interest in the subject matter in controversy." Code of Judicial Conduct, Canon 3C(1)(c) (1972).

Rule 26.1(a) has been amended to require that nongovernmental corporate parties who currently do not have to file a corporate disclosure statement—that is, nongovernmental corporate parties who do not have any parent corporations and at least 10% of whose stock is not owned by any publicly held corporation—inform the court of that fact. At present, when a corporate disclosure statement is not filed, courts do not know whether it has not been filed because there was nothing to report or because of ignorance of Rule 26.1(a).

Rule 26.1(a) does not require the disclosure of all information that could conceivably be relevant to a judge who is trying to decide whether he or she has a "financial interest" in a case. Experience with divergent disclosure practices and improving technology may provide the foundation for more comprehensive disclosure requirements. The Judicial Conference, supported by the committees that work regularly with the Code of Judicial Conduct and by the Administrative Office of the United States Courts, is in the best position to develop any additional requirements and to adjust those requirements as technology and other developments warrant. Thus, Rule 26.1(a) has been amended to authorize the Judicial Conference to promulgate more detailed financial disclosure requirements—requirements that might apply beyond nongovernmental corporate parties.

Rule 26.1 Corporate Disclosure Statement

As has been true in the past, Rule 26.1(a) does not forbid the promulgation of local rules that require disclosures in addition to those required by Rule 26.1(a) itself. However, along with the authority provided to the Judicial Conference to require additional disclosures is the authority to preempt any local rulemaking on the topic of financial disclosure.

Subdivision (b). Rule 26.1(b) has been amended to require parties to file supplemental disclosure statements whenever there is a change in the information that Rule 26.1(a) requires the parties to disclose. For example, if a publicly held corporation acquires 10% or more of a party's stock after the party has filed its disclosure statement, the party should file a supplemental statement identifying that publicly held corporation.

Subdivision (c). Rule 26.1(c) has been amended to provide that a party who is required to file a supplemental disclosure statement must file an original and 3 copies, unless a local rule or an order entered in a particular case provides otherwise.

b. *Alternative Two* [At its June 7–8, 2001, meeting, the Committee on Rules of Practice and Procedure voted to approve Alternative Two.]

Subdivision (a). Rule 26.1(a) requires nongovernmental corporate parties to file a "corporate disclosure statement." In that statement, a nongovernmental corporate party is required to identify all of its parent corporations and all publicly held corporations that own 10% or more of its stock. The corporate disclosure statement is intended to assist judges in determining whether they must recuse themselves by reason of "a financial interest in the subject matter in controversy." Code of Judicial Conduct, Canon 3C(1)(c) (1972).

Rule 26.1(a) has been amended to require that nongovernmental corporate parties who have not been required to file a corporate disclosure statement—that is, nongovernmental corporate parties who do not have any parent corporations and at least 10% of whose stock is not owned by any publicly held corporation—inform the court of that fact. At present, when a corporate disclosure statement is not filed, courts do not know whether it has not been filed because there was nothing to report or because of ignorance of Rule 26.1.

Subdivision (b). Rule 26.1(b) has been amended to require parties to file supplemental disclosure statements whenever there is a change in the information that Rule 26.1(a) requires the parties to disclose. For example, if a publicly held corporation acquires 10% or more of a party's stock after the party has filed its disclosure statement, the party should file a supplemental statement identifying that publicly held corporation.

Subdivision (c). Rule 26.1(c) has been amended to provide that a party who is required to file a supplemental disclosure statement must file an original and 3 copies, unless a local rule or an order entered in a particular case provides otherwise.

Changes Made After Publication and Comments. The Committee is submitting two versions of proposed Rule 26.1 for the consideration of the Standing Committee.

The first version—"Alternative One"—is the same as the version that was published, except that the rule has been amended to refer to "any information that may be *publicly designated* by the Judicial Conference" instead of to "any information that may be *required* by the Judicial Conference." At its April meeting, the Committee gave unconditional approval to all of "Alternative One," except the Judicial Conference provisions. The Committee conditioned its approval of the Judicial Conference provisions on the Standing Committee's assuring itself that lawyers would have ready access to any standards promulgated by the Judicial Conference and that the Judicial Conference provisions were consistent with the Rules Enabling Act.

The second version—"Alternative Two"—is the same as the version that was published, except that the Judicial Conference provisions have been eliminated. The Civil Rules Committee met several days after the Appellate Rules Committee and joined the Bankruptcy Rules Committee in disapproving the Judicial Conference provisions. Given the decreasing likelihood that the Judicial Conference provisions will be approved by the Standing Committee, I asked Prof. Schiltz to draft, and the Appellate Rules Committee to approve, a version of Rule 26.1 that omitted those provisions. "Alternative Two" was circulated to and approved by the Committee in late April.

I should note that, at its April meeting, the Appellate Rules Committee discussed the financial disclosure provision that was approved by the Bankruptcy Rules Committee. That provision defines the scope of the financial disclosure obligation much differently than the provisions approved by the Appellate, Civil, and Criminal Rules Committees, which are based on existing Rule 26.1. For example, the bankruptcy provision requires disclosure when a party "directly or indirectly" owns 10 percent or more of "any class" of a publicly *or* privately held corporation's "equity interests." Members of the Appellate Rules Committee expressed several concerns about the provision approved by the Bankruptcy Rules Committee, objecting both to its substance and to its ambiguity.

Rule 27. Motions

(a) In General.
  (1) *Application for Relief.* An application for an order or other relief is made by motion unless these rules prescribe another form. A motion must be in writing unless the court permits otherwise.
  (2) *Contents of a Motion.*
    (A) *Grounds and Relief Sought.* A motion must state with particularity the grounds for the motion, the relief sought, and the legal argument necessary to support it.
    (B) *Accompanying Documents.*
      (i) Any affidavit or other paper necessary to support a motion must be served and filed with the motion.
      (ii) An affidavit must contain only factual information, not legal argument.
      (iii) A motion seeking substantive relief must include a copy of the trial court's opinion or agency's decision as a separate exhibit.
    (C) *Documents Barred or Not Required.*
      (i) A separate brief supporting or responding to a motion must not be filed.
      (ii) A notice of motion is not required.
      (iii) A proposed order is not required.
  (3) *Response.*
    (A) *Time to file.* Any party may file a response to a motion; Rule 27(a)(2) governs its contents. The response must be filed within 10 days after service of the motion unless the court shortens or extends the time. A motion authorized by Rules 8, 9, 18, or 41 may be granted before the 10-day period runs only if the court gives reasonable notice to the parties that it intends to act sooner.
    (B) *Request for Affirmative Relief.* A response may include a motion for affirmative relief. The time to respond to the new motion, and to reply to that response, are governed by Rule 27(a)(3)(A) and (a)(4). The title of the response must alert the court to the request for relief.
  (4) *Reply to Response.* Any reply to a response must be filed within 7 days after service of the response. A reply must not present matters that do not relate to the response.

(b) Disposition of a Motion for a Procedural Order. The court may act on a motion for a procedural order—including a motion under Rule 26(b)—at any time without awaiting a response, and may, by rule or by order in a particular case, authorize its clerk to act on specified types of procedural motions. A party adversely affected by the court's, or the clerk's, action may file a motion to reconsider, vacate, or modify that action. Timely opposition filed after the motion is granted in whole or in part does not constitute a request to reconsider, vacate, or modify the disposition; a motion requesting that relief must be filed.

(c) Power of a Single Judge to Entertain a Motion. A circuit judge may act alone on any motion, but may not dismiss or otherwise determine an appeal or other proceeding. A court of appeals may provide by rule or by order in a particular case that only the court may act on any motion or class of motions. The court may review the action of a single judge.

(d) Form of Papers; Page Limits; and Number of Copies.
  (1) *Format.*
    (A) *Reproduction.* A motion, response, or reply may be reproduced by any process that yields a clear black image on light paper. The paper must be opaque and unglazed. Only one side of the paper may be used.
    (B) *Cover.* A cover is not required, but there must be a caption that includes the case number, the name of the court, the title of the case, and a brief descriptive title indicating the purpose of the motion and identifying the party or parties for whom it is filed. If a cover is used, it must be white.
    (C) *Binding.* The document must be bound in any manner that is secure, does not obscure the text, and permits the document to lie reasonably flat when open.
    (D) *Paper Size, Line Spacing, and Margins.* The document must be on 8 1/2 by 11 inch paper. The text must be double-spaced, but quotations more than two lines long may be indented and single-spaced. Headings and footnotes may be single-spaced. Margins must be at least one inch on all four sides. Page numbers may be placed in the margins, but no text may appear there.

Rule 27. Motions

(E) *Typeface and Type Styles.* The document must comply with the typeface requirements of Rule 32(a)(5) and the type-style requirements of Rule 32(a)(6).

[The following text of subdivision (2) was effective until December 1, 2016.]

(2) *Page Limits.* A motion or a response to a motion must not exceed 20 pages, exclusive of the corporate disclosure statement and accompanying documents authorized by Rule 27(a)(2)(B), unless the court permits or directs otherwise. A reply to a response must not exceed 10 pages.

[The following text of subdivision (2) became effective December 1, 2016.]

(2) *Length Limits.* Except by the court's permission, and excluding the accompanying documents authorized by Rule 27(a)(2)(B):
   (A) a motion or response to a motion produced using a computer must not exceed 5,200 words;
   (B) a handwritten or typewritten motion or response to a motion must not exceed 20 pages;
   (C) a reply produced using a computer must not exceed 2,600 words; and
   (D) a handwritten or typewritten reply to a response must not exceed 10 pages.

(3) *Number of Copies.* An original and 3 copies must be filed unless the court requires a different number by local rule or by order in a particular case.

(e) Oral Argument. A motion will be decided without oral argument unless the court orders otherwise.
(As amended Apr. 1, 1979, eff. Aug. 1, 1979; Apr. 25, 1989, eff. Dec. 1, 1989; Apr. 29, 1994, eff. Dec. 1, 1994; Apr. 24, 1998, eff. Dec. 1, 1998; Apr. 29, 2002, eff. Dec. 1, 2002; Apr. 25, 2005, eff. Dec. 1, 2005; Mar. 26, 2009, eff. Dec. 1, 2009.)

Notes of Advisory Committee on Rules—1967

Subdivisions (a) and (b). Many motions seek relief of a sort which is ordinarily unopposed or which is granted as of course. The provision of subdivision (a) which permits any party to file a response in opposition to a motion within 7 days after its service upon him assumes that the motion is one of substance which ought not be acted upon without affording affected parties an opportunity to reply. A motion to dismiss or otherwise determine an appeal is clearly such a motion. Motions authorized by Rules 8, 9, 18 and 41 are likewise motions of substance; but in the nature of the relief sought, to afford an adversary an automatic delay of at least 7 days is undesirable, thus such motions may be acted upon after notice which is reasonable under the circumstances.

The term "motions for procedural orders" is used in subdivision (b) to describe motions which do not substantially affect the rights of the parties or the ultimate disposition of the appeal. To prevent delay in the disposition of such motions, subdivision (b) provides that they may be acted upon immediately without awaiting a response, subject to the right of any party who is adversely affected by the action to seek reconsideration.

Subdivision (c). Within the general consideration of procedure on motions is the problem of the power of a single circuit judge. Certain powers are granted to a single judge of a court of appeals by statute. Thus, under 28 U.S.C. §2101(f) a single judge may stay execution and enforcement of a judgment to enable a party aggrieved to obtain certiorari; under 28 U.S.C. §2251 a judge before whom a habeas corpus proceeding involving a person detained by state authority is pending may stay any proceeding against the person; under 28 U.S.C. §2253 a single judge may issue a certificate of probable cause. In addition, certain of these rules expressly grant power to a single judge. See Rules 8, 9 and 18.

This subdivision empowers a single circuit judge to act upon virtually all requests for intermediate relief which may be made during the course of an appeal or other proceeding. By its terms he may entertain and act upon any motion other than a motion to dismiss or otherwise determine an appeal or other proceeding. But the relief sought must be "relief which under these rules may properly be sought by motion."

Examples of the power conferred on a single judge by this subdivision are: to extend the time for transmitting the record or docketing the appeal (Rules 11 and 12); to permit intervention in agency cases (Rule 15), or substitution in any case (Rule 43); to permit an appeal in forma pauperis (Rule 24); to enlarge any time period fixed by the rules other than that for initiating a proceeding in the court of appeals (Rule 26(b)); to permit the filing of a brief by amicus curiae (Rule 29); to authorize the filing of a deferred appendix (Rule 30(c)), or dispense with the requirement of an appendix in a specific case (Rule 30(f)), or permit carbon copies of briefs or appendices to be used (Rule 32(a)); to permit the filing of additional briefs (Rule 28(c)), or the filing of briefs of extraordinary length (Rule 28(g)); to postpone oral argument (Rule

Rule 27. Motions

34(a)), or grant additional time therefor (Rule 34(b)).

Certain rules require that application for the relief or orders which they authorize be made by petition. Since relief under those rules may not properly be sought by motion, a single judge may not entertain requests for such relief. Thus a single judge may not act upon requests for permission to appeal (see Rules 5 and 6); or for mandamus or other extraordinary writs (see Rule 21), other than for stays or injunctions *pendente lite*, authority to grant which is "expressly conferred by these rules" on a single judge under certain circumstances (see Rules 8 and 18); or upon petitions for rehearing (see Rule 40).

A court of appeals may by order or rule abridge the power of a single judge if it is of the view that a motion or a class of motions should be disposed of by a panel. Exercise of any power granted a single judge is discretionary with the judge. The final sentence in this subdivision makes the disposition of any matter by a single judge subject to review by the court.

Notes of Advisory Committee on Rules—1979 Amendment

The proposed amendment would give sanction to local rules in a number of circuits permitting the clerk to dispose of specified types of procedural motions.

Notes of Advisory Committee on Rules—1989 Amendment

The amendment is technical. No substantive change is intended.

Notes of Advisory Committee on Rules—1994 Amendment

Subdivision (d). The amendment makes it clear that a court may require a different number of copies either by rule or by order in an individual case. The number of copies of any document that a court of appeals needs varies depending upon the way in which the court conducts business. The internal operation of the courts of appeals necessarily varies from circuit to circuit because of differences in the number of judges, the geographic area included within the circuit, and other such factors. Uniformity could be achieved only by setting the number of copies artificially high so that parties in all circuits file enough copies to satisfy the needs of the court requiring the greatest number. Rather than do that, the Committee decided to make it clear that local rules may require a greater or lesser number of copies and that, if the circumstances of a particular case indicate the need for a different number of copies in that case, the court may so order.

Committee Notes on Rules—1998 Amendment

In addition to amending Rule 27 to conform to uniform drafting standards, several substantive amendments are made. The Advisory Committee had been working on substantive amendments to Rule 27 just prior to completion of this larger project.

Subdivision (a). Paragraph (1) retains the language of the existing rule indicating that an application for an order or other relief is made by filing a motion unless another form is required by some other provision in the rules.

Paragraph (1) also states that a motion must be in writing unless the court permits otherwise. The writing requirement has been implicit in the rule; the Advisory Committee decided to make it explicit. There are, however, instances in which a court may permit oral motions. Perhaps the most common such instance would be a motion made during oral argument in the presence of opposing counsel; for example, a request for permission to submit a supplemental brief on an issue raised by the court for the first time at oral argument. Rather than limit oral motions to those made during oral argument or, conversely, assume the propriety of making even extremely complex motions orally during argument, the Advisory Committee decided that it is better to leave the determination of the propriety of an oral motion to the court's discretion. The provision does not disturb the practice in those circuits that permit certain procedural motions, such as a motion for extension of time for filing a brief, to be made by telephone and ruled upon by the clerk.

Paragraph (2) outlines the contents of a motion. It begins with the general requirement from the current rule that a motion must state with particularity the grounds supporting it and the relief requested. It adds a requirement that all legal arguments should be presented in the body of the motion; a separate brief or memorandum supporting or responding to a motion must not be filed. The Supreme Court uses this single document approach. Sup. Ct. R. 21.1. In furtherance of the requirement that all legal argument must be contained in the body of the motion, paragraph (2) also states that an affidavit that is attached to a motion should contain only factual information and not legal argument.

Paragraph (2) further states that whenever a motion requests substantive relief, a copy of the trial court's opinion or agency's decision must be attached.

Although it is common to present a district court with a proposed order along with the motion requesting relief, that is not the practice in the courts of appeals. A proposed order is not required and is not expected or desired. Nor is a notice of

Rule 27. Motions

motion required.

Paragraph (3) retains the provisions of the current rule concerning the filing of a response to a motion except that the time for responding has been expanded to 10 days rather than 7 days. Because the time periods in the rule apply to a substantive motion as well as a procedural motion, the longer time period may help reduce the number of motions for extension of time, or at least provide a more realistic time frame within which to make and dispose of such a motion.

A party filing a response in opposition to a motion may also request affirmative relief. It is the Advisory Committee's judgment that it is permissible to combine the response and the new motion in the same document. Indeed, because there may be substantial overlap of arguments in the response and in the request for affirmative relief, a combined document may be preferable. If a request for relief is combined with a response, the caption of the document must alert the court to the request for relief. The time for a response to such a new request and for reply to that response are governed by the general rules regulating responses and replies.

Paragraph (4) is new. Two circuits currently have rules authorizing a reply. As a general matter, a reply should not reargue propositions presented in the motion or present matters that do not relate to the response. Sometimes matters relevant to the motion arise after the motion is filed; treatment of such matters in the reply is appropriate even though strictly speaking it may not relate to the response.

Subdivision (b). The material in this subdivision remains substantively unchanged except to clarify that one may file a motion for reconsideration, etc., of a disposition by either the court or the clerk. A new sentence is added indicating that if a motion is granted in whole or in part before the filing of timely opposition to the motion, the filing of the opposition is not treated as a request for reconsideration, etc. A party wishing to have the court reconsider, vacate, or modify the disposition must file a new motion that addresses the order granting the motion.

Although the rule does not require a court to do so, it would be helpful if, whenever a motion is disposed of before receipt of any response from the opposing party, the ruling indicates that it was issued without awaiting a response. Such a statement will aid the opposing party in deciding whether to request reconsideration. The opposing party may have mailed a response about the time of the ruling and be uncertain whether the court has considered it.

Subdivision (c). The changes in this subdivision are stylistic only. No substantive changes are intended.

Subdivision (d). This subdivision has been substantially revised.

The format requirements have been moved from Rule 32(b) to paragraph (1) of this subdivision. No cover is required, but a caption is needed as well as a descriptive title indicating the purpose of the motion and identifying the party or parties for whom it is filed. Spiral binding or secure stapling at the upper left-hand corner satisfies the binding requirement. But they are not intended to be the exclusive methods of binding.

Paragraph (2) establishes page limits; twenty pages for a motion or a response, and ten pages for a reply. Three circuits have established page limits by local rule. This rule does not establish special page limits for those instances in which a party combines a response to a motion with a new request for affirmative relief. Because a combined document most often will be used when there is substantial overlap in the argument in opposition to the motion and in the argument for the affirmative relief, twenty pages may be sufficient in most instances. If it is not, the party may request additional pages. If ten pages is insufficient for the original movant to both reply to the response, and respond to the new request for affirmative relief, two separate documents may be used or a request for additional pages may be made.

The changes in paragraph (4) are stylistic only. No substantive changes are intended.

Subdivision (e). This new provision makes it clear that there is no right to oral argument on a motion. Seven circuits have local rules stating that oral argument of motions will not be held unless the court orders it.

Committee Notes on Rules—2002 Amendment

Subdivision (a)(3)(A). Subdivision (a)(3)(A) presently requires that a response to a motion be filed within 10 days after service of the motion. Intermediate Saturdays, Sundays, and legal holidays are counted in computing that 10-day deadline, which means that, except when the 10-day deadline ends on a weekend or legal holiday, parties generally must respond to motions within 10 actual days.

Fed. R. App. P. 26 (a)(2) has been amended to provide that, in computing any period of time, a litigant should "[e]xclude intermediate Saturdays, Sundays, and legal holidays when the period is less than 11 days, unless stated in calendar days." This change in the method of computing deadlines means that 10-day deadlines (such as that in subdivision (a)(3)(A)) have been lengthened as a practical matter. Under the new computation method, parties would never have less than 14 actual days to respond to motions, and legal holidays could extend that period to as much as 18 days.

Permitting parties to take two weeks or more to respond to motions would introduce significant and unwarranted delay into appellate proceedings. For that reason, the 10-day deadline in subdivision (a)(3)(A) has been reduced to 8 days. This change will, as a practical matter, ensure that every party will have at least 10 actual days—but, in the absence of a legal holiday, no more than 12 actual days—to respond to motions. The court continues to have discretion to shorten or

Rule 27. Motions

extend that time in appropriate cases.

Changes Made After Publication and Comments. In response to the objections of commentators, the time to respond to a motion was increased from the proposed 7 days to 8 days. No other changes were made to the text of the proposed amendment or to the Committee Note.

Subdivision (a)(4). Subdivision (a)(4) presently requires that a reply to a response to a motion be filed within 7 days after service of the response. Intermediate Saturdays, Sundays, and legal holidays are counted in computing that 7-day deadline, which means that, except when the 7-day deadline ends on a weekend or legal holiday, parties generally must reply to responses to motions within one week.

Fed. R. App. P. 26 (a)(2) has been amended to provide that, in computing any period of time, a litigant should "[e]xclude intermediate Saturdays, Sundays, and legal holidays when the period is less than 11 days, unless stated in calendar days." This change in the method of computing deadlines means that 7-day deadlines (such as that in subdivision (a)(4)) have been lengthened as a practical matter. Under the new computation method, parties would never have less than 9 actual days to reply to responses to motions, and legal holidays could extend that period to as much as 13 days.

Permitting parties to take 9 or more days to reply to a response to a motion would introduce significant and unwarranted delay into appellate proceedings. For that reason, the 7-day deadline in subdivision (a)(4) has been reduced to 5 days. This change will, as a practical matter, ensure that every party will have 7 actual days to file replies to responses to motions (in the absence of a legal holiday).

Changes Made After Publication and Comments. No changes were made to the text of the proposed amendment or to the Committee Note.

Subdivision (d)(1)(B). A cover is not required on motions, responses to motions, or replies to responses to motions. However, Rule 27(d)(1)(B) has been amended to provide that if a cover is nevertheless used on such a paper, the cover must be white. The amendment is intended to promote uniformity in federal appellate practice.

Changes Made After Publication and Comments. No changes were made to the text of the proposed amendment or to the Committee Note.

Committee Notes on Rules—2005 Amendment

Subdivision (d)(1)(E). A new subdivision (E) has been added to Rule 27(d)(1) to provide that a motion, a response to a motion, and a reply to a response to a motion must comply with the typeface requirements of Rule 32(a)(5) and the type-style requirements of Rule 32(a)(6). The purpose of the amendment is to promote uniformity in federal appellate practice and to prevent the abuses that might occur if no restrictions were placed on the size of typeface used in motion papers.

Changes Made After Publication and Comments. No changes were made to the text of the proposed amendment or to the Committee Note.

Committee Notes on Rules—2009 Amendment

Subdivision (a)(3)(A). Subdivision (a)(3)(A) formerly required that a response to a motion be filed "within 8 days after service of the motion unless the court shortens or extends the time." Prior to the 2002 amendments to Rule 27, subdivision (a)(3)(A) set this period at 10 days rather than 8 days. The period was changed in 2002 to reflect the change from a time-computation approach that counted intermediate weekends and holidays to an approach that did not.(Prior to the 2002 amendments, intermediate weekends and holidays were excluded only if the period was less than 7 days; after those amendments, such days were excluded if the period was less than 11 days.) Under current Rule 26(a), intermediate weekends and holidays are counted for all periods. Accordingly, revised subdivision (a)(3)(A) once again sets the period at 10 days.

Subdivision (a)(4). Subdivision (a)(4) formerly required that a reply to a response be filed "within 5 days after service of the response." Prior to the 2002 amendments, this period was set at 7 days; in 2002 it was shortened in the light of the 2002 change in time-computation approach (discussed above). Under current Rule 26(a), intermediate weekends and holidays are counted for all periods, and revised subdivision (a)(4) once again sets the period at 7 days.

Committee Notes on Rules – 2016 Amendment

The page limits previously employed in Rules 5, 21, 27, 35, and 40 have been largely overtaken by changes in technology. For papers produced using a computer, those page limits are now replaced by word limits. The word limits were derived from the current page limits using the assumption that one page is equivalent to 260 words. Papers produced using a computer must include the certificate of compliance required by Rule 32(g); Form 6 in the Appendix of Forms suffices to meet that requirement. Page limits are retained for papers prepared without the aid of a computer (i.e., handwritten or typewritten papers). For both the word limit and the page limit, the calculation excludes the accompanying documents required by Rule 27(a)(2)(B) and any items listed in Rule 32(f).

Rule 28. Briefs

(a) Appellant's Brief. The appellant's brief must contain, under appropriate headings and in the order indicated:

    (1) a corporate disclosure statement if required by Rule 26.1;
    (2) a table of contents, with page references;
    (3) a table of authorities—cases (alphabetically arranged), statutes, and other authorities—with references to the pages of the brief where they are cited;
    (4) a jurisdictional statement, including:
        (A) the basis for the district court's or agency's subject-matter jurisdiction, with citations to applicable statutory provisions and stating relevant facts establishing jurisdiction;
        (B) the basis for the court of appeals' jurisdiction, with citations to applicable statutory provisions and stating relevant facts establishing jurisdiction;
        (C) the filing dates establishing the timeliness of the appeal or petition for review; and
        (D) an assertion that the appeal is from a final order or judgment that disposes of all parties' claims, or information establishing the court of appeals' jurisdiction on some other basis;
    (5) a statement of the issues presented for review;
    (6) a concise statement of the case setting out the facts relevant to the issues submitted for review, describing the relevant procedural history, and identifying the rulings presented for review, with appropriate references to the record (see Rule 28(e));
    (7) a summary of the argument, which must contain a succinct, clear, and accurate statement of the arguments made in the body of the brief, and which must not merely repeat the argument headings;
    (8) the argument, which must contain:
        (A) appellant's contentions and the reasons for them, with citations to the authorities and parts of the record on which the appellant relies; and
        (B) for each issue, a concise statement of the applicable standard of review (which may appear in the discussion of the issue or under a separate heading placed before the discussion of the issues);
    (9) a short conclusion stating the precise relief sought; and

[The following text of subdivision (10) was effective until December 1, 2016.]

    (10) the certificate of compliance, if required by Rule 32(a)(7).

[The following text of subdivision (10) became effective December 1, 2016.]

    (10) the certificate of compliance, if required by Rule 32(g)(1).

(b) Appellee's Brief. The appellee's brief must conform to the requirements of Rule 28(a)(1)–(8) and (10), except that none of the following need appear unless the appellee is dissatisfied with the appellant's statement:

    (1) the jurisdictional statement;
    (2) the statement of the issues;
    (3) the statement of the case; and
    (4) the statement of the standard of review.

(c) Reply Brief. The appellant may file a brief in reply to the appellee's brief. Unless the court permits, no further briefs may be filed. A reply brief must contain a table of contents, with page references, and a table of authorities—cases (alphabetically arranged), statutes, and other authorities—with references to the pages of the reply brief where they are cited.

Rule 28. Briefs

(d) References to Parties. In briefs and at oral argument, counsel should minimize use of the terms "appellant" and "appellee." To make briefs clear, counsel should use the parties' actual names or the designations used in the lower court or agency proceeding, or such descriptive terms as "the employee," "the injured person," "the taxpayer," "the ship," "the stevedore."

(e) References to the Record. References to the parts of the record contained in the appendix filed with the appellant's brief must be to the pages of the appendix. If the appendix is prepared after the briefs are filed, a party referring to the record must follow one of the methods detailed in Rule 30(c). If the original record is used under Rule 30(f) and is not consecutively paginated, or if the brief refers to an unreproduced part of the record, any reference must be to the page of the original document. For example:

- Answer p. 7;
- Motion for Judgment p. 2;
- Transcript p. 231.

Only clear abbreviations may be used. A party referring to evidence whose admissibility is in controversy must cite the pages of the appendix or of the transcript at which the evidence was identified, offered, and received or rejected.

(f) Reproduction of Statutes, Rules, Regulations, etc. If the court's determination of the issues presented requires the study of statutes, rules, regulations, etc., the relevant parts must be set out in the brief or in an addendum at the end, or may be supplied to the court in pamphlet form.

(g) [Reserved]

(h) [Reserved]

(i) Briefs in a Case Involving Multiple Appellants or Appellees. In a case involving more than one appellant or appellee, including consolidated cases, any number of appellants or appellees may join in a brief, and any party may adopt by reference a part of another's brief. Parties may also join in reply briefs.

(j) Citation of Supplemental Authorities. If pertinent and significant authorities come to a party's attention after the party's brief has been filed—or after oral argument but before decision—a party may promptly advise the circuit clerk by letter, with a copy to all other parties, setting forth the citations. The letter must state the reasons for the supplemental citations, referring either to the page of the brief or to a point argued orally. The body of the letter must not exceed 350 words. Any response must be made promptly and must be similarly limited.

(As amended Apr. 30, 1979, eff. Aug. 1, 1979; Mar. 10, 1986, eff. July 1, 1986; Apr. 25, 1989, eff. Dec. 1, 1989; Apr. 30, 1991, eff. Dec. 1, 1991; Apr. 22, 1993, eff. Dec. 1, 1993; Apr. 29, 1994, eff. Dec. 1, 1994; Apr. 24, 1998, eff. Dec. 1, 1998; Apr. 29, 2002, eff. Dec. 1, 2002; Apr. 25, 2005, eff. Dec. 1, 2005; Apr. 16, 2013, eff. Dec. 1, 2013; Apr. 28, 2016, eff. Dec. 1, 2016.)

Notes of Advisory Committee on Rules—1967

This rule is based upon Supreme Court Rule 40. For variations in present circuit rules on briefs see 2d Cir. Rule 17, 3d Cir. Rule 24, 5th Cir. Rule 24, and 7th Cir. Rule 17. All circuits now limit the number of pages of briefs, a majority limiting the brief to 50 pages of standard typographic printing. Fifty pages of standard typographic printing is the approximate equivalent of 70 pages of typewritten text, given the page sizes required by Rule 32 and the requirement set out there that text produced by a method other than standard typographic must be double spaced.

Notes of Advisory Committee on Rules—1979 Amendment

The proposed amendment eliminates the distinction appearing in the present rule between the permissible length in pages of printed and typewritten briefs, investigation of the matter having disclosed that the number of words on the printed page is little if any larger than the number on a page typed in standard elite type.

The provision is made subject to local rule to permit the court of appeals to require that typewritten briefs be typed in larger type and permit a correspondingly larger number of pages.

Subdivision (j). Proposed new Rule 28(j) makes provision for calling the court's attention to authorities that come to the party's attention after the brief has been filed. It is patterned after the practice under local rule in some of the circuits.

Rule 28. Briefs

Notes of Advisory Committee on Rules—1986 Amendment

While Rule 28(g) can be read as requiring that tables of authorities be included in a reply brief, such tables are often not included. Their absence impedes efficient use of the reply brief to ascertain the appellant's response to a particular argument of the appellee or to the appellee's use of a particular authority. The amendment to Rule 28(c) is intended to make it clear that such tables are required in reply briefs.

The amendment to Rule 28(j) is technical. No substantive change is intended.

Notes of Advisory Committee on Rules—1989 Amendment

The amendment provides that the corporate disclosure statement required by new rule 26.1 shall be treated similarly to tables of contents and tables of citations and shall not be counted for purposes of the number of pages allowed in a brief.

Notes of Advisory Committee on Rules—1991 Amendment

Subdivision (a). The amendment adds a new subparagraph (2) that requires an appellant to include a specific jurisdictional statement in the appellant's brief to aid the court of appeals in determining whether it has both federal subject matter and appellate jurisdiction.

Subdivision (b). The amendment requires the appellee to include a jurisdictional statement in the appellee's brief except that the appellee need not include the statement if the appellee is satisfied with the appellant's jurisdictional statement.

Subdivision (h). The amendment provides that when more than one party appeals from a judgment or order, the party filing the first appeal is normally treated as the appellant for purposes of this rule and Rules 30 and 31. The party who first files an appeal usually is the principal appellant and should be treated as such. Parties who file a notice of appeal after the first notice often bring protective appeals and they should be treated as cross appellants. Local rules in the Fourth and Federal Circuits now take that approach. If notices of appeal are filed on the same day, the rule follows the old approach of treating the plaintiff below as the appellant. For purposes of this rule, in criminal cases "the plaintiff" means the United States. In those instances where the designations provided by the rule are inappropriate, they may be altered by agreement of the parties or by an order of the court.

Notes of Advisory Committee on Rules—1993 Amendment

Note to paragraph (a)(5). The amendment requires an appellant's brief to state the standard of review applicable to each issue on appeal. Five circuits currently require these statements. Experience in those circuits indicates that requiring a statement of the standard of review generally results in arguments that are properly shaped in light of the standard.

Notes of Advisory Committee on Rules—1994 Amendment

Subdivision (a). The amendment adds a requirement that an appellant's brief contain a summary of the argument. A number of circuits have local rules requiring a summary and the courts report that they find the summary useful. *See*, D.C. Cir. R. 11(a)(5); 5th Cir. R. 28.2.2; 8th Cir. R. 28A(i)(6); 11th Cir. R. 28–2(i); and Fed. Cir. R. 28.

Subdivision (b). The amendment adds a requirement that an appellee's brief contain a summary of the argument.

Subdivision (g). The amendment adds proof of service to the list of items in a brief that do not count for purposes of the page limitation. The concurrent amendment to Rule 25(d) requires a certificate of service to list the addresses to which a paper was mailed or at which it was delivered. When a number of parties must be served, the listing of addresses may run to several pages and those pages should not count for purposes of the page limitation.

Committee Notes on Rules—1998 Amendment

The language and organization of the rule are amended to make the rule more easily understood. In additional to changes made to improve the understanding, the Advisory Committee has changed language to make style and terminology consistent throughout the appellate rules. These changes are intended to be stylistic only.
Several substantive changes are made in this rule, however. Most of them are necessary to conform Rule 28 with changes recommended in Rule 32.

Subdivision (a). The current rule requires a brief to include a statement of the case which includes a description of the nature of the case, the course of proceedings, the disposition of the case—all of which might be described as the procedural history—as well as a statement of the facts. The amendments separate this into two statements: one procedural, called the

Rule 28. Briefs

statement of the case; and one factual, called the statement of the facts. The Advisory Committee believes that the separation will be helpful to the judges. The table of contents and table of authorities have also been separated into two distinct items.

An additional amendment of subdivision (a) is made to conform it with an amendment being made to Rule 32. Rule 32(a)(7) generally requires a brief to include a certificate of compliance with type-volume limitations contained in that rule. (No certificate is required if a brief does not exceed 30 pages, or 15 pages for a reply brief.) Rule 28(a) is amended to include that certificate in the list of items that must be included in a brief whenever it is required by Rule 32.

Subdivision (g). The amendments delete subdivision (g) that limited a principal brief to 50 pages and a reply brief to 25 pages. The length limitations have been moved to Rule 32. Rule 32 deals generally with the format for a brief or appendix.

Subdivision (h). The amendment requires an appellee's brief to comply with Rule 28(a)(1) through (11) with regard to a cross-appeal. The addition of separate paragraphs requiring a corporate disclosure statement, table of authorities, statement of facts, and certificate of compliance increased the relevant paragraphs of subdivision (a) from (7) to (11). The other changes are stylistic; no substantive changes are intended.

Committee Notes on Rules—2002 Amendment

Subdivision (j). In the past, Rule 28(j) has required parties to describe supplemental authorities "without argument." Enforcement of this restriction has been lax, in part because of the difficulty of distinguishing "state[ment] . . . [of] the reasons for the supplemental citations," which is required, from "argument" about the supplemental citations, which is forbidden.

As amended, Rule 28(j) continues to require parties to state the reasons for supplemental citations, with reference to the part of a brief or oral argument to which the supplemental citations pertain. But Rule 28(j) no longer forbids "argument." Rather, Rule 28(j) permits parties to decide for themselves what they wish to say about supplemental authorities. The only restriction upon parties is that the body of a Rule 28(j) letter—that is, the part of the letter that begins with the first word after the salutation and ends with the last word before the complimentary close—cannot exceed 350 words. All words found in footnotes will count toward the 350-word limit.

Changes Made After Publication and Comments. No changes were made to the text of the proposed amendment or to the Committee Note, except that the word limit was increased from 250 to 350 in response to the complaint of some commentators that parties would have difficulty bringing multiple supplemental authorities to the attention of the court in one 250-word letter.

Committee Notes on Rules—2005 Amendment

Subdivision (c). Subdivision (c) has been amended to delete a sentence that authorized an appellee who had cross-appealed to file a brief in reply to the appellant's response. All rules regarding briefing in cases involving cross-appeals have been consolidated into new Rule 28.1.

Subdivision (h). Subdivision (h)—regarding briefing in cases involving cross-appeals—has been deleted. All rules regarding such briefing have been consolidated into new Rule 28.1.

Committee Notes on Rules—2013 Amendment

Subdivision (a). Rule 28(a) is amended to remove the requirement of separate statements of the case and of the facts. Currently Rule 28(a)(6) provides that the statement of the case must "indicat[e] the nature of the case, the course of proceedings, and the disposition below," and it precedes Rule 28(a)(7)'s requirement that the brief include "a statement of facts." Experience has shown that these requirements have generated confusion and redundancy. Rule 28(a) is amended to consolidate subdivisions (a)(6) and (a)(7) into a new subdivision (a)(6) that provides for one "statement," much like Supreme Court Rule 24.1(g) (which requires "[a] concise statement of the case, setting out the facts material to the consideration of the questions presented, with appropriate references to the joint appendix..."). This permits but does not require the lawyer to present the factual and procedural history chronologically. Conforming changes are made by renumbering Rules 28(a)(8) through (11) as Rules 28(a)(7) through (10).

The statement of the case should describe the nature of the case, which includes (1) the facts relevant to the issues submitted for review; (2) those aspects of the case's procedural history that are necessary to understand the posture of the appeal or are relevant to the issues submitted for review; and (3) the rulings presented for review. The statement should be concise, and can include subheadings, particularly for the purpose of highlighting the rulings presented for review.

Subdivision (b). Rule 28(b) is amended to accord with the amendment to Rule 28(a). Current Rules 28(b)(3) and (4) are consolidated into new Rule 28(b)(3), which refers to "The statement of the case." Rule 28(b)(5) becomes Rule 28(b)(4). And

Rule 28(b)'s reference to certain subdivisions of Rule 28(a) is updated to reflect the renumbering of those subdivisions.

Changes Made After Publication and Comments. After publication and comment, the Committee made one change to the text of the proposal and two changes to the Committee Note.

During the comment period, concerns were raised that the deletion of current Rule 28(b)(6)'s reference to "the nature of the case, the course of proceedings, and the disposition below" might lead readers to conclude that those items may no longer be included in the statement of the case. The Committee rejected that concern with respect to the "nature of the case" and the "disposition below," because the Rule as published would naturally be read to permit continued inclusion of those items in the statement of the case. The Committee adhered to its view that the deletion of "course of proceedings" is useful because that phrase tends to elicit unnecessary detail; but to address the commenters' concerns, the Committee added, to the revised Rule text, the phrase "describing the relevant procedural history."

The Committee augmented the Note to Rule 28(a) in two respects. It added a reference to Supreme Court Rule 24.1(g), upon which the proposed revision to Rule 28(a)(6) is modeled. And it added—as a second paragraph in the Note—a discussion of the contents of the statement of the case.

Committee Notes on Rules – 2016 Amendment

Rule 28(a)(10) is revised to refer to Rule 32(g)(1) instead of Rule 32(a)(7), to reflect the relocation of the certificate-of-compliance requirement.

Rule 28.1 Cross-Appeals

(a) Applicability. This rule applies to a case in which a cross-appeal is filed. Rules 28(a)–(c), 31(a)(1), 32(a)(2), and 32(a)(7)(A)–(B) do not apply to such a case, except as otherwise provided in this rule.

(b) Designation of Appellant. The party who files a notice of appeal first is the appellant for the purposes of this rule and Rules 30 and 34. If notices are filed on the same day, the plaintiff in the proceeding below is the appellant. These designations may be modified by the parties' agreement or by court order.

(c) Briefs. In a case involving a cross-appeal:

(1) *Appellant's Principal Brief.* The appellant must file a principal brief in the appeal. That brief must comply with Rule 28(a).

(2) *Appellee's Principal and Response Brief.* The appellee must file a principal brief in the cross-appeal and must, in the same brief, respond to the principal brief in the appeal. That appellee's brief must comply with Rule 28(a), except that the brief need not include a statement of the case unless the appellee is dissatisfied with the appellant's statement.

(3) *Appellant's Response and Reply Brief.* The appellant must file a brief that responds to the principal brief in the cross-appeal and may, in the same brief, reply to the response in the appeal. That brief must comply with Rule 28(a)(2)–(8) and (10), except that none of the following need appear unless the appellant is dissatisfied with the appellee's statement in the cross-appeal:

(A) the jurisdictional statement;
(B) the statement of the issues;
(C) the statement of the case; and
(D) the statement of the standard of review.

(4) *Appellee's Reply Brief.* The appellee may file a brief in reply to the response in the cross-appeal. That brief must comply with Rule 28(a)(2)–(3) and (10) and must be limited to the issues presented by the cross-appeal.

(5) *No Further Briefs.* Unless the court permits, no further briefs may be filed in a case involving a cross-appeal.

(d) Cover. Except for filings by unrepresented parties, the cover of the appellant's principal brief must be blue; the appellee's principal and response brief, red; the appellant's response and reply brief, yellow; the appellee's reply brief, gray; an intervenor's or amicus curiae's brief, green; and any supplemental brief, tan. The front cover of a brief must contain the information required by Rule 32(a)(2).

(e) Length.

Rule 28.1 Cross-Appeals

[The following text of subdivision (e) was effective until December 1, 2016.]

(1) *Page Limitation.* Unless it complies with Rule 28.1(e)(2) and (3), the appellant's principal brief must not exceed 30 pages; the appellee's principal and response brief, 35 pages; the appellant's response and reply brief, 30 pages; and the appellee's reply brief, 15 pages.
(2) *Type-Volume Limitation.*
    (A) The appellant's principal brief or the appellant's response and reply brief is acceptable if:
        (i) it contains no more than 14,000 words; or
        (ii) it uses a monospaced face and contains no more than 1,300 lines of text.
    (B) The appellee's principal and response brief is acceptable if:
        (i) it contains no more than 16,500 words; or
        (ii) it uses a monospaced face and contains no more than 1,500 lines of text.
    (C) The appellee's reply brief is acceptable if it contains no more than half of the type volume specified in Rule 28.1(e)(2)(A).

[The following text of subdivision (e) became effective December 1, 2016.]

(1) *Page Limitation.* Unless it complies with Rule 28.1(e)(2), the appellant's principal brief must not exceed 30 pages; the appellee's principal and response brief, 35 pages; the appellant's response and reply brief, 30 pages; and the appellee's reply brief, 15 pages.
(2) *Type-Volume Limitation.*
    (A) The appellant's principal brief or the appellant's response and reply brief is acceptable if it:
        (i) contains no more than 13,000 words; or
        (ii) uses a monospaced face and contains no more than 1,300 lines of text.
    (B) The appellee's principal and response brief is acceptable if it:
        (i) contains no more than 15,300 words; or
        (ii) uses a monospaced face and contains no more than 1,500 lines of text.
    (C) The appellee's reply brief is acceptable if it contains no more than half of the type volume specified in Rule 28.1(e)(2)(A).

(3) *Certificate of Compliance.* A brief submitted under Rule 28.1(e)(2) must comply with Rule 32(a)(7)(C).
(f) Time to Serve and File a Brief. Briefs must be served and filed as follows:
    (1) the appellant's principal brief, within 40 days after the record is filed;
    (2) the appellee's principal and response brief, within 30 days after the appellant's principal brief is served;
    (3) the appellant's response and reply brief, within 30 days after the appellee's principal and response brief is served; and
    (4) the appellee's reply brief, within 14 days after the appellant's response and reply brief is served, but at least 7 days before argument unless the court, for good cause, allows a later filing.
(As added Apr. 25, 2005, eff. Dec. 1, 2005; amended Mar. 26, 2009, eff. Dec. 1, 2009; Apr. 16, 2013, eff. Dec. 1, 2013; Apr. 28, 2016, eff. Dec. 1, 2016.)

Committee Notes on Rules—2005

The Federal Rules of Appellate Procedure have said very little about briefing in cases involving cross-appeals. This vacuum has frustrated judges, attorneys, and parties who have sought guidance in the rules. More importantly, this vacuum has been filled by conflicting local rules regarding such matters as the number and length of briefs, the colors of the covers of briefs, and the deadlines for serving and filing briefs. These local rules have created a hardship for attorneys who practice in more than one circuit.

New Rule 28.1 provides a comprehensive set of rules governing briefing in cases involving cross-appeals. The few existing provisions regarding briefing in such cases have been moved into new Rule 28.1, and several new provisions have been added to fill the gaps in the existing rules. The new provisions reflect the practices of the large majority of circuits and, to a significant extent, the new provisions have been patterned after the requirements imposed by Rules 28, 31, and

32 on briefs filed in cases that do not involve cross-appeals.

Subdivision (a). Subdivision (a) makes clear that, in a case involving a cross-appeal, briefing is governed by new Rule 28.1, and not by Rules 28(a), 28(b), 28(c), 31(a)(1), 32(a)(2), 32(a)(7)(A), and 32(a)(7)(B), except to the extent that Rule 28.1 specifically incorporates those rules by reference.

Subdivision (b). Subdivision (b) defines who is the "appellant" and who is the "appellee" in a case involving a cross-appeal. Subdivision (b) is taken directly from former Rule 28(h), except that subdivision (b) refers to a party being designated as an appellant "for the purposes of this rule and Rules 30 and 34," whereas former Rule 28(h) also referred to Rule 31. Because the matter addressed by Rule 31(a)(1)—the time to serve and file briefs—is now addressed directly in new Rule 28.1(f), the cross-reference to Rule 31 is no longer necessary. In Rule 31 and in all rules other than Rules 28.1, 30, and 34, references to an "appellant" refer both to the appellant in an appeal and to the cross-appellant in a cross-appeal, and references to an "appellee" refer both to the appellee in an appeal and to the cross-appellee in a cross-appeal. Cf. Rule 31(c).

Subdivision (c). Subdivision (c) provides for the filing of four briefs in a case involving a cross-appeal. This reflects the practice of every circuit except the Seventh. See 7th Cir. R. 28(d)(1)(a).

The first brief is the "appellant's principal brief." That brief—like the appellant's principal brief in a case that does not involve a cross-appeal—must comply with Rule 28(a).

The second brief is the "appellee's principal and response brief." Because this brief serves as the appellee's principal brief on the merits of the cross-appeal, as well as the appellee's response brief on the merits of the appeal, it must also comply with Rule 28(a), with the limited exceptions noted in the text of the rule.

The third brief is the "appellant's response and reply brief." Like a response brief in a case that does not involve a cross-appeal—that is, a response brief that does not also serve as a principal brief on the merits of a cross-appeal—the appellant's response and reply brief must comply with Rule 28(a)(2)–(9) and (11), with the exceptions noted in the text of the rule. See Rule 28(b). The one difference between the appellant's response and reply brief, on the one hand, and a response brief filed in a case that does not involve a cross-appeal, on the other, is that the latter must include a corporate disclosure statement. See Rule 28(a)(1) and (b). An appellant filing a response and reply brief in a case involving a cross-appeal has already filed a corporate disclosure statement with its principal brief on the merits of the appeal.

The fourth brief is the "appellee's reply brief." Like a reply brief in a case that does not involve a cross-appeal, it must comply with Rule 28(c), which essentially restates the requirements of Rule 28(a)(2)–(3) and (11). (Rather than restating the requirements of Rule 28(a)(2)–(3) and (11), as Rule 28(c) does, Rule 28.1(c)(4) includes a direct cross-reference.) The appellee's reply brief must also be limited to the issues presented by the cross-appeal.

Subdivision (d). Subdivision (d) specifies the colors of the covers on briefs filed in a case involving a cross-appeal. It is patterned after Rule 32(a)(2), which does not specifically refer to cross-appeals.

Subdivision (e). Subdivision (e) sets forth limits on the length of the briefs filed in a case involving a cross-appeal. It is patterned after Rule 32(a)(7), which does not specifically refer to cross-appeals. Subdivision (e) permits the appellee's principal and response brief to be longer than a typical principal brief on the merits because this brief serves not only as the principal brief on the merits of the cross-appeal, but also as the response brief on the merits of the appeal. Likewise, subdivision (e) permits the appellant's response and reply brief to be longer than a typical reply brief because this brief serves not only as the reply brief in the appeal, but also as the response brief in the cross-appeal. For purposes of determining the maximum length of an amicus curiae's brief filed in a case involving a cross-appeal, Rule 29(d)'s reference to "the maximum length authorized by these rules for a party's principal brief" should be understood to refer to subdivision (e)'s limitations on the length of an appellant's principal brief.

Subdivision (f). Subdivision (f) provides deadlines for serving and filing briefs in a cross-appeal. It is patterned after Rule 31(a)(1), which does not specifically refer to cross-appeals.

Changes Made After Publication and Comments. The Committee adopted the recommendation of the Style Subcommittee that the text of Rule 28.1 be changed in a few minor respects to improve clarity. (That recommendation is described below.) The Committee also adopted three suggestions made by the Department of Justice: (1) A sentence was added to the Committee Note to Rule 28.1(b) to clarify that the term "appellant" (and "appellee") as used by rules other than Rules 28.1, 30, and 34, refers to both the appellant in an appeal and the cross-appellant in a cross-appeal (and to both the appellee in an appeal and the cross-appellee in a cross-appeal). (2) Rule 28.1(d) was amended to prescribe cover colors for supplemental briefs and briefs filed by an intervenor or amicus curiae. (3) A few words were added to the Committee Note to Rule 28.1(e) to clarify the length of an amicus curiae's brief.

Committee Notes on Rules—2009 Amendment

Subdivision (f)(4). Subdivision (f)(4) formerly required that the appellee's reply brief be served "at least 3 days before argument unless the court, for good cause, allows a later filing." Under former Rule 26(a), "3 days" could mean as many as 5 or even 6 days. See the Note to Rule 26. Under revised Rule 26(a), intermediate weekends and holidays are counted.

Rule 29. Brief of an Amicus Curiae

Changing "3 days" to "7 days" alters the period accordingly. Under revised Rule 26(a), when a period ends on a weekend or holiday, one must continue to count in the same direction until the next day that is not a weekend or holiday; the choice of the 7-day period for subdivision (f)(4) will minimize such occurrences.

Committee Notes on Rules—2013 Amendment

Subdivision (c). Subdivision (c) is amended to accord with the amendments to Rule 28(a). Rule 28(a) is amended to consolidate subdivisions (a)(6) and (a)(7) into a new subdivision (a)(6) that provides for one "statement of the case setting out the facts relevant to the issues submitted for review, describing the relevant procedural history, and identifying the rulings presented to review. . . ." Rule 28.1(c) is amended to refer to that consolidated "statement of the case," and references to subdivisions of Rule 28(a) are revised to reflect the re0numbering of those subdivisions.

Changes Made After Publication and Comment. No changes were made to the text of the proposed amendment to Rule 28.1 after publication and comment. The Committee revised a quotation in the Committee Note to Rule 28.1(c) to conform to the changes (described above) to the text of proposed Rule 28(a)(6).

Committee Notes on Rules – 2016 Amendment

When Rule 28.1 was adopted in 2005, it modeled its type-volume limits on those set forth in Rule 32(a)(7) for briefs in cases that did not involve a cross-appeal. At that time, Rule 32(a)(7)(B) set word limits based on an estimate of 280 words per page.

In the course of adopting word limits for the length limits in Rules 5, 21, 27, 35, and 40, and responding to concern about the length of briefs, the Committee has reevaluated the conversion ratio (from pages to words) and decided to apply a conversion ratio of 260 words per page. Rules 28.1 and 32(a)(7)(B) are amended to reduce the word limits accordingly.

In a complex case, a party may need to file a brief that exceeds the type-volume limitations specified in these rules, such as to include unusually voluminous information explaining relevant background or legal provisions or to respond to multiple briefs by opposing parties or amici. The Committee expects that courts will accommodate those situations by granting leave to exceed the type-volume limitations as appropriate.

Rule 29. Brief of an Amicus Curiae

[The following text of subdivision (a) was effective until December 1, 2016.]

(a) When Permitted. The United States or its officer or agency or a state may file an amicus-curiae brief without the consent of the parties or leave of court. Any other amicus curiae may file a brief only by leave of court or if the brief states that all parties have consented to its filing.

[The following text of subdivision (a) became effective December 1, 2016.]

(a) During Initial Consideration of a Case on the Merits.
(1) *Applicability.* This Rule 29(a) governs amicus filings during a court's initial consideration of a case on the merits.
(2) *When Permitted.* The United States or its officer or agency or a state may file an amicus curiae brief without the consent of the parties or leave of court. Any other amicus curiae may file a brief only by leave of court or if the brief states that all parties have consented to its filing.
(3) *Motion for Leave to File.* The motion must be accompanied by the proposed brief and state:
    (A) the movant's interest; and
    (B) the reason why an amicus brief is desirable and why the matters asserted are relevant to the disposition of the case.
(4) *Contents and Form.* An amicus brief must comply with Rule 32. In addition to the requirements of Rule 32, the cover must identify the party or parties supported and indicate whether the brief supports affirmance or reversal.
An amicus brief need not comply with Rule 28, but must include the following:

Rule 29. Brief of an Amicus Curiae

(A) if the amicus curiae is a corporation, a disclosure statement like that required of parties by Rule 26.1;
(B) a table of contents, with page references;
(C) a table of authorities—cases (alphabetically arranged), statutes, and other authorities—with references to the pages of the brief where they are cited;
(D) a concise statement of the identity of the amicus curiae, its interest in the case, and the source of its authority to file;
(E) unless the amicus curiae is one listed in the first sentence of Rule 29(a)(2), a statement that indicates whether:
    (i) a party's counsel authored the brief in whole or in part;
    (ii) a party or a party's counsel contributed money that was intended to fund preparing or submitting the brief; and
    (iii) a person—other than the amicus curiae, its members, or its counsel—contributed money that was intended to fund preparing or submitting the brief and, if so, identifies each such person;
(F) an argument, which may be preceded by a summary and which need not include a statement of the applicable standard of review; and
(G) a certificate of compliance under Rule 32(g)(1), if length is computed using a word or line limit.
(5) *Length*. Except by the court's permission, an amicus brief may be no more than one-half the maximum length authorized by these rules for a party's principal brief. If the court grants a party permission to file a longer brief, that extension does not affect the length of an amicus brief.
(6) *Time for Filing*. An amicus curiae must file its brief, accompanied by a motion for filing when necessary, no later than 7 days after the principal brief of the party being supported is filed. An amicus curiae that does not support either party must file its brief no later than 7 days after the appellant's or petitioner's principal brief is filed. A court may grant leave for later filing, specifying the time within which an opposing party may answer.
(7) *Reply Brief*. Except by the court's permission, an amicus curiae may not file a reply brief.
(8) *Oral Argument*. An amicus curiae may participate in oral argument only with the court's permission.

[The following text of subdivision (b) was effective until December 1, 2016.]

(b) Motion for Leave to File. The motion must be accompanied by the proposed brief and state:
(1) the movant's interest; and
(2) the reason why an amicus brief is desirable and why the matters asserted are relevant to the disposition of the case.

[The following text of subdivision (b) became effective December 1, 2016.]

(b) During Consideration of Whether to Grant Rehearing.
(1) *Applicability*. This Rule 29(b) governs amicus filings during a court's consideration of whether to grant panel rehearing or rehearing en banc, unless a local rule or order in a case provides otherwise.
(2) *When Permitted*. The United States or its officer or agency or a state may file an amicus curiae brief without the consent of the parties or leave of court. Any other amicus curiae may file a brief only by leave of court.
(3) *Motion for Leave to File*. Rule 29(a)(3) applies to a motion for leave.
(4) *Contents, Form, and Length*. Rule 29(a)(4) applies to the amicus brief. The brief must not exceed 2,600 words.
(5) *Time for Filing*. An amicus curiae supporting the petition for rehearing or supporting neither party must file its brief, accompanied by a motion for filing when necessary, no later than 7 days after the petition is filed. An amicus curiae opposing the petition must file its brief, accompanied by a motion for filing when necessary, no later than the date set by the court for the response.

Rule 29. Brief of an Amicus Curiae

(c) Contents and Form. An amicus brief must comply with Rule 32. In addition to the requirements of Rule 32, the cover must identify the party or parties supported and indicate whether the brief supports affirmance or reversal. An amicus brief need not comply with Rule 28, but must include the following:

(1) if the amicus curiae is a corporation, a disclosure statement like that required of parties by Rule 26.1;

(2) a table of contents, with page references;

(3) a table of authorities—cases (alphabetically arranged), statutes and other authorities—with references to the pages of the brief where they are cited;

(4) a concise statement of the identity of the amicus curiae, its interest in the case, and the source of its authority to file;

(5) unless the amicus curiae is one listed in the first sentence of Rule 29(a), a statement that indicates whether:

(A) a party's counsel authored the brief in whole or in part;

(B) a party or party's counsel contributed money that was intended to fund preparing or submitting the brief; and

(C) a person—other than the amicus curiae, its members, or its counsel—contributed money that was intended to fund preparing or submitting the brief and, if so, identifies each such person;

(6) an argument, which may be preceded by a summary and which need not include a statement of the applicable standard of review; and

(7) a certificate of compliance, if required by Rule 32(a)(7).

(d) Length. Except by the court's permission, an amicus brief may be no more than one-half the maximum length authorized by these rules for a party's principal brief. If the court grants a party permission to file a longer brief, that extension does not affect the length of an amicus brief.

(e) Time for Filing. An amicus curiae must file its brief, accompanied by a motion for filing when necessary, no later than 7 days after the principal brief of the party being supported is filed. An amicus curiae that does not support either party must file its brief no later than 7 days after the appellant's or petitioner's principal brief is filed. A court may grant leave for later filing, specifying the time within which an opposing party may answer.

(f) Reply Brief. Except by the court's permission, an amicus curiae may not file a reply brief.

(g) Oral Argument. An amicus curiae may participate in oral argument only with the court's permission.

(As amended Apr. 24, 1998, eff. Dec. 1, 1998; Apr. 28, 2010, eff. Dec. 1, 2010; Apr. 28, 2016, eff. Dec. 1, 2016.)

Notes of Advisory Committee on Rules—1967

Only five circuits presently regulate the filing of the brief of an amicus curiae. See D.C. Cir. Rule 18(j); 1st Cir. Rule 23(10); 6th Cir. Rule 17(4); 9th Cir. Rule 18(9); 10th Cir. Rule 20. This rule follows the practice of a majority of circuits in requiring leave of court to file an amicus brief except under the circumstances stated therein. Compare Supreme Court Rule 42.

Committee Notes on Rules—1998 Amendment

The language and organization of the rule are amended to make the rule more easily understood. In addition to changes made to improve the understanding, the Advisory Committee has changed language to make style and terminology consistent throughout the appellate rules. These changes are intended to be stylistic only.

Several substantive changes are made in this rule, however.

Subdivision (a). The major change in this subpart is that when a brief is filed with the consent of all parties, it is no longer necessary to obtain the parties' written consent and to file the consents with the brief. It is sufficient to obtain the parties' oral consent and to state in the brief that all parties have consented. It is sometimes difficult to obtain all the written consents by the filing deadline and it is not unusual for counsel to represent that parties have consented; for example, in a motion for extension of time to file a brief it is not unusual for the movant to state that the other parties have been consulted and they do not object to the extension. If a party's consent has been misrepresented, the party will be able to take action before the court considers the amicus brief.

The District of Columbia is added to the list of entities allowed to file an amicus brief without consent of all parties. The other changes in this material are stylistic.

Rule 29. Brief of an Amicus Curiae

Subdivision (b). The provision in the former rule, granting permission to conditionally file the brief with the motion, is changed to one requiring that the brief accompany the motion. Sup. Ct. R. 37.4 requires that the proposed brief be presented with the motion.

The former rule only required the motion to identify the applicant's interest and to generally state the reasons why an amicus brief is desirable. The amended rule additionally requires that the motion state the relevance of the matters asserted to the disposition of the case. As Sup. Ct. R. 37.1 states:

An *amicus curiae* brief which brings relevant matter to the attention of the Court that has not already been brought to its attention by the parties is of considerable help to the Court. An *amicus curiae* brief which does not serve this purpose simply burdens the staff and facilities of the Court and its filing is not favored.

Because the relevance of the matters asserted by an amicus is ordinarily the most compelling reason for granting leave to file, the Committee believes that it is helpful to explicitly require such a showing.

Subdivision (c). The provisions in this subdivision are entirely new. Previously there was confusion as to whether an amicus brief must include all of the items listed in Rule 28. Out of caution practitioners in some circuits included all those items. Ordinarily that is unnecessary.

The requirement that the cover identify the party supported and indicate whether the amicus supports affirmance or reversal is an administrative aid.

Paragraph (c)(3) requires an amicus to state the source of its authority to file. The amicus simply must identify which of the provisions in Rule 29(a) provides the basis for the amicus to file its brief.

Subdivision (d). This new provision imposes a shorter page limit for an amicus brief than for a party's brief. This is appropriate for two reasons. First, an amicus may omit certain items that must be included in a party's brief. Second, an amicus brief is supplemental. It need not address all issues or all facets of a case. It should treat only matter not adequately addressed by a party.

Subdivision (e). The time limit for filing is changed. An amicus brief must be filed no later than 7 days after the principal brief of the party being supported is filed. Occasionally, an amicus supports neither party; in such instances, the amendment provides that the amicus brief must be filed no later than 7 days after the appellant's or petitioner's principal brief is filed. Note that in both instances the 7-day period runs from when a brief is filed. The passive voice—"is filed"—is used deliberately. A party or amicus can send its brief to a court for filing and, under Rule 25, the brief is timely if mailed within the filing period. Although the brief is timely if mailed within the filing period, it is not "filed" until the court receives it and file stamps it. "Filing" is done by the court, not by the party. It may be necessary for an amicus to contact the court to ascertain the filing date.

The 7-day stagger was adopted because it is long enough to permit an amicus to review the completed brief of the party being supported and avoid repetitious argument. A 7-day period also is short enough that no adjustment need be made in the opposing party's briefing schedule. The opposing party will have sufficient time to review arguments made by the amicus and address them in the party's responsive pleading. The timetable for filing the parties' briefs is unaffected by this change.

A court may grant permission to file an amicus brief in a context in which the party does not file a "principal brief"; for example, an amicus may be permitted to file in support of a party's petition for rehearing. In such instances the court will establish the filing time for the amicus.

The former rule's statement that a court may, for cause shown, grant leave for later filing is unnecessary. Rule 26(b) grants general authority to enlarge the time prescribed in these rules for good cause shown. This new rule, however, states that when a court grants permission for later filing, the court must specify the period within which an opposing party may answer the arguments of the amicus.

Subdivision (f). This subdivision generally prohibits the filing a a reply brief by an amicus curiae. Sup. Ct. R. 37 and local rules of the D.C., Ninth, and Federal Circuits state that an amicus may not file a reply brief. The role of an amicus should not require the use of a reply brief.

Subdivision (g). The language of this subdivision stating that an amicus will be granted permission to participate in oral argument "only for extraordinary reasons" has been deleted. The change is made to reflect more accurately the current practice in which it is not unusual for a court to permit an amicus to argue when a party is willing to share its argument time with the amicus. The Committee does not intend, however, to suggest that in other instances an amicus will be permitted to argue absent extraordinary circumstances.

Committee Notes on Rules—2010 Amendment

Subdivision (a). New Rule 1(b) defines the term "state" to include "the District of Columbia and any United States commonwealth or territory." That definition renders subdivision (a)'s reference to a "Territory, Commonwealth, or the District of Columbia" redundant. Accordingly, subdivision (a) is amended to refer simply to "[t]he United States or its officer or agency or a state."

Rule 29. Brief of an Amicus Curiae

Subdivision (c). The subparts of subdivision (c) are renumbered due to the relocation of an existing provision in new subdivision (c)(1) and the addition of a new provision in new subdivision (c)(5). Existing subdivisions (c)(1) through (c)(5) are renumbered, respectively, (c)(2), (c)(3), (c)(4), (c)(6) and (c)(7). The new ordering of the subdivisions tracks the order in which the items should appear in the brief.

Subdivision (c)(1). The requirement that corporate amici include a disclosure statement like that required of parties by Rule 26.1 was previously stated in the third sentence of subdivision (c). The requirement has been moved to new subdivision (c)(1) for ease of reference.

Subdivision (c)(5). New subdivision (c)(5) sets certain disclosure requirements concerning authorship and funding. Subdivision (c)(5) exempts from the authorship and funding disclosure requirements entities entitled under subdivision (a) to file an amicus brief without the consent of the parties or leave of court. Subdivision (c)(5) requires amicus briefs to disclose whether counsel for a party authored the brief in whole or in part and whether a party or a party's counsel contributed money with the intention of funding the preparation or submission of the brief. A party's or counsel's payment of general membership dues to an amicus need not be disclosed. Subdivision (c)(5) also requires amicus briefs to state whether any other "person" (other than the amicus, its members, or its counsel) contributed money with the intention of funding the brief's preparation or submission, and, if so, to identify all such persons. "Person," as used in subdivision (c)(5), includes artificial persons as well as natural persons.

The disclosure requirement, which is modeled on Supreme Court Rule 37.6, serves to deter counsel from using an amicus brief to circumvent page limits on parties' briefs. *See Glassroth v. Moore*, 347 F.3d 916, 919 (11th Cir. 2003) (noting the majority's suspicion "that amicus briefs are often used as a means of evading the page limitations on a party's briefs"). It also may help judges to assess whether the amicus itself considers the issue important enough to sustain the cost and effort of filing an amicus brief.

It should be noted that coordination between the amicus and the party whose position the amicus supports is desirable, to the extent that it helps to avoid duplicative arguments. This was particularly true prior to the 1998 amendments, when deadlines for amici were the same as those for the party whose position they supported. Now that the filing deadlines are staggered, coordination may not always be essential in order to avoid duplication. In any event, mere coordination—in the sense of sharing drafts of briefs—need not be disclosed under subdivision (c)(5). Cf. Eugene Gressman et al., Supreme Court Practice 739 (9th ed. 2007) (Supreme Court Rule 37.6 does not "require disclosure of any coordination and discussion between party counsel and amici counsel regarding their respective arguments....").

Changes Made After Publication and Comment. No changes were made to the proposed amendment to Rule 29(a). However, the Committee made a number of changes to Rule 29(c).

One change concerns the third subdivision of the authorship and funding disclosure requirement. As published, that third subdivision would have directed the filer to "identif[y] every person – other than the amicus curiae, its members, or its counsel – who contributed money that was intended to fund preparing or submitting the brief." A commentator criticized this language as ambiguous, because the commentator argued that the provision as drafted did not make clear whether it is necessary for the brief to state that no such persons exist (if that is the case). The Committee revised this portion of the requirement to require a statement that indicates whether "a person – other than the amicus curiae, its members, or its counsel – contributed money that was intended to fund preparing or submitting the brief and, if so, identifies each such person."

Another set of changes concerns the placement of the disclosure requirement. As published, the Rule 29(c) proposal would have placed the new authorship and funding disclosure requirement in a new subdivision (c)(7) and would have moved the requirement of a corporate disclosure statement from the initial block of text in Rule 29(c) to a new subdivision (c)(6). New subdivision (c)(7) would have directed that the authorship and funding disclosure be made "in the first footnote on the first page." Commentators criticized this directive as ambiguous and suggested that a better approach would be to direct that the authorship and funding disclosure follow the statement currently required by existing Rule 29(c)(3). The Committee found merit in these suggestions and decided to add the authorship and funding disclosure provision to existing subdivision (c)(3). However, a further revision to the structure of subdivision (c) was later made in response to style guidance from Professor Kimble, as discussed below.

Subsequent to the Appellate Rules Committee's meeting, the language adopted by the advisory committee was circulated to Professor Kimble for style review. Professor Kimble argued that the authorship and funding disclosure provision should be placed in a separate subdivision rather than being placed in existing subdivision (c)(3). In the light of the Appellate Rules Committee's goal of listing the required components in the order in which they should appear in the brief, the decision was made to place the authorship and funding disclosure provision in a new subdivision following existing subdivision (c)(3). Though this requires renumbering the subparts of Rule 29(c), those subparts have only existed for about a decade (since the 1998 restyling) and citations to the specific subparts of Rule 29(c) do not appear in the caselaw. Given that this change entails renumbering some subparts of Rule 29(c), it also seems advisable to move the corporate disclosure provision into a new subdivision (c)(1) and to renumber the subsequent subdivisions accordingly. Professor Kimble also suggested two stylistic changes to the language of what will now become new subdivision (c)(5).

First, instead of using the language "unless filed by an amicus curiae listed in the first sentence of Rule 29(a)," the provision now reads "unless the amicus curiae is one listed in the first sentence of Rule 29(a)." Second, the words "indicates whether" have been moved up into the introductory text in 29(c)(5) instead of being repeated at the outset of the three subsections (29(c)(5)(A), (B) and (C). Also, a comma has been added to what will become Rule 29(c)(3).

Committee Notes on Rules – 2016 Amendment

Rule 29 is amended to address amicus filings in connection with requests for panel rehearing and rehearing en banc.

Existing Rule 29 is renumbered Rule 29(a), and language is added to that subdivision (a) to state that its provisions apply to amicus filings during the court's initial consideration of a case on the merits. Rule 29(c)(7) becomes Rule 29(a)(4)(G) and is revised to accord with the relocation and revision of the certificate-of-compliance requirement. New Rule 32(g)(1) states that "[a] brief submitted under Rules 28.1(e)(2), 29(b)(4), or 32(a)(7)(B) . . . must include" a certificate of compliance. An amicus brief submitted during initial consideration of a case on the merits counts as a "brief submitted under Rule[] . . . 32(a)(7)(B)" if the amicus computes Rule 29(a)(5)'s length limit by taking half of a type-volume limit in Rule 32(a)(7)(B). Rule 29(a)(4)(G) restates Rule 32(g)(1)'s requirement functionally, by providing that a certificate of compliance is required if an amicus brief's length is computed using a word or line limit.

New subdivision (b) is added to address amicus filings in connection with a petition for panel rehearing or rehearing en banc. Subdivision (b) sets default rules that apply when a court does not provide otherwise by local rule or by order in a case. A court remains free to adopt different rules governing whether amicus filings are permitted in connection with petitions for rehearing, and governing the procedures when such filings are permitted.

Rule 30. Appendix to the Briefs
(a) Appellant's Responsibility.
(1) *Contents of the Appendix.* The appellant must prepare and file an appendix to the briefs containing:
    (A) the relevant docket entries in the proceeding below;
    (B) the relevant portions of the pleadings, charge, findings, or opinion;
    (C) the judgment, order, or decision in question; and
    (D) other parts of the record to which the parties wish to direct the court's attention.

(2) *Excluded Material.* Memoranda of law in the district court should not be included in the appendix unless they have independent relevance. Parts of the record may be relied on by the court or the parties even though not included in the appendix.

(3) *Time to File; Number of Copies.* Unless filing is deferred under Rule 30(c), the appellant must file 10 copies of the appendix with the brief and must serve one copy on counsel for each party separately represented. An unrepresented party proceeding in forma pauperis must file 4 legible copies with the clerk, and one copy must be served on counsel for each separately represented party. The court may by local rule or by order in a particular case require the filing or service of a different number.

(b) All Parties' Responsibilities.

(1) *Determining the Contents of the Appendix.* The parties are encouraged to agree on the contents of the appendix. In the absence of an agreement, the appellant must, within 14 days after the record is filed, serve on the appellee a designation of the parts of the record the appellant intends to include in the appendix and a statement of the issues the appellant intends to present for review. The appellee may, within 14 days after receiving the designation, serve on the appellant a designation of additional parts to which it wishes to direct the court's attention. The appellant must include the designated parts in the appendix. The parties must not engage in unnecessary designation of parts of the record, because the entire record is available to the court. This paragraph applies also to a cross-appellant and a cross-appellee.

(2) *Costs of Appendix.* Unless the parties agree otherwise, the appellant must pay the cost of the appendix. If the appellant considers parts of the record designated by the appellee to be unnecessary, the appellant may advise the appellee, who must then advance the cost of including those parts. The cost of the appendix is a taxable cost. But if any party causes unnecessary parts of the record to be included in the appendix, the court may impose the cost of those parts on that party. Each circuit must, by local rule, provide for sanctions against attorneys who unreasonably and vexatiously increase litigation costs by including

Rule 30. Appendix to the Briefs

unnecessary material in the appendix.

(c) Deferred Appendix.

(1) *Deferral Until After Briefs Are Filed.* The court may provide by rule for classes of cases or by order in a particular case that preparation of the appendix may be deferred until after the briefs have been filed and that the appendix may be filed 21 days after the appellee's brief is served. Even though the filing of the appendix may be deferred, Rule 30(b) applies; except that a party must designate the parts of the record it wants included in the appendix when it serves its brief, and need not include a statement of the issues presented.

(2) *References to the Record.*

(A) If the deferred appendix is used, the parties may cite in their briefs the pertinent pages of the record. When the appendix is prepared, the record pages cited in the briefs must be indicated by inserting record page numbers, in brackets, at places in the appendix where those pages of the record appear.

(B) A party who wants to refer directly to pages of the appendix may serve and file copies of the brief within the time required by Rule 31(a), containing appropriate references to pertinent pages of the record. In that event, within 14 days after the appendix is filed, the party must serve and file copies of the brief, containing references to the pages of the appendix in place of or in addition to the references to the pertinent pages of the record. Except for the correction of typographical errors, no other changes may be made to the brief.

(d) Format of the Appendix. The appendix must begin with a table of contents identifying the page at which each part begins. The relevant docket entries must follow the table of contents. Other parts of the record must follow chronologically. When pages from the transcript of proceedings are placed in the appendix, the transcript page numbers must be shown in brackets immediately before the included pages. Omissions in the text of papers or of the transcript must be indicated by asterisks. Immaterial formal matters (captions, subscriptions, acknowledgments, etc.) should be omitted.

(e) Reproduction of Exhibits. Exhibits designated for inclusion in the appendix may be reproduced in a separate volume, or volumes, suitably indexed. Four copies must be filed with the appendix, and one copy must be served on counsel for each separately represented party. If a transcript of a proceeding before an administrative agency, board, commission, or officer was used in a district-court action and has been designated for inclusion in the appendix, the transcript must be placed in the appendix as an exhibit.

(f) Appeal on the Original Record Without an Appendix. The court may, either by rule for all cases or classes of cases or by order in a particular case, dispense with the appendix and permit an appeal to proceed on the original record with any copies of the record, or relevant parts, that the court may order the parties to file.

(As amended Mar. 30, 1970, eff. July 1, 1970; Mar. 10, 1986, eff. July 1, 1986; Apr. 30, 1991, eff. Dec. 1, 1991; Apr. 29, 1994, eff. Dec. 1, 1994; Apr. 24, 1998, eff. Dec. 1, 1998; Mar. 26, 2009, eff. Dec. 1, 2009.)

Notes of Advisory Committee on Rules—1967

Subdivision (a). Only two circuits presently require a printed record (5th Cir. Rule 23(a); 8th Cir. Rule 10 (in civil appeals only)), and the rules and practice in those circuits combine to make the difference between a printed record and the appendix, which is now used in eight circuits and in the Supreme Court in lieu of the printed record, largely nominal. The essential characteristics of the appendix method are: (1) the entire record may not be reproduced; (2) instead, the parties are to set out in an appendix to the briefs those parts of the record which in their judgment the judges must consult in order to determine the issues presented by the appeal; (3) the appendix is not the record but merely a selection therefrom for the convenience of the judges of the court of appeals; the record is the actual trial court record, and the record itself is always available to supply inadvertent omissions from the appendix. These essentials are incorporated, either by rule or by practice, in the circuits that continue to require the printed record rather than the appendix. See 5th Cir. Rule 23(a)(9) and 8th Cir. Rule 10(a)–(d).

Subdivision (b). Under the practice in six of the eight circuits which now use the appendix method, unless the parties agree to use a single appendix, the appellant files with his brief an appendix containing the parts of the record which he deems it essential that the court read in order to determine the questions presented. If the appellee deems additional parts of the record necessary he must include such parts as an appendix to his brief. The proposed rules differ from that

Rule 30. Appendix to the Briefs

practice. By the new rule a single appendix is to be filed. It is to be prepared by the appellant, who must include therein those parts which he deems essential and those which the appellee designates as essential.

Under the practice by which each party files his own appendix the resulting reproduction of essential parts of the record is often fragmentary; it is not infrequently necessary to piece several appendices together to arrive at a usable reproduction. Too, there seems to be a tendency on the part of some appellants to reproduce less than what is necessary for a determination of the issues presented (see *Moran Towing Corp. v. M. A. Gammino Construction Co.*, 363 F.2d 108 (1st Cir. 1966); *Walters v. Shari Music Publishing Corp.*, 298 F.2d 206 (2d Cir. 1962) and cases cited therein; *Morrison v. Texas Co.*, 289 F.2d 382 (7th Cir. 1961) and cases cited therein), a tendency which is doubtless encouraged by the requirement in present rules that the appellee reproduce in his separately prepared appendix such necessary parts of the record as are not included by the appellant.

Under the proposed rule responsibility for the preparation of the appendix is placed on the appellant. If the appellee feels that the appellant has omitted essential portions of the record, he may require the appellant to include such portions in the appendix. The appellant is protected against a demand that he reproduce parts which he considers unnecessary by the provisions entitling him to require the appellee to advance the costs of reproducing such parts and authorizing denial of costs for matter unnecessarily reproduced.

Subdivision (c). This subdivision permits the appellant to elect to defer the production of the appendix to the briefs until the briefs of both sides are written, and authorizes a court of appeals to require such deferred filing by rule or order. The advantage of this method of preparing the appendix is that it permits the parties to determine what parts of the record need to be reproduced in the light of the issues actually presented by the briefs. Often neither side is in a position to say precisely what is needed until the briefs are completed. Once the argument on both sides is known, it should be possible to confine the matter reproduced in the appendix to that which is essential to a determination of the appeal or review. This method of preparing the appendix is presently in use in the Tenth Circuit (Rule 17) and in other circuits in review of agency proceedings, and it has proven its value in reducing the volume required to be reproduced. When the record is long, use of this method is likely to result in substantial economy to the parties.

Subdivision (e). The purpose of this subdivision is to reduce the cost of reproducing exhibits. While subdivision (a) requires that 10 copies of the appendix be filed, unless the court requires a lesser number, subdivision (e) permits exhibits necessary for the determination of an appeal to be bound separately, and requires only 4 copies of such a separate volume or volumes to be filed and a single copy to be served on counsel.

Subdivision (f). This subdivision authorizes a court of appeals to dispense with the appendix method of reproducing parts of the record and to hear appeals on the original record and such copies of it as the court may require.

Since 1962 the Ninth Circuit has permitted all appeals to be heard on the original record and a very limited number of copies. Under the practice as adopted in 1962, any party to an appeal could elect to have the appeal heard on the original record and two copies thereof rather than on the printed record theretofore required. The resulting substantial saving of printing costs led to the election of the new practice in virtually all cases, and by 1967 the use of printed records had ceased. By a recent amendment, the Ninth Circuit has abolished the printed record altogether. Its rules now provide that all appeals are to be heard on the original record, and it has reduced the number of copies required to two sets of copies of the transmitted original papers (excluding copies of exhibits, which need not be filed unless specifically ordered). See 9 Cir. Rule 10, as amended June 2, 1967, effective September 1, 1967. The Eighth Circuit permits appeals in criminal cases and in habeas corpus and 28 U.S.C. §2255 proceedings to be heard on the original record and two copies thereof. See 8 Cir. Rule 8 (i)–(j). The Tenth Circuit permits appeals in all cases to be heard on the original record and four copies thereof whenever the record consists of two hundred pages or less. See 10 Cir. Rule 17(a). This subdivision expressly authorizes the continuation of the practices in the Eighth, Ninth and Tenth Circuits.

The judges of the Court of Appeals for the Ninth Circuit have expressed complete satisfaction with the practice there in use and have suggested that attention be called to the advantages which it offers in terms of reducing cost.

Notes of Advisory Committee on Rules—1970 Amendment

Subdivision (a). The amendment of subdivision (a) is related to the amendment of Rule 31(a), which authorizes a court of appeals to shorten the time for filing briefs. By virtue of this amendment, if the time for filing the brief of the appellant is shortened the time for filing the appendix is likewise shortened.

Subdivision (c). As originally written, subdivision (c) permitted the appellant to elect to defer filing of the appendix until 21 days after service of the brief of the appellee. As amended, subdivision (c) requires that an order of court be obtained before filing of the appendix can be deferred, unless a court permits deferred filing by local rule. The amendment should not cause use of the deferred appendix to be viewed with disfavor. In cases involving lengthy records, permission to defer filing of the appendix should be freely granted as an inducement to the parties to include in the appendix only matter that the briefs show to be necessary for consideration by the judges. But the Committee is advised that appellants have elected to defer filing of the appendix in cases involving brief records merely to obtain the 21 day delay. The

Rule 30. Appendix to the Briefs

subdivision is amended to prevent that practice.

Notes of Advisory Committee on Rules—1986 Amendment

Subdivision (a). During its study of the separate appendix [see Report on the Advisory Committee on the Federal Appellate Rules on the Operation of Rule 30, — FRD — (1985)], the Advisory Committee found that this document was frequently encumbered with memoranda submitted to the trial court. *United States v. Noall,* 587 F.2d 123, 125 n. 1 (2nd Cir. 1978). See generally *Drewett v. Aetna Cas. & Sur. Co.,* 539 F.2d 496, 500 (5th Cir. 1976); *Volkswagenwerk Aktiengesellschaft v. Church,* 413 F.2d 1126, 1128 (9th Cir. 1969). Inclusion of such material makes the appendix more bulky and therefore less useful to the appellate panel. It also can increase significantly the costs of litigation.

There are occasions when such trial court memoranda have independent relevance in the appellate litigation. For instance, there may be a dispute as to whether a particular point was raised or whether a concession was made in the district court. In such circumstances, it is appropriate to include pertinent sections of such memoranda in the appendix.

Subdivision (b). The amendment to subdivision (b) is designed to require the circuits, by local rule, to establish a procedural mechanism for the imposition of sanctions against those attorneys who conduct appellate litigation in bad faith. Both 28 U.S.C. §1927 and the inherent power of the court authorized such sanctions. See *Brennan v. Local 357, International Brotherhood of Teamsters,* 709 F.2d 611 (9th Cir. 1983). See generally *Roadway Express, Inc. v. Piper,* 447 U.S. 752 (1980). While considerations of uniformity are important and doubtless will be taken into account by the judges of the respective circuits, the Advisory Committee believes that, at this time, the circuits need the flexibility to tailor their approach to the conditions of local practice. The local rule shall provide for notice and opportunity to respond before the imposition of any sanction.

Technical amendments also are made to subdivisions (a), (b) and (c) which are not intended to be substantive changes.

Taxation of Fees in Appeals in Which the Requirement of an Appendix Is Dispensed With

The Judicial Conference of the United States at its session on October 28th and 29th approved the following resolution relating to fees to be taxed in the courts of appeals as submitted by the Judicial Council of the Ninth Circuit with the proviso that its application to any court of appeals shall be at the election of each such court:

For some time it has been the practice in the Ninth Circuit Court of Appeals to dispense with an appendix in an appellate record and to hear the appeal on the original record, with a number of copies thereof being supplied (Rule 30f, Federal Rules of Appellate Procedure). It has been the practice of the Court to tax a fee of $5 in small records and $10 in large records for the time of the clerk involved in preparing such appeals and by way of reimbursement for postage expense. Judicial Conference approval heretofore has not been secured and the Judicial Council of the Ninth Circuit now seeks to fix a flat fee of $15 to be charged as fees for costs to be charged by *any* court of appeals "in any appeal in which the requirement of an appendix is dispensed with pursuant to Rule 30f, Federal Rules of Appellate Procedure."

Notes of Advisory Committee on Rules—1991 Amendment

Subdivision (b). The amendment requires a cross appellant to serve the appellant with a statement of the issues that the cross appellant intends to pursue on appeal. No later than ten days after the record is filed, the appellant and cross appellant must serve each other with a statement of the issues each intends to present for review and with a designation of the parts of the record that each wants included in the appendix. Within the next ten days, both the appellee and the cross appellee may designate additional materials for inclusion in the appendix. The appellant must then include in the appendix the parts thus designated for both the appeal and any cross appeals. The Committee expects that simultaneous compliance with this subdivision by an appellant and a cross appellant will be feasible in most cases. If a cross appellant cannot fairly be expected to comply until receipt of the appellant's statement of issues, relief may be sought by motion in the court of appeals.

Notes of Advisory Committee on Rules—1994 Amendment

Subdivision (a). The only substantive change is to allow a court to require the filing of a greater number of copies of an appendix as well as a lesser number.

Committee Notes on Rules—1998 Amendment

The language and organization of the rule are amended to make the rule more easily understood. In addition to changes made to improve the understanding, the Advisory Committee has changed language to make style and

Rule 31. Serving and Filing Briefs

terminology consistent throughout the appellate rules. These changes are intended to be stylistic only.

Subdivision (a). Paragraph (a)(3) is amended so that it is consistent with Rule 31(b). An unrepresented party proceeding in forma pauperis is only required to file 4 copies of the appendix rather than 10.

Subdivision (c). When a deferred appendix is used, a brief must make reference to the original record rather than to the appendix because it does not exist when the briefs are prepared. Unless a party later files an amended brief with direct references to the pages of the appendix (as provided in subparagraph (c)(2)(B)), the material in the appendix must indicate the pages of the original record from which it was drawn so that a reader of the brief can make meaningful use of the appendix. The instructions in the current rule for cross-referencing the appendix materials to the original record are unclear. The language in paragraph (c)(2) has been amended to try to clarify the procedure.

Subdivision (d). In recognition of the fact that use of a typeset appendix is exceedingly rare in the courts of appeals, the last sentence—permitting a question and answer (as from a transcript) to be in a single paragraph—has been omitted.

Committee Notes on Rules—2009 Amendment

Subdivision (b)(1). The times set in the former rule at 10 days have been revised to 14 days. See the Note to Rule 26.

Rule 31. Serving and Filing Briefs

(a) Time to Serve and File a Brief.

(1) The appellant must serve and file a brief within 40 days after the record is filed. The appellee must serve and file a brief within 30 days after the appellant's brief is served. The appellant may serve and file a reply brief within 14 days after service of the appellee's brief but a reply brief must be filed at least 7 days before argument, unless the court, for good cause, allows a later filing.

(2) A court of appeals that routinely considers cases on the merits promptly after the briefs are filed may shorten the time to serve and file briefs, either by local rule or by order in a particular case.

(b) Number of Copies. Twenty-five copies of each brief must be filed with the clerk and 2 copies must be served on each unrepresented party and on counsel for each separately represented party. An unrepresented party proceeding in forma pauperis must file 4 legible copies with the clerk, and one copy must be served on each unrepresented party and on counsel for each separately represented party. The court may by local rule or by order in a particular case require the filing or service of a different number.

(c) Consequence of Failure to File. If an appellant fails to file a brief within the time provided by this rule, or within an extended time, an appellee may move to dismiss the appeal. An appellee who fails to file a brief will not be heard at oral argument unless the court grants permission.

(As amended Mar. 30, 1970, eff. July 1, 1970; Mar. 10, 1986, eff. July 1, 1986; Apr. 29, 1994, eff. Dec. 1, 1994; Apr. 24, 1998, eff. Dec. 1, 1998; Apr. 29, 2002, eff. Dec. 1, 2002; Mar. 26, 2009, eff. Dec. 1, 2009.)

Notes of Advisory Committee on Rules—1967

A majority of the circuits now require the brief of the appellant to be filed within 30 days from the date on which the record is filed. But in those circuits an exchange of designations is unnecessary in the preparation of the appendix. The appellant files with his brief an appendix containing the parts of the record which he deems essential. If the appellee considers other parts essential, he includes those parts in his own appendix. Since the proposed rule requires the appellant to file with his brief an appendix containing necessary parts of the record as designated by both parties, the rule allows the appellant 40 days in order to provide time for the exchange of designations respecting the content of the appendix (see Rule 30(b)).

Notes of Advisory Committee on Rules—1970 Amendment

The time prescribed by Rule 31(a) for preparing briefs—40 days to the appellant, 30 days to the appellee—is well within the time that must ordinarily elapse in most circuits before an appeal can be reached for consideration. In those circuits, the time prescribed by the Rule should not be disturbed. But if a court of appeals maintains a current calendar, that is, if an appeal can be heard as soon as the briefs have been filed, or if the practice of the court permits the submission of appeals for preliminary consideration as soon as the briefs have been filed, the court should be free to prescribe shorter periods in the interest of expediting decision.

Rule 32. Form of Briefs, Appendices, and Other Papers

Notes of Advisory Committee on Rules—1986 Amendment

The amendments to Rules 31(a) and (c) are technical. No substantive change is intended.

Notes of Advisory Committee on Rules—1994 Amendment

Subdivision (b). The amendment allows a court of appeals to require the filing of a greater, as well as a lesser, number of copies of briefs. The amendment also allows the required number to be prescribed by local rule as well as by order in a particular case.

Committee Notes on Rules—1998 Amendment

The language and organization of the rule are amended to make the rule more easily understood. In addition to changes made to improve the understanding, the Advisory Committee has changed language to make style and terminology consistent throughout the appellate rules. These changes are intended to be stylistic only; a substantive change is made, however, in subdivision (b).

Subdivision (a). Paragraph (a)(2) explicitly authorizes a court of appeals to shorten a briefing schedule if the court routinely considers cases on the merits promptly after the briefs are filed. Extensions of the briefing schedule, by order, are permitted under the general provisions of Rule 26(b).

Subdivision (b). The current rule says that a party who is permitted to file "typewritten ribbon and carbon copies of the brief" need only file an original and three copies of the brief. The quoted language, in conjunction with current rule 24(c), means that a party allowed to proceed in forma pauperis need not file 25 copies of the brief. Two changes are made in this subdivision. First, it is anachronistic to refer to a party who is allowed to file a typewritten brief as if that would distinguish the party from all other parties; any party is permitted to file a typewritten brief. The amended rule states directly that it applies to a party permitted to proceed in forma pauperis. Second, the amended rule does not generally permit parties who are represented by counsel to file the lesser number of briefs. Inexpensive methods of copying are generally available. Unless it would impose hardship, in which case a motion to file a lesser number should be filed, a represented party must file the usual number of briefs.

Committee Notes on Rules—2002 Amendment

Subdivision (b). In requiring that two copies of each brief "must be served on counsel for each separately represented party," Rule 31(b) may be read to imply that copies of briefs need not be served on unrepresented parties. The Rule has been amended to clarify that briefs must be served on all parties, including those who are not represented by counsel.

Changes Made After Publication and Comments. No changes were made to the text of the proposed amendment or to the Committee Note.

Committee Notes on Rules—2009 Amendment

Subdivision (a)(1). Subdivision (a)(1) formerly required that the appellant's reply brief be served "at least 3 days before argument, unless the court, for good cause, allows a later filing." Under former Rule 26(a), "3 days" could mean as many as 5 or even 6 days. See the Note to Rule 26. Under revised Rule 26(a), intermediate weekends and holidays are counted. Changing "3 days" to "7 days" alters the period accordingly. Under revised Rule 26(a), when a period ends on a weekend or holiday, one must continue to count in the same direction until the next day that is not a weekend or holiday; the choice of the 7-day period for subdivision (a)(1) will minimize such occurrences.

Rule 32. Form of Briefs, Appendices, and Other Papers
(a) Form of a Brief.
(1) *Reproduction.*
    (A) A brief may be reproduced by any process that yields a clear black image on light paper. The paper must be opaque and unglazed. Only one side of the paper may be used.
    (B) Text must be reproduced with a clarity that equals or exceeds the output of a laser printer.
    (C) Photographs, illustrations, and tables may be reproduced by any method that results in a good copy of the original; a glossy finish is acceptable if the original is glossy.

Rule 32. Form of Briefs, Appendices, and Other Papers

(2) *Cover.* Except for filings by unrepresented parties, the cover of the appellant's brief must be blue; the appellee's, red; an intervenor's or amicus curiae's, green; any reply brief, gray; and any supplemental brief, tan. The front cover of a brief must contain:

    (A) the number of the case centered at the top;

    (B) the name of the court;

    (C) the title of the case (see Rule 12(a));

    (D) the nature of the proceeding (e.g., Appeal, Petition for Review) and the name of the court, agency, or board below;

    (E) the title of the brief, identifying the party or parties for whom the brief is filed; and

    (F) the name, office address, and telephone number of counsel representing the party for whom the brief is filed.

(3) *Binding.* The brief must be bound in any manner that is secure, does not obscure the text, and permits the brief to lie reasonably flat when open.

(4) *Paper Size, Line Spacing, and Margins.* The brief must be on 8 1/2 by 11 inch paper. The text must be double-spaced, but quotations more than two lines long may be indented and single-spaced. Headings and footnotes may be single-spaced. Margins must be at least one inch on all four sides. Page numbers may be placed in the margins, but no text may appear there.

(5) *Typeface.* Either a proportionally spaced or a monospaced face may be used.

    (A) A proportionally spaced face must include serifs, but sans-serif type may be used in headings and captions. A proportionally spaced face must be 14-point or larger.

    (B) A monospaced face may not contain more than 10 1/2 characters per inch.

(6) *Type Styles.* A brief must be set in a plain, roman style, although italics or boldface may be used for emphasis. Case names must be italicized or underlined.

[The following text of subdivision (7) was effective until December 1, 2016.]

(7) *Length.*

    (A) *Page Limitation.* A principal brief may not exceed 30 pages, or a reply brief 15 pages, unless it complies with Rule 32(a)(7)(B) and (C).

    (B) *Type-Volume Limitation.*

        (i) A principal brief is acceptable if:

        • it contains no more than 14,000 words; or

        • it uses a monospaced face and contains no more than 1,300 lines of text.

        (ii) A reply brief is acceptable if it contains no more than half of the type volume specified in Rule 32(a)(7)(B)(i).

        (iii) Headings, footnotes, and quotations count toward the word and line limitations. The corporate disclosure statement, table of contents, table of citations, statement with respect to oral argument, any addendum containing statutes, rules or regulations, and any certificates of counsel do not count toward the limitation.

[The following text of subdivision (7) became effective December 1, 2016.]

(7) *Length.*

    (A) Page Limitation. A principal brief may not exceed 30 pages, or a reply brief 15 pages, unless it complies with Rule 32(a)(7)(B).

    (B) Type-Volume Limitation.

        (i) A principal brief is acceptable if it:

        • contains no more than 13,000 words; or

        • uses a monospaced face and contains no more than 1,300 lines of text.

        (ii) A reply brief is acceptable if it contains no more than half of the type volume specified in Rule 32(a)(7)(B)(i).

Rule 32. Form of Briefs, Appendices, and Other Papers

     (C) *Certificate of Compliance.*
        (i) A brief submitted under Rules 28.1(e)(2) or 32(a)(7)(B) must include a certificate by the attorney, or an unrepresented party, that the brief complies with the type-volume limitation. The person preparing the certificate may rely on the word or line count of the word-processing system used to prepare the brief. The certificate must state either:
         • the number of words in the brief; or
         • the number of lines of monospaced type in the brief.
        (ii) Form 6 in the Appendix of Forms is a suggested form of a certificate of compliance. Use of Form 6 must be regarded as sufficient to meet the requirements of Rules 28.1(e)(3) and 32(a)(7)(C)(i).

(b) Form of an Appendix. An appendix must comply with Rule 32(a)(1), (2), (3), and (4), with the following exceptions:
    (1) The cover of a separately bound appendix must be white.
    (2) An appendix may include a legible photocopy of any document found in the record or of a printed judicial or agency decision.
    (3) When necessary to facilitate inclusion of odd-sized documents such as technical drawings, an appendix may be a size other than 8 1/2 by 11 inches, and need not lie reasonably flat when opened.

(c) Form of Other Papers.
    (1) *Motion.* The form of a motion is governed by Rule 27(d).
    (2) *Other Papers.* Any other paper, including a petition for panel rehearing and a petition for hearing or rehearing en banc, and any response to such a petition, must be reproduced in the manner prescribed by Rule 32(a), with the following exceptions:
        (A) A cover is not necessary if the caption and signature page of the paper together contain the information required by Rule 32(a)(2). If a cover is used, it must be white.
        (B) Rule 32(a)(7) does not apply.

(d) Signature. Every brief, motion, or other paper filed with the court must be signed by the party filing the paper or, if the party is represented, by one of the party's attorneys.

[The following text of subdivision (e) was effective until December 1, 2016.]

(e) Local Variation. Every court of appeals must accept documents that comply with the form requirements of this rule. By local rule or order in a particular case a court of appeals may accept documents that do not meet all of the form requirements of this rule.

[The following text of subdivisions (e), (f) and (g) became effective December 1, 2016.]

(e) Local Variation. Every court of appeals must accept documents that comply with the form requirements of this rule and the length limits set by these rules. By local rule or order in a particular case, a court of appeals may accept documents that do not meet all the form requirements of this rule or the length limits set by these rules.

(f) Items Excluded from Length. In computing any length limit, headings, footnotes, and quotations count toward the limit but the following items do not:
- the cover page;
- a corporate disclosure statement;
- a table of contents;
- a table of citations;
- a statement regarding oral argument;
- an addendum containing statutes, rules, or regulations;
- certificates of counsel;
- the signature block;
- the proof of service; and

Rule 32. Form of Briefs, Appendices, and Other Papers

- any item specifically excluded by these rules or by local rule.

(g) Certificate of Compliance.

(1) Briefs and Papers That Require a Certificate. A brief submitted under Rules 28.1(e)(2), 29(b)(4), or 32(a)(7)(B)—and a paper submitted under Rules 5(c)(1), 21(d)(1), 27(d)(2)(A), 27(d)(2)(C), 35(b)(2)(A), or 40(b)(1)—must include a certificate by the attorney, or an unrepresented party, that the document complies with the type-volume limitation. The person preparing the certificate may rely on the word or line count of the word-processing system used to prepare the document. The certificate must state the number of words—or the number of lines of monospaced type—in the document.

(2) Acceptable Form. Form 6 in the Appendix of Forms meets the requirements for a certificate of compliance.

(As amended Apr. 24, 1998, eff. Dec. 1, 1998; Apr. 29, 2002, eff. Dec. 1, 2002; Apr. 25, 2005, eff. Dec. 1, 2005; Apr. 28, 2016, eff. Dec. 1, 2016.)

Notes of Advisory Committee on Rules—1967

Only two methods of printing are now generally recognized by the circuits—standard typographic printing and the offset duplicating process (multilith). A third, mimeographing, is permitted in the Fifth Circuit. The District of Columbia, Ninth, and Tenth Circuits permit records to be reproduced by copying processes. The Committee feels that recent and impending advances in the arts of duplicating and copying warrant experimentation with less costly forms of reproduction than those now generally authorized. The proposed rule permits, in effect, the use of any process other than the carbon copy process which produces a clean, readable page. What constitutes such is left in first instance to the parties and ultimately to the court to determine. The final sentence of the first paragraph of subdivision (a) is added to allow the use of multilith, mimeograph, or other forms of copies of the reporter's original transcript whenever such are available.

Committee Notes on Rules—1998 Amendment

In addition to amending Rule 32 to conform to uniform drafting standards, several substantive amendments are made. The Advisory Committee had been working on substantive amendments to Rule 32 for some time prior to completion of this larger project.

Subdivison (a). Form of a Brief.

Paragraph (a)(1). Reproduction.

The rule permits the use of "light" paper, not just "white" paper. Cream and buff colored paper, including recycled paper, are acceptable. The rule permits printing on only one side of the paper. Although some argue that paper could be saved by allowing double-sided printing, others argue that in order to preserve legibility a heavier weight paper would be needed, resulting in little, if any, paper saving. In addition, the blank sides of a brief are commonly used by judges and their clerks for making notes about the case.

Because photocopying is inexpensive and widely available and because use of carbon paper is now very rare, all references to the use of carbon copies have been deleted.

The rule requires that the text be reproduced with a clarity that equals or exceeds the output of a laser printer. That means that the method used must have a print resolution of 300 dots per inch (dpi) or more. This will ensure the legibility of the brief. A brief produced by a typewriter or a daisy wheel printer, as well as one produced by a laser printer, has a print resolution of 300 dpi or more. But a brief produced by a dot-matrix printer, fax machine, or portable printer that uses heat or dye transfer methods does not. Some ink jet printers are 300 dpi or more, but some are 216 dpi and would not be sufficient.

Photographs, illustrations, and tables may be reproduced by any method that results in a good copy.

Paragraph (a)(2). Cover.

The rule requires that the number of the case be centered at the top of the front cover of a brief. This will aid in identification of the brief. The idea was drawn from a local rule. The rule also requires that the title of the brief identify the party or parties on whose behalf the brief is filed. When there are multiple appellants or appellees, the information is necessary to the court. If, however, the brief is filed on behalf of all appellants or appellees, it may so indicate. Further, it may be possible to identify the class of parties on whose behalf the brief is filed. Otherwise, it may be necessary to name each party. The rule also requires that attorney's telephone numbers appear on the front cover of a brief or appendix.

Paragraph (a)(3). Binding.

The rule requires a brief to be bound in any manner that is secure, does not obscure the text, and that permits the brief to lie reasonably flat when open. Many judges and most court employees do much of their work at computer

Rule 32. Form of Briefs, Appendices, and Other Papers

keyboards and a brief that lies flat when open is significantly more convenient. One circuit already has such a requirement and another states a preference for it. While a spiral binding would comply with this requirement, it is not intended to be the exclusive method of binding. Stapling a brief at the upper left-hand corner also satisfies this requirement as long as it is sufficiently secure.

Paragraph (a)(4). Paper Size, Line Spacing, and Margins.

The provisions for pamphlet-size briefs are deleted because their use is so rare. If a circuit wishes to authorize their use, it has authority to do so under subdivision (d) of this rule.

Paragraph (a)(5). Typeface.

This paragraph and the next one, governing type style, are new. The existing rule simply states that a brief produced by the standard typographic process must be printed in at least 11 point type, or if produced in any other manner, the lines of text must be double spaced. Today few briefs are produced by commercial printers or by typewriters; most are produced on and printed by computer. The availability of computer fonts in a variety of sizes and styles has given rise to local rules limiting type styles. The Advisory Committee believes that some standards are needed both to ensure that all litigants have an equal opportunity to present their material and to ensure that the briefs are easily legible.

With regard to typeface there are two options: proportionally-spaced typeface or monospaced typeface.

A proportionally-spaced typeface gives a different amount of horizontal space to characters depending upon the width of the character. A capital "M" is given more horizontal space than a lower case "i." The rule requires that a proportionally-spaced typeface have serifs. Serifs are small horizontal or vertical strokes at the ends of the lines that make up the letters and numbers. Studies have shown that long passages of serif type are easier to read and comprehend than long passages of sans-serif type. The rule accordingly limits the principal sections of submissions to serif type, although sans-serif type may be used in headings and captions. This is the same approach magazines, newspapers, and commercial printers take. Look at a professionally printed brief; you will find sans-serif type confined to captions, if it is used at all. The next line shows two characters enlarged for detail. The first has serifs, the second does not.

Y Y

So that the type is easily legible, the rule requires a minimum type size of 14 points for proportionally-spaced typeface.

A monospaced typeface is one in which all characters have the same advance width. That means that each character is given the same horizontal space on the line. A wide letter such as a capital "M" and a narrow letter such as a lower case "i" are given the same space. Most typewriters produce mono-spaced type, and most computers also can do so using fonts with names such as "Courier."

This sentence is in a proportionally spaced font; as you can see, the m and i have different widths.

This sentence is in a monospaced font; as you can see, the m and i have the same width.

The rule requires use of a monospaced typeface that produces no more than 10 1/2 characters per inch. A standard typewriter with pica type produces a monospaced typeface with 10 characters per inch (cpi). That is the ideal monospaced typeface. The rule permits up to 10 1/2 cpi because some computer software programs contain monospaced fonts that purport to produce 10 cpi but that in fact produce slightly more than 10 cpi. In order to avoid the need to reprint a brief produced in good faith reliance upon such a program, the rule permits a bit of leeway. A monospace typeface with no more than 10 cpi is preferred.

Paragraph (a)(6). Type Styles.

The rule requires use of plain roman, that is not italic or script, type. Italics and boldface may be used for emphasis. Italicizing case names is preferred but underlining may be used.

Paragraph (a)(7). Type-Volume Limitation.

Subparagraph (a)(7)(A) contains a safe-harbor provision. A principal brief that does not exceed 30 pages complies with the type-volume limitation without further question or certification. A reply brief that does not exceed 15 pages is similarly treated. The current limit is 50 pages but that limit was established when most briefs were produced on typewriters. The widespread use of personal computers has made a multitude of printing options available to practitioners. Use of a proportional typeface alone can greatly increase the amount of material per page as compared with use of a monospace typeface. Even though the rule requires use of 14-point proportional type, there is great variation in the x-height of different 14-point typefaces. Selection of a typeface with a small x-height increases the amount of text per page. Computers also make possible fine gradations in spacing between lines and tight tracking between letters and words. All of this, and more, have made the 50-page limit virtually meaningless. Establishing a safe-harbor of 50 pages would permit a person who makes use of the multitude of printing "tricks" available with most personal computers to file a brief far longer than the "old" 50-page brief. Therefore, as to those briefs not subject to any other volume control than a page limit, a 30-page limit is imposed.

The limits in subparagraph (B) approximate the current 50-page limit and compliance with them is easy even for a person without a personal computer. The aim of these provisions is to create a level playing field. The rule gives every party an equal opportunity to make arguments, without permitting those with the best in-house typesetting an opportunity to expand their submissions.

Rule 32. Form of Briefs, Appendices, and Other Papers

The length can be determined either by counting words or lines. That is, the length of a brief is determined not by the number of pages but by the number of words or lines in the brief. This gives every party the same opportunity to present an argument without regard to the typeface used and eliminates any incentive to use footnotes or typographical "tricks" to squeeze more material onto a page.

The word counting method can be used with any typeface.

A monospaced brief can meet the volume limitation by using the word or a line count. If the line counting method is used, the number of lines may not exceed 1,300—26 lines per page in a 50-page brief. The number of lines is easily counted manually. Line counting is not sufficient if a proportionally spaced typeface is used, because the amount of material per line can vary widely.

A brief using the type-volume limitations in subparagraph (B) must include a certificate by the attorney, or party proceeding pro se, that the brief complies with the limitation. The rule permits the person preparing the certification to rely upon the word or line count of the word-processing system used to prepare the brief.

Currently, Rule 28(g) governs the length of a brief. Rule 28(g) begins with the words "[e]xcept by permission of the court," signaling that a party may file a motion to exceed the limits established in the rule. The absence of similar language in Rule 32 does not mean that the Advisory Committee intends to prohibit motions to deviate from the requirements of the rule. The Advisory Committee does not believe that any such language is needed to authorize such a motion.

Subdivision (b). Form of an Appendix.

The provisions governing the form of a brief generally apply to an appendix. The rule recognizes, however, that an appendix is usually produced by photocopying existing documents. The rule requires that the photocopies be legible.

The rule permits inclusion not only of documents from the record but also copies of a printed judicial or agency decision. If a decision that is part of the record in the case has been published, it is helpful to provide a copy of the published decision in place of a copy of the decision from the record.

Subdivision (c). Form of Other Papers.

The old rule required a petition for rehearing to be produced in the same manner as a brief or appendix. The new rule also requires that a petition for rehearing en banc and a response to either a petition for panel rehearing or a petition for rehearing en banc be prepared in the same manner. But the length limitations of paragraph (a)(7) do not apply to those documents and a cover is not required if all the information needed by the court to properly identify the document and the parties is included in the caption or signature page.

Existing subdivision (b) states that other papers may be produced in like manner, or "they may be typewritten upon opaque, unglazed paper 8 1/2 by 11 inches in size." The quoted language is deleted but that method of preparing documents is not eliminated because (a)(5)(B) permits use of standard pica type. The only change is that the new rule now specifies margins for typewritten documents.

Subdivision (d). Local Variation.

A brief that complies with the national rule should be acceptable in every court. Local rules may move in one direction only; they may authorize noncompliance with certain of the national norms. For example, a court that wishes to do so may authorize printing of briefs on both sides of the paper, or the use of smaller type size or sans-serif proportional type. A local rule may not, however, impose requirements that are not in the national rule.

Committee Notes on Rules—2002 Amendment

Subdivision (a)(2). On occasion, a court may permit or order the parties to file supplemental briefs addressing an issue that was not addressed—or adequately addressed—in the principal briefs. Rule 32(a)(2) has been amended to require that tan covers be used on such supplemental briefs. The amendment is intended to promote uniformity in federal appellate practice. At present, the local rules of the circuit courts conflict. *See, e.g.,* D.C. Cir. R. 28(g) (requiring yellow covers on supplemental briefs); 11th Cir. R. 32, I.O.P. 1 (requiring white covers on supplemental briefs).

Changes Made After Publication and Comments. No changes were made to the text of the proposed amendment or to the Committee Note.

Subdivision (a)(7)(C). If the principal brief of a party exceeds 30 pages, or if the reply brief of a party exceeds 15 pages, Rule 32(a)(7)(C) provides that the party or the party's attorney must certify that the brief complies with the type-volume limitation of Rule 32(a)(7)(B). Rule 32(a)(7)(C) has been amended to refer to Form 6 (which has been added to the Appendix of Forms) and to provide that a party or attorney who uses Form 6 has complied with Rule 32(a)(7)(C). No court may provide to the contrary, in its local rules or otherwise.

Form 6 requests not only the information mandated by Rule 32(a)(7)(C), but also information that will assist courts in enforcing the typeface requirements of Rule 32(a)(5) and the type style requirements of Rule 32(a)(6). Parties and attorneys are not required to use Form 6, but they are encouraged to do so.

Subdivision (c)(2)(A). Under Rule 32(c)(2)(A), a cover is not required on a petition for panel rehearing, petition for

Rule 32. Form of Briefs, Appendices, and Other Papers

hearing or rehearing en banc, answer to a petition for panel rehearing, response to a petition for hearing or rehearing en banc, or any other paper. Rule 32(d) makes it clear that no court can require that a cover be used on any of these papers. However, nothing prohibits a court from providing in its local rules that if a cover on one of these papers is "voluntarily" used, it must be a particular color. Several circuits have adopted such local rules. *See, e.g.*, Fed. Cir. R. 35(c) (requiring yellow covers on petitions for hearing or rehearing en banc and brown covers on responses to such petitions); Fed. Cir. R. 40(a) (requiring yellow covers on petitions for panel rehearing and brown covers on answers to such petitions); 7th Cir. R. 28 (requiring blue covers on petitions for rehearing filed by appellants or answers to such petitions, and requiring red covers on petitions for rehearing filed by appellees or answers to such petitions); 9th Cir. R. 40–1 (requiring blue covers on petitions for panel rehearing filed by appellants and red covers on answers to such petitions, and requiring red covers on petitions for panel rehearing filed by appellees and blue covers on answers to such petitions); 11th Cir. R. 35–6 (requiring white covers on petitions for hearing or rehearing en banc).

These conflicting local rules create a hardship for counsel who practice in more than one circuit. For that reason, Rule 32(c)(2)(A) has been amended to provide that if a party chooses to use a cover on a paper that is not required to have one, that cover must be white. The amendment is intended to preempt all local rulemaking on the subject of cover colors and thereby promote uniformity in federal appellate practice.

Changes Made After Publication and Comments. No changes were made to the text of the proposed amendment or to the Committee Note.

Subdivisions (d) and (e). Former subdivision (d) has been redesignated as subdivision (e), and a new subdivision (d) has been added. The new subdivision (d) requires that every brief, motion, or other paper filed with the court be signed by the attorney or unrepresented party who files it, much as Fed. R. Civ. P. 11 (a) imposes a signature requirement on papers filed in district court. Only the original copy of every paper must be signed. An appendix filed with the court does not have to be signed at all.

By requiring a signature, subdivision (d) ensures that a readily identifiable attorney or party takes responsibility for every paper. The courts of appeals already have authority to sanction attorneys and parties who file papers that contain misleading or frivolous assertions, *see, e.g.*, 28 U.S.C. §1912, Fed. R. App. P. 38 & 46(b)(1)(B), and thus subdivision (d) has not been amended to incorporate provisions similar to those found in Fed. R. Civ. P. 11 (b) and 11(c).

Changes Made After Publication and Comments. No changes were made to the text of the proposed amendment. A line was added to the Committee Note to clarify that only the original copy of a paper needs to be signed.

Committee Notes on Rules—2005 Amendment

Subdivision (a)(7)(C). Rule 32(a)(7)(C) has been amended to add cross-references to new Rule 28.1, which governs briefs filed in cases involving cross-appeals. Rule 28.1(e)(2) prescribes type-volume limitations that apply to such briefs, and Rule 28.1(e)(3) requires parties to certify compliance with those type-volume limitations under Rule 32(a)(7)(C).

Committee Notes on Rules – 2016 Amendment

When Rule 32(a)(7)(B)'s type-volume limits for briefs were adopted in 1998, the word limits were based on an estimate of 280 words per page. In the course of adopting word limits for the length limits in Rules 5, 21, 27, 35, and 40, and responding to concern about the length of briefs, the Committee has reevaluated the conversion ratio (from pages to words) and decided to apply a conversion ratio of 260 words per page. Rules 28.1 and 32(a)(7)(B) are amended to reduce the word limits accordingly.

In a complex case, a party may need to file a brief that exceeds the type-volume limitations specified in these rules, such as to include unusually voluminous information explaining relevant background or legal provisions or to respond to multiple briefs by opposing parties or amici. The Committee expects that courts will accommodate those situations by granting leave to exceed the type-volume limitations as appropriate.

Subdivision (e) is amended to make clear a court's ability (by local rule or order in a case) to increase the length limits for briefs and other documents. Subdivision (e) already established this authority as to the length limits in Rule 32(a)(7); the amendment makes clear that this authority extends to all length limits in the Appellate Rules.

A new subdivision (f) is added to set out a global list of items excluded from length computations, and the list of exclusions in former subdivision (a)(7)(B)(iii) is deleted. The certificate-of-compliance provision formerly in Rule 32(a)(7)(C) is relocated to a new Rule 32(g) and now applies to filings under all type-volume limits (other than Rule 28(j)'s word limit)—including the new word limits in Rules 5, 21, 27, 29, 35, and 40. Conforming amendments are made to Form 6.

Rule 32.1 Citing Judicial Dispositions

(a) Citation Permitted. A court may not prohibit or restrict the citation of federal judicial opinions, orders, judgments, or other written dispositions that have been:

(i) designated as "unpublished," "not for publication," "non-precedential," "not precedent," or the like; and

(ii) issued on or after January 1, 2007.

(b) Copies Required. If a party cites a federal judicial opinion, order, judgment, or other written disposition that is not available in a publicly accessible electronic database, the party must file and serve a copy of that opinion, order, judgment, or disposition with the brief or other paper in which it is cited.

(As added Apr. 12, 2006, eff. Dec. 1, 2006.)

Committee Notes on Rules—2006

Rule 32.1 is a new rule addressing the citation of judicial opinions, orders, judgments, or other written dispositions that have been designated by a federal court as "unpublished," "not for publication," "non-precedential," "not precedent," or the like. This Committee Note will refer to these dispositions collectively as "unpublished" opinions.

Rule 32.1 is extremely limited. It does not require any court to issue an unpublished opinion or forbid any court from doing so. It does not dictate the circumstances under which a court may choose to designate an opinion as "unpublished" or specify the procedure that a court must follow in making that determination. It says nothing about what effect a court must give to one of its unpublished opinions or to the unpublished opinions of another court. Rule 32.1 addresses only the *citation* of federal judicial dispositions that have been *designated* as "unpublished" or "non-precedential"—whether or not those dispositions have been published in some way or are precedential in some sense.

Subdivision (a). Every court of appeals has allowed unpublished opinions to be cited in some circumstances, such as to support a contention of issue preclusion or claim preclusion. But the circuits have differed dramatically with respect to the restrictions that they have placed on the citation of unpublished opinions for their persuasive value. Some circuits have freely permitted such citation, others have discouraged it but permitted it in limited circumstances, and still others have forbidden it altogether.

Rule 32.1(a) is intended to replace these inconsistent standards with one uniform rule. Under Rule 32.1(a), a court of appeals may not prohibit a party from citing an unpublished opinion of a federal court for its persuasive value or for any other reason. In addition, under Rule 32.1(a), a court may not place any restriction on the citation of such opinions. For example, a court may not instruct parties that the citation of unpublished opinions is discouraged, nor may a court forbid parties to cite unpublished opinions when a published opinion addresses the same issue.

Rule 32.1(a) applies only to unpublished opinions issued on or after January 1, 2007. The citation of unpublished opinions issued before January 1, 2007, will continue to be governed by the local rules of the circuits.

Subdivision (b). Under Rule 32.1(b), a party who cites an opinion of a federal court must provide a copy of that opinion to the court of appeals and to the other parties, unless that opinion is available in a publicly accessible electronic database—such as a commercial database maintained by a legal research service or a database maintained by a court. A party who is required under Rule 32.1(b) to provide a copy of an opinion must file and serve the copy with the brief or other paper in which the opinion is cited. Rule 32.1(b) applies to all unpublished opinions, regardless of when they were issued.

Changes Made After Publication and Comment. (At its June 15–16, 2005, meeting, the Standing Rules Committee with the advisory committee chair's concurrence agreed to delete sections of the Committee Note, which provided background information on the justification of the proposal.) The changes made by the Advisory Committee after publication are described in my May 14, 2004 report to the Standing Committee. At its April 2005 meeting, the Advisory Committee directed that two additional changes be made.

First, the Committee decided to add "federal" before "judicial opinions" in subdivision (a) and before "judicial opinion" in subdivision (b) to make clear that Rule 32.1 applies only to the unpublished opinions of federal courts. Conforming changes were made to the Committee Note. These changes address the concern of some state court judges—conveyed by Chief Justice Wells at the June 2004 Standing Committee meeting—that Rule 32.1 might have an impact on state law.

Second, the Committee decided to insert into the Committee Note references to the studies conducted by the Federal Judicial Center ("FJC") and the Administrative Office ("AO"). (The studies are described below. [Omitted]) These references make clear that the arguments of Rule 32.1's opponents were taken seriously and studied carefully, but ultimately rejected because they were unsupported by or, in some instances, actually refuted by the best available empirical evidence.

Rule 33. Appeal Conferences

Rule 33. Appeal Conferences

The court may direct the attorneys—and, when appropriate, the parties—to participate in one or more conferences to address any matter that may aid in disposing of the proceedings, including simplifying the issues and discussing settlement. A judge or other person designated by the court may preside over the conference, which may be conducted in person or by telephone. Before a settlement conference, the attorneys must consult with their clients and obtain as much authority as feasible to settle the case. The court may, as a result of the conference, enter an order controlling the course of the proceedings or implementing any settlement agreement.
(As amended Apr. 29, 1994, eff. Dec. 1, 1994; Apr. 24, 1998, eff. Dec. 1, 1998.)

Notes of Advisory Committee on Rules—1967

The uniform rule for review or enforcement of orders of administrative agencies, boards, commissions or officers (see the general note following Rule 15) authorizes a prehearing conference in agency review proceedings. The same considerations which make a prehearing conference desirable in such proceedings may be present in certain cases on appeal from the district courts. The proposed rule is based upon subdivision 11 of the present uniform rule for review of agency orders.

Notes of Advisory Committee on Rules—1994 Amendment

Rule 33 has been entirely rewritten. The new rule makes several changes.

The caption of the rule has been changed from "Prehearing Conference" to "Appeal Conferences" to reflect the fact that occasionally a conference is held after oral argument.

The rule permits the court to require the parties to attend the conference in appropriate cases. The Committee does not contemplate that attendance of the parties will become routine, but in certain instances the parties' presence can be useful. The language of the rule is broad enough to allow a court to determine that an executive or employee (other than the general counsel) of a corporation or government agency with authority regarding the matter at issue, constitutes "the party."

The rule includes the possibility of settlement among the possible conference topics.

The rule recognizes that conferences are often held by telephone.

The rule allows a judge or other person designated by the court to preside over a conference. A number of local rules permit persons other than judges to preside over conferences. 1st Cir. R. 47.5; 6th Cir. R. 18; 8th Cir. R. 33A; 9th Cir. R. 33–1; and 10th Cir. R. 33.

The rule requires an attorney to consult with his or her client before a settlement conference and obtain as much authority as feasible to settle the case. An attorney can never settle a case without his or her client's consent. Certain entities, especially government entities, have particular difficulty obtaining authority to settle a case. The rule requires counsel to obtain only as much authority "as feasible."

Committee Notes on Rules—1998 Amendment

The language of the rule is amended to make the rule more easily understood. In addition to changes made to improve the understanding, the Advisory Committee has changed language to make style and terminology consistent throughout the appellate rules. These changes are intended to be stylistic only.

Rule 34. Oral Argument

(a) In General.

(1) *Party's Statement.* Any party may file, or a court may require by local rule, a statement explaining why oral argument should, or need not, be permitted.

(2) *Standards.* Oral argument must be allowed in every case unless a panel of three judges who have examined the briefs and record unanimously agrees that oral argument is unnecessary for any of the following reasons:

(A) the appeal is frivolous;

(B) the dispositive issue or issues have been authoritatively decided; or

Rule 34. Oral Argument

(C) the facts and legal arguments are adequately presented in the briefs and record, and the decisional process would not be significantly aided by oral argument.

(b) Notice of Argument; Postponement. The clerk must advise all parties whether oral argument will be scheduled, and, if so, the date, time, and place for it, and the time allowed for each side. A motion to postpone the argument or to allow longer argument must be filed reasonably in advance of the hearing date.

(c) Order and Contents of Argument. The appellant opens and concludes the argument. Counsel must not read at length from briefs, records, or authorities.

(d) Cross-Appeals and Separate Appeals. If there is a cross-appeal, Rule 28.1(b) determines which party is the appellant and which is the appellee for purposes of oral argument. Unless the court directs otherwise, a cross-appeal or separate appeal must be argued when the initial appeal is argued. Separate parties should avoid duplicative argument.

(e) Nonappearance of a Party. If the appellee fails to appear for argument, the court must hear appellant's argument. If the appellant fails to appear for argument, the court may hear the appellee's argument. If neither party appears, the case will be decided on the briefs, unless the court orders otherwise.

(f) Submission on Briefs. The parties may agree to submit a case for decision on the briefs, but the court may direct that the case be argued.

(g) Use of Physical Exhibits at Argument; Removal. Counsel intending to use physical exhibits other than documents at the argument must arrange to place them in the courtroom on the day of the argument before the court convenes. After the argument, counsel must remove the exhibits from the courtroom, unless the court directs otherwise. The clerk may destroy or dispose of the exhibits if counsel does not reclaim them within a reasonable time after the clerk gives notice to remove them.

(As amended Apr. 1, 1979, eff. Aug. 1, 1979; Mar. 10, 1986, eff. July 1, 1986; Apr. 30, 1991, eff. Dec. 1, 1991; Apr. 22, 1993, eff. Dec. 1, 1993; Apr. 24, 1998, eff. Dec. 1, 1998; Apr. 25, 2005, eff. Dec. 1, 2005.)

Notes of Advisory Committee on Rules—1967

A majority of circuits now limit oral argument to thirty minutes for each side, with the provision that additional time may be made available upon request. The Committee is of the view that thirty minutes to each side is sufficient in most cases, but that where additional time is necessary it should be freely granted on a proper showing of cause therefor. It further feels that the matter of time should be left ultimately to each court of appeals, subject to the spirit of the rule that a reasonable time should be allowed for argument. The term "side" is used to indicate that the time allowed by the rule is afforded to opposing interests rather than to individual parties. Thus if multiple appellants or appellees have a common interest, they constitute only a single side. If counsel for multiple parties who constitute a single side feel that additional time is necessary, they may request it. In other particulars this rule follows the usual practice among the circuits. See 3d Cir. Rule 31; 6th Cir. Rule 20; 10th Cir. Rule 23.

Notes of Advisory Committee on Rules—1979 Amendment

The proposed amendment, patterned after the recommendations in the Report of the Commission on Revision of the Federal Court Appellate System, Structure and Internal Procedures: Recommendations for Change, 1975, created by Public Law 489 of the 92nd Cong. 2nd Sess., 86 Stat. 807, sets forth general principles and minimum standards to be observed in formulating any local rule.

Notes of Advisory Committee on Rules—1986 Amendment

The amendments to Rules 34(a) and (e) are technical. No substantive change is intended.

Notes of Advisory Committee on Rules—1991 Amendment

Subdivision (d). The amendment of subdivision (d) conforms this rule with the amendment of Rule 28(h).

Notes of Advisory Committee on Rules—1993 Amendment

Subdivision (c). The amendment deletes the requirement that the opening argument must include a fair statement of

Rule 35. En Banc Determination

the case. The Committee proposed the change because in some circuits the court does not want appellants to give such statements. In those circuits, the rule is not followed and is misleading. Nevertheless, the Committee does not want the deletion of the requirement to indicate disapproval of the practice. Those circuits that desire a statement of the case may continue the practice.

Committee Notes on Rules—1998 Amendment

The language of the rule is amended to make the rule more easily understood. In addition to changes made to improve the understanding, the Advisory Committee has changed language to make style and terminology consistent throughout the appellate rules. These changes are intended to be stylistic only. Substantive changes are made in subdivision (a).

Subdivision (a). Currently subdivision (a) says that oral argument must be permitted unless, applying a local rule, a panel of three judges unanimously agrees that oral argument is not necessary. Rule 34 then outlines the criteria to be used to determine whether oral argument is needed and requires any local rule to "conform substantially" to the "minimum standard[s]" established in the national rule. The amendments omit the local rule requirement and make the criteria applicable by force of the national rule. The local rule is an unnecessary instrument.

Paragraph (a)(2) states that one reason for deciding that oral argument is unnecessary is that the dispositive issue has been authoritatively decided. The amended language no longer states that the issue must have been "recently" decided. The Advisory Committee does not intend any substantive change, but thinks that the use of "recently" may be misleading.

Subdivision (d). A cross-reference to Rule 28(h) has been substituted for a reiteration of the provisions of Rule 28(h).

Committee Notes on Rules—2005 Amendment

Subdivision (d). A cross-reference in subdivision (d) has been changed to reflect the fact that, as part of an effort to collect within one rule all provisions regarding briefing in cases involving cross-appeals, former Rule 28(h) has been abrogated and its contents moved to new Rule 28.1(b).

Rule 35. En Banc Determination

(a) When Hearing or Rehearing En Banc May Be Ordered. A majority of the circuit judges who are in regular active service and who are not disqualified may order that an appeal or other proceeding be heard or reheard by the court of appeals en banc. An en banc hearing or rehearing is not favored and ordinarily will not be ordered unless:

(1) en banc consideration is necessary to secure or maintain uniformity of the court's decisions; or

(2) the proceeding involves a question of exceptional importance.

(b) Petition for Hearing or Rehearing En Banc. A party may petition for a hearing or rehearing en banc.

(1) The petition must begin with a statement that either:

(A) the panel decision conflicts with a decision of the United States Supreme Court or of the court to which the petition is addressed (with citation to the conflicting case or cases) and consideration by the full court is therefore necessary to secure and maintain uniformity of the court's decisions; or

(B) the proceeding involves one or more questions of exceptional importance, each of which must be concisely stated; for example, a petition may assert that a proceeding presents a question of exceptional importance if it involves an issue on which the panel decision conflicts with the authoritative decisions of other United States Courts of Appeals that have addressed the issue.

[The following text of subdivisions (2) and (3) were effective until December 1, 2016.]

(2) Except by the court's permission, a petition for an en banc hearing or rehearing must not exceed 15 pages, excluding material not counted under Rule 32.

(3) For purposes of the page limit in Rule 35(b)(2), if a party files both a petition for panel rehearing and a petition for rehearing en banc, they are considered a single document even if they are filed separately, unless separate filing is required by local rule.

Rule 35. En Banc Determination

[The following text of subdivisions (2) and (3) became effective December 1, 2016.]

(2) Except by the court's permission:
  (A) a petition for an en banc hearing or rehearing produced using a computer must not exceed 3,900 words; and
  (B) a handwritten or typewritten petition for an en banc hearing or rehearing must not exceed 15 pages.
(3) For purposes of the limits in Rule 35(b)(2), if a party files both a petition for panel rehearing and a petition for rehearing en banc, they are considered a single document even if they are filed separately, unless separate filing is required by local rule.

(c) Time for Petition for Hearing or Rehearing En Banc. A petition that an appeal be heard initially en banc must be filed by the date when the appellee's brief is due. A petition for a rehearing en banc must be filed within the time prescribed by Rule 40 for filing a petition for rehearing.

(d) Number of Copies. The number of copies to be filed must be prescribed by local rule and may be altered by order in a particular case.

(e) Response. No response may be filed to a petition for an en banc consideration unless the court orders a response.

(f) Call for a Vote. A vote need not be taken to determine whether the case will be heard or reheard en banc unless a judge calls for a vote.

(As amended Apr. 1, 1979, eff. Aug. 1, 1979; Apr. 29, 1994, eff. Dec. 1, 1994; Apr. 24, 1998, eff. Dec. 1, 1998; Apr. 25, 2005, eff. Dec. 1, 2005; Apr. 28, 2016, eff. Dec. 1, 2016.)

Notes of Advisory Committee on Rules—1967

Statutory authority for in banc hearings is found in 28 U.S.C. §46(c). The proposed rule is responsive to the Supreme Court's view in *Western Pacific Ry. Corp. v. Western Pacific Ry. Co.*, 345 U.S. 247, 73 S.Ct. 656, 97 L.Ed. 986 (1953), that litigants should be free to suggest that a particular case is appropriate for consideration by all the judges of a court of appeals. The rule is addressed to the procedure whereby a party may suggest the appropriateness of convening the court in banc. It does not affect the power of a court of appeals to initiate in banc hearings *sua sponte*.

The provision that a vote will not be taken as a result of the suggestion of the party unless requested by a judge of the court in regular active service or by a judge who was a member of the panel that rendered a decision sought to be reheard is intended to make it clear that a suggestion of a party as such does not require any action by the court. See *Western Pacific Ry. Corp. v. Western Pacific Ry. Co.*, supra, 345 U.S. at 262, 73 S.Ct. 656. The rule merely authorizes a suggestion, imposes a time limit on suggestions for rehearings in banc, and provides that suggestions will be directed to the judges of the court in regular active service.

In practice, the suggestion of a party that a case be reheard in banc is frequently contained in a petition for rehearing, commonly styled "petition for rehearing in banc." Such a petition is in fact merely a petition for a rehearing, with a suggestion that the case be reheard in banc. Since no response to the suggestion, as distinguished from the petition for rehearing, is required, the panel which heard the case may quite properly dispose of the petition without reference to the suggestion. In such a case the fact that no response has been made to the suggestion does not affect the finality of the judgment or the issuance of the mandate, and the final sentence of the rule expressly so provides.

Notes of Advisory Committee on Rules—1979 Amendment

Under the present rule there is no specific provision for a response to a suggestion that an appeal be heard in banc. This has led to some uncertainty as to whether such a response may be filed. The proposed amendment would resolve this uncertainty.

While the present rule provides a time limit for suggestions for rehearing in banc, it does not deal with the timing of a request that the appeal be heard in banc initially. The proposed amendment fills this gap as well, providing that the suggestion must be made by the date of which the appellee's brief is filed.

Provision is made for circulating the suggestions to members of the panel despite the fact that senior judges on the panel would not be entitled to vote on whether a suggestion will be granted.

Rule 35. En Banc Determination

Notes of Advisory Committee on Rules—1994 Amendment

Subdivision (d). Subdivision (d) is added; it authorizes the courts of appeals to prescribe the number of copies of suggestions for hearing or rehearing in banc that must be filed. Because the number of copies needed depends directly upon the number of judges in the circuit, local rules are the best vehicle for setting the required number of copies.

Committee Notes on Rules—1998 Amendment

The language and organization of the rule are amended to make the rule more easily understood. In addition to changes made to improve the understanding, the Advisory Committee has changed language to make style and terminology consistent throughout the appellate rules. These changes are intended to be stylistic only.

Several substantive changes are made in this rule, however.

One of the purposes of the substantive amendments is to treat a request for a rehearing en banc like a petition for panel rehearing so that a request for a rehearing en banc will suspend the finality of the court of appeals' judgment and delay the running of the period for filing a petition for writ of certiorari. Companion amendments are made to Rule 41.

Subdivision (a). The title of this subdivision is changed from "when hearing or rehearing in banc *will* be ordered" to "When Hearing or Rehearing En Banc *May* Be Ordered." The change emphasizes the discretion a court has with regard to granting en banc review.

Subdivision (b). The term "petition" for rehearing en banc is substituted for the term "suggestion" for rehearing en banc. The terminology change reflects the Committee's intent to treat similarly a petition for panel rehearing and a request for a rehearing en banc. The terminology change also delays the running of the time for filing a petition for a writ of certiorari because Sup. Ct. R. 13.3 says:

if a petition for rehearing is timely filed in the lower court by any party, the time to file the petition for a writ of certiorari for all parties . . . runs from the date of the denial of the petition for rehearing or, if the petition for rehearing is granted, the subsequent entry of judgment.

The amendments also require each petition for en banc consideration to begin with a statement concisely demonstrating that the case meets the usual criteria for en banc consideration. It is the Committee's hope that requiring such a statement will cause the drafter of a petition to focus on the narrow grounds that support en banc consideration and to realize that a petition should not be filed unless the case meets those rigid standards.

Intercircuit conflict is cited as one reason for asserting that a proceeding involves a question of "exceptional importance." Intercircuit conflicts create problems. When the circuits construe the same federal law differently, parties' rights and duties depend upon where a case is litigated. Given the increase in the number of cases decided by the federal courts and the limitation on the number of cases the Supreme Court can hear, conflicts between the circuits may remain unresolved by the Supreme Court for an extended period of time. The existence of an intercircuit conflict often generates additional litigation in the other circuits as well as in the circuits that are already in conflict. Although an en banc proceeding will not necessarily prevent intercircuit conflicts, an en banc proceeding provides a safeguard against unnecessary intercircuit conflicts.

Some circuits have had rules or internal operating procedures that recognize a conflict with another circuit as a legitimate basis for granting a rehearing en banc. An intercircuit conflict may present a question of "exceptional importance" because of the costs that intercircuit conflicts impose on the system as a whole, in addition to the significance of the issues involved. It is not, however, the Committee's intent to make the granting of a hearing or rehearing en banc mandatory whenever there is an intercircuit conflict.

The amendment states that "a petition may assert that a proceeding presents a question of exceptional importance if it involves an issue on which the panel decision conflicts with the authoritative decisions of every other United States Court of Appeals that has addressed the issue." [The Supreme Court revised the proposed amendment to Rule 35(b)(1)(B) by deleting "every" before "other United States Court of Appeals".] That language contemplates two situations in which a rehearing en banc may be appropriate. The first is when a panel decision creates a conflict. A panel decision creates a conflict when it conflicts with the decisions of all other circuits that have considered the issue. If a panel decision simply joins one side of an already existing conflict, a rehearing en banc may not be as important because it cannot avoid the conflict. The second situation that may be a strong candidate for a rehearing en banc is one in which the circuit persists in a conflict created by a pre-existing decision of the same circuit and no other circuits have joined on that side of the conflict. The amendment states that the conflict must be with an "authoritative" decision of another circuit. "Authoritative" is used rather than "published" because in some circuits unpublished opinions may be treated as authoritative.

Counsel are reminded that their duty is fully discharged without filing a petition for rehearing en banc unless the case meets the rigid standards of subdivision (a) of this rule and even then the granting of a petition is entirely within the court's discretion.

Paragraph (2) of this subdivision establishes a maximum length for a petition. Fifteen pages is the length currently

Rule 35. En Banc Determination

used in several circuits. Each request for en banc consideration must be studied by every active judge of the court and is a serious call on limited judicial resources. The extraordinary nature of the issue or the threat to uniformity of the court's decision can be established in most cases in less than fifteen pages. A court may shorten the maximum length on a case by case basis but the rule does not permit a circuit to shorten the length by local rule. The Committee has retained page limits rather than using word or line counts similar to those in amended Rule 32 because there has not been a serious enough problem to justify importing the word and line-count and typeface requirements that are applicable to briefs into other contexts.

Paragraph (3), although similar to (2), is separate because it deals with those instances in which a party files both a petition for rehearing en banc under this rule and a petition for panel rehearing under Rule 40.

To improve the clarity of the rule, the material dealing with filing a response to a petition and with voting on a petition have been moved to new subdivisions (e) and (f).

Subdivision (c). Two changes are made in this subdivision. First, the sentence stating that a request for a rehearing en banc does not affect the finality of the judgment or stay the issuance of the mandate is deleted. Second, the language permitting a party to include a request for rehearing en banc in a petition for panel rehearing is deleted. The Committee believes that those circuits that want to require two separate documents should have the option to do so.

Subdivision (e). This is a new subdivision. The substance of the subdivision, however, was drawn from former subdivision (b). The only changes are stylistic; no substantive changes are intended.

Subdivision (f). This is a new subdivision. The substance of the subdivision, however, was drawn from former subdivision (b).

Because of the discretionary nature of the en banc procedure, the filing of a suggestion for rehearing en banc has not required a vote; a vote is taken only when requested by a judge. It is not the Committee's intent to change the discretionary nature of the procedure or to require a vote on a petition for rehearing en banc. The rule continues, therefore, to provide that a court is not obligated to vote on such petitions. It is necessary, however, that each court develop a procedure for disposing of such petitions because they will suspend the finality of the court's judgment and toll the time for filing a petition for certiorari.

Former subdivision (b) contained language directing the clerk to distribute a "suggestion" to certain judges and indicating which judges may call for a vote. New subdivision (f) does not address those issues because they deal with internal court procedures.

Committee Notes on Rules—2005 Amendment

Subdivision (a). Two national standards— 28 U.S.C. §46(c) and Rule 35(a)—provide that a hearing or rehearing en banc may be ordered by "a majority of the circuit judges who are in regular active service." Although these standards apply to all of the courts of appeals, the circuits are deeply divided over the interpretation of this language when one or more active judges are disqualified.

The Supreme Court has never addressed this issue. In *Shenker v. Baltimore & Ohio R.R. Co.*, 374 U.S. 1 (1963), the Court rejected a petitioner's claim that his rights under §46(c) had been violated when the Third Circuit refused to rehear his case en banc. The Third Circuit had 8 active judges at the time; 4 voted in favor of rehearing the case, 2 against, and 2 abstained. No judge was disqualified. The Supreme Court ruled against the petitioner, holding, in essence, that §46(c) did not provide a cause of action, but instead simply gave litigants "the right to know the administrative machinery that will be followed and the right to suggest that the *en banc* procedure be set in motion in his case." *Id.* at 5. *Shenker* did stress that a court of appeals has broad discretion in establishing internal procedures to handle requests for rehearings—or, as *Shenker* put it, " 'to devise its own administrative machinery to provide the *means* whereby a majority may order such a hearing.' " *Id.* (quoting *Western Pac. R.R. Corp. v. Western Pac. R.R. Co.*, 345 U.S. 247, 250 (1953) (emphasis added)). But *Shenker* did not address what is meant by "a majority" in §46(c) (or Rule 35(a), which did not yet exist)—and *Shenker* certainly did not suggest that the phrase should have different meanings in different circuits.

In interpreting that phrase, 7 of the courts of appeals follow the "absolute majority" approach. *See* Marie Leary, Defining the "Majority" Vote Requirement in Federal Rule of Appellate Procedure 35 (a) for Rehearings En Banc in the United States Courts of Appeals 8 tbl.1 (Federal Judicial Center 2002). Under this approach, disqualified judges are counted in the base in calculating whether a majority of judges have voted to hear a case en banc. Thus, in a circuit with 12 active judges, 7 must vote to hear a case en banc. If 5 of the 12 active judges are disqualified, all 7 non-disqualified judges must vote to hear the case en banc. The votes of 6 of the 7 non-disqualified judges are not enough, as 6 is not a majority of 12.

Six of the courts of appeals follow the "case majority" approach. *Id.* Under this approach, disqualified judges are not counted in the base in calculating whether a majority of judges have voted to hear a case en banc. Thus, in a case in which 5 of a circuit's 12 active judges are disqualified, only 4 judges (a majority of the 7 non-disqualified judges) must vote to hear a case en banc. (The First and Third Circuits explicitly qualify the case majority approach by providing that a case

Rule 35. En Banc Determination

cannot be heard en banc unless a majority of all active judges—disqualified and non-disqualified—are eligible to participate.)

Rule 35(a) has been amended to adopt the case majority approach as a uniform national interpretation of §46(c). The federal rules of practice and procedure exist to "maintain consistency," which Congress has equated with "promot[ing] the interest of justice." 28 U.S.C. §2073(b). The courts of appeals should not follow two inconsistent approaches in deciding whether sufficient votes exist to hear a case en banc, especially when there is a governing statute and governing rule that apply to all circuits and that use identical terms, and especially when there is nothing about the local conditions of each circuit that justifies conflicting approaches.

The case majority approach represents the better interpretation of the phrase "the circuit judges . . . in regular active service" in the first sentence of §46(c). The second sentence of §46(c)—which defines which judges are eligible to participate in a case being heard or reheard en banc—uses the similar expression "all circuit judges in regular active service." It is clear that "all circuit judges in regular active service" in the second sentence does not include disqualified judges, as disqualified judges clearly cannot participate in a case being heard or reheard en banc. Therefore, assuming that two nearly identical phrases appearing in adjacent sentences in a statute should be interpreted in the same way, the best reading of "the circuit judges . . . in regular active service" in the first sentence of §46(c) is that it, too, does not include disqualified judges.

This interpretation of §46(c) is bolstered by the fact that the case majority approach has at least two major advantages over the absolute majority approach:

First, under the absolute majority approach, a disqualified judge is, as a practical matter, counted as voting against hearing a case en banc. This defeats the purpose of recusal. To the extent possible, the disqualification of a judge should not result in the equivalent of a vote for or against hearing a case en banc.

Second, the absolute majority approach can leave the en banc court helpless to overturn a panel decision with which almost all of the circuit's active judges disagree. For example, in a case in which 5 of a circuit's 12 active judges are disqualified, the case cannot be heard en banc even if 6 of the 7 non-disqualified judges strongly disagree with the panel opinion. This permits one active judge—perhaps sitting on a panel with a visiting judge—effectively to control circuit precedent, even over the objection of all of his or her colleagues. *See Gulf Power Co. v. FCC*, 226 F.3d 1220, 1222-23 (11th Cir. 2000) (Carnes, J., concerning the denial of reh'g en banc), *rev'd sub nom. National Cable & Telecomm. Ass'n, Inc. v. Gulf Power Co.*, 534 U.S. 327 (2002). Even though the en banc court may, in a future case, be able to correct an erroneous legal interpretation, the en banc court will never be able to correct the injustice inflicted by the panel on the parties to the case. Morever [sic], it may take many years before sufficient non-disqualified judges can be mustered to overturn the panel's erroneous legal interpretation. In the meantime, the lower courts of the circuit must apply—and the citizens of the circuit must conform their behavior to—an interpretation of the law that almost all of the circuit's active judges believe is incorrect.

The amendment to Rule 35(a) is not meant to alter or affect the quorum requirement of 28 U.S.C. §46(d). In particular, the amendment is not intended to foreclose the possibility that §46(d) might be read to require that more than half of all circuit judges in regular active service be eligible to participate in order for the court to hear or rehear a case en banc.

Changes Made After Publication and Comments. No changes were made to the text of the proposed amendment. The Committee Note was modified in three respects. First, the Note was changed to put more emphasis on the fact that the case majority rule is the best interpretation of §46(c). Second, the Note now clarifies that nothing in the proposed amendment is intended to foreclose courts from interpreting 28 U.S.C. §46(d) to provide that a case cannot be heard or reheard en banc unless a majority of all judges in regular active service—disqualified or not—are eligible to participate. Finally, a couple of arguments made by supporters of the amendment to Rule 35(a) were incorporated into the Note.

Committee Notes on Rules – 2016 Amendment

The page limits previously employed in Rules 5, 21, 27, 35, and 40 have been largely overtaken by changes in technology. For papers produced using a computer, those page limits are now replaced by word limits. The word limits were derived from the current page limits using the assumption that one page is equivalent to 260 words. Papers produced using a computer must include the certificate of compliance required by Rule 32(g); Form 6 in the Appendix of Forms suffices to meet that requirement. Page limits are retained for papers prepared without the aid of a computer (i.e., handwritten or typewritten papers). For both the word limit and the page limit, the calculation excludes any items listed in Rule 32(f).

Rule 36. Entry of Judgment; Notice

(a) Entry. A judgment is entered when it is noted on the docket. The clerk must prepare, sign, and enter the judgment:

(1) after receiving the court's opinion—but if settlement of the judgment's form is required, after final settlement; or

(2) if a judgment is rendered without an opinion, as the court instructs.

(b) Notice. On the date when judgment is entered, the clerk must serve on all parties a copy of the opinion—or the judgment, if no opinion was written—and a notice of the date when the judgment was entered.

(As amended Apr. 24, 1998, eff. Dec. 1, 1998; Apr. 29, 2002, eff. Dec. 1, 2002.)

Notes of Advisory Committee on Rules—1967

This is the typical rule. See 1st Cir. Rule 29; 3rd Cir. Rule 32; 6th Cir. Rule 21. At present, uncertainty exists as to the date of entry of judgment when the opinion directs subsequent settlement of the precise terms of the judgment, a common practice in cases involving enforcement of agency orders. See Stern and Gressman, Supreme Court Practice, p. 203 (3d Ed., 1962). The principle of finality suggests that in such cases entry of judgment should be delayed until approval of the judgment in final form.

Committee Notes on Rules—1998 Amendment

The language and organization of the rule are amended to make the rule more easily understood. In addition to changes made to improve the understanding, the Advisory Committee has changed language to make style and terminology consistent throughout the appellate rules. These changes are intended to be stylistic only.

Committee Notes on Rules—2002 Amendment

Subdivision (b). Subdivision (b) has been amended so that the clerk may use electronic means to serve a copy of the opinion or judgment or to serve notice of the date when judgment was entered upon parties who have consented to such service.

Changes Made After Publication and Comments. No changes were made to the text of the proposed amendment or to the Committee Note.

Rule 37. Interest on Judgment

(a) When the Court Affirms. Unless the law provides otherwise, if a money judgment in a civil case is affirmed, whatever interest is allowed by law is payable from the date when the district court's judgment was entered.

(b) When the Court Reverses. If the court modifies or reverses a judgment with a direction that a money judgment be entered in the district court, the mandate must contain instructions about the allowance of interest.

(As amended Apr. 24, 1998, eff. Dec. 1, 1998.)

Notes of Advisory Committee on Rules—1967

The first sentence makes it clear that if a money judgment is affirmed in the court of appeals, the interest which attaches to money judgments by force of law (see 28 U.S.C. §1961 and §2411) upon their initial entry is payable as if no appeal had been taken, whether or not the mandate makes mention of interest. There has been some confusion on this point. See *Blair v. Durham*, 139 F.2d 260 (6th Cir., 1943) and cases cited therein.

In reversing or modifying the judgment of the district court, the court of appeals may direct the entry of a money judgment, as, for example, when the court of appeals reverses a judgment notwithstanding the verdict and directs entry of judgment on the verdict. In such a case the question may arise as to whether interest is to run from the date of entry of the judgment directed by the court of appeals or from the date on which the judgment would have been entered in the district court except for the erroneous ruling corrected on appeal. In *Briggs v. Pennsylvania R. Co.*, 334 U.S. 304, 68 S.Ct. 1039, 92 L.Ed. 1403 (1948), the Court held that where the mandate of the court of appeals directed entry of judgment upon

Rule 38. Frivolous Appeal

a verdict but made no mention of interest from the date of the verdict to the date of the entry of the judgment directed by the mandate, the district court was powerless to add such interest. The second sentence of the proposed rule is a reminder to the court, the clerk and counsel of the *Briggs* rule. Since the rule directs that the matter of interest be disposed of by the mandate, in cases where interest is simply overlooked, a party who conceives himself entitled to interest from a date other than the date of entry of judgment in accordance with the mandate should be entitled to seek recall of the mandate for determination of the question.

Committee Notes on Rules—1998 Amendment

The language and organization of the rule are amended to make the rule more easily understood. In addition to changes made to improve the understanding, the Advisory Committee has changed language to make style and terminology consistent throughout the appellate rules. These changes are intended to be stylistic only.

Rule 38. Frivolous Appeal

If a court of appeals determines that an appeal is frivolous, it may, after a separately filed motion or notice from the court and reasonable opportunity to respond, award just damages and single or double costs to the appellee.

(As amended Apr. 29, 1994, eff. Dec. 1, 1994; Apr. 24, 1998, eff. Dec. 1, 1998.)

Notes of Advisory Committee on Rules—1967

Compare 28 U.S.C. §1912. While both the statute and the usual rule on the subject by courts of appeals (Fourth Circuit Rule 20 is a typical rule) speak of "damages for delay," the courts of appeals quite properly allow damages, attorney's fees and other expenses incurred by an appellee if the appeal is frivolous without requiring a showing that the appeal resulted in delay. See *Dunscombe v. Sayle*, 340 F.2d 311 (5th Cir., 1965), *cert. den.*, 382 U.S. 814, 86 S.Ct. 32, 15 L.Ed.2d 62 (1965); *Lowe v. Willacy*, 239 F.2d 179 (9th Cir., 1956); *Griffith Wellpoint Corp. v. Munro-Langstroth, Inc.*, 269 F.2d 64 (1st Cir., 1959); *Ginsburg v. Stern*, 295 F.2d 698 (3d Cir., 1961). The subjects of interest and damages are separately regulated, contrary to the present practice of combining the two (see Fourth Circuit Rule 20) to make it clear that the awards are distinct and independent. Interest is provided for by law; damages are awarded by the court in its discretion in the case of a frivolous appeal as a matter of justice to the appellee and as a penalty against the appellant.

Notes of Advisory Committee on Rules—1994 Amendment

The amendment requires that before a court of appeals may impose sanctions, the person to be sanctioned must have notice and an opportunity to respond. The amendment reflects the basic principle enunciated in the Supreme Court's opinion in *Roadway Express, Inc. v. Piper*, 447 U.S. 752, 767 (1980), that notice and opportunity to respond must precede the imposition of sanctions. A separately filed motion requesting sanctions constitutes notice. A statement inserted in a party's brief that the party moves for sanctions is not sufficient notice. Requests in briefs for sanctions have become so commonplace that it is unrealistic to expect careful responses to such requests without any indication that the court is actually contemplating such measures. Only a motion, the purpose of which is to request sanctions, is sufficient. If there is no such motion filed, notice must come from the court. The form of notice from the court and of the opportunity for comment purposely are left to the court's discretion.

Committee Notes on Rules—1998 Amendment

Only the caption of this rule has been amended. The changes are intended to be stylistic only.

Rule 39. Costs

(a) Against Whom Assessed. The following rules apply unless the law provides or the court orders otherwise:

    (1) if an appeal is dismissed, costs are taxed against the appellant, unless the parties agree otherwise;

    (2) if a judgment is affirmed, costs are taxed against the appellant;

    (3) if a judgment is reversed, costs are taxed against the appellee;

Rule 39. Costs

(4) if a judgment is affirmed in part, reversed in part, modified, or vacated, costs are taxed only as the court orders.

(b) Costs For and Against the United States. Costs for or against the United States, its agency, or officer will be assessed under Rule 39(a) only if authorized by law.

(c) Costs of Copies. Each court of appeals must, by local rule, fix the maximum rate for taxing the cost of producing necessary copies of a brief or appendix, or copies of records authorized by Rule 30(f). The rate must not exceed that generally charged for such work in the area where the clerk's office is located and should encourage economical methods of copying.

(d) Bill of Costs: Objections; Insertion in Mandate.

(1) A party who wants costs taxed must—within 14 days after entry of judgment—file with the circuit clerk, with proof of service, an itemized and verified bill of costs.

(2) Objections must be filed within 14 days after service of the bill of costs, unless the court extends the time.

(3) The clerk must prepare and certify an itemized statement of costs for insertion in the mandate, but issuance of the mandate must not be delayed for taxing costs. If the mandate issues before costs are finally determined, the district clerk must—upon the circuit clerk's request—add the statement of costs, or any amendment of it, to the mandate.

(e) Costs on Appeal Taxable in the District Court. The following costs on appeal are taxable in the district court for the benefit of the party entitled to costs under this rule:

(1) the preparation and transmission of the record;

(2) the reporter's transcript, if needed to determine the appeal;

(3) premiums paid for a supersedeas bond or other bond to preserve rights pending appeal; and

(4) the fee for filing the notice of appeal.

(As amended Apr. 30, 1979, eff. Aug. 1, 1979; Mar. 10, 1986, eff. July 1, 1986; Apr. 24, 1998, eff. Dec. 1, 1998; Mar. 26, 2009, eff. Dec. 1, 2009.)

Notes on Advisory Committee on Rules—1967

Subdivision (a). Statutory authorization for taxation of costs is found in 28 U.S.C. §1920. The provisions of this subdivision follow the usual practice in the circuits. A few statutes contain specific provisions in derogation of these general provisions. (See 28 U.S.C. §1928, which forbids the award of costs to a successful plaintiff in a patent infringement action under the circumstances described by the statute). These statutes are controlling in cases to which they apply.

Subdivision (b). The rules of the courts of appeals at present commonly deny costs to the United States except as allowance may be directed by statute. Those rules were promulgated at a time when the United States was generally invulnerable to an award of costs against it, and they appear to be based on the view that if the United States is not subject to costs if it loses, it ought not be entitled to recover costs if it wins.

The number of cases affected by such rules has been greatly reduced by the Act of July 18, 1966, 80 Stat. 308 (1 U.S. Code Cong. & Ad. News, p. 349 (1966), 89th Cong., 2d Sess., which amended 28 U.S.C. §2412, the former general bar to the award of costs against the United States. Section 2412 as amended generally places the United States on the same footing as private parties with respect to the award of costs in civil cases. But the United States continues to enjoy immunity from costs in certain cases. By its terms amended section 2412 authorizes an award of costs against the United States only in civil actions, and it excepts from its general authorization of an award of costs against the United States cases which are "otherwise specifically provided (for) by statute." Furthermore, the Act of July 18, 1966, *supra*, provides that the amendments of section 2412 which it effects shall apply only to actions filed subsequent to the date of its enactment. The second clause continues in effect, for these and all other cases in which the United States enjoys immunity from costs, the presently prevailing rule that the United States may recover costs as the prevailing party only if it would have suffered them as the losing party.

Subdivision (c). While only five circuits (D.C. Cir. Rule 20(d); 1st Cir. Rule 31(4); 3d Cir. Rule 35(4); 4th Cir. Rule 21(4); 9th Cir. Rule 25, as amended June 2, 1967) presently tax the cost of printing briefs, the proposed rule makes the cost taxable in keeping with the principle of this rule that all cost items expended in the prosecution of a proceeding should be borne by the unsuccessful party.

Subdivision (e). The costs described in this subdivision are costs of the appeal and, as such, are within the undertaking of the appeal bond. They are made taxable in the district court for general convenience. Taxation of the cost of the reporter's transcript is specifically authorized by 28 U.S.C. §1920, but in the absence of a rule some district courts have

Rule 40. Petition for Panel Rehearing

held themselves without authority to tax the cost (*Perlman v. Feldmann*, 116 F.Supp. 102 (D.Conn., 1953); *Firtag v. Gendleman*, 152 F.Supp. 226 (D.D.C., 1957); *Todd Atlantic Shipyards Corps. v. The Southport*, 100 F.Supp. 763 (E.D.S.C., 1951). Provision for taxation of the cost of premiums paid for supersedeas bonds is common in the local rules of district courts and the practice is established in the Second, Seventh, and Ninth Circuits. *Berner v. British Commonwealth Pacific Air Lines, Ltd.*, 362 F.2d 799 (2d Cir. 1966); *Land Oberoesterreich v. Gude*, 93 F.2d 292 (2d Cir., 1937); *In re Northern Ind. Oil Co.*, 192 F.2d 139 (7th Cir., 1951); *Lunn v. F. W. Woolworth*, 210 F.2d 159 (9th Cir., 1954).

Notes of Advisory Committee on Rules—1979 Amendment

Subdivision (c). The proposed amendment would permit variations among the circuits in regulating the maximum rates taxable as costs for printing or otherwise reproducing briefs, appendices, and copies of records authorized by Rule 30(f). The present rule has had a different effect in different circuits depending upon the size of the circuit, the location of the clerk's office, and the location of other cities. As a consequence there was a growing sense that strict adherence to the rule produces some unfairness in some of the circuits and the matter should be made subject to local rule.

Subdivision (d). The present rule makes no provision for objections to a bill of costs. The proposed amendment would allow 10 days for such objections. Cf. Rule 54(d) of the F.R.C.P. It provides further that the mandate shall not be delayed for taxation of costs.

Notes of Advisory Committee on Rules—1986 Amendment

The amendment to subdivision (c) is intended to increase the degree of control exercised by the courts of appeals over rates for printing and copying recoverable as costs. It further requires the courts of appeals to encourage cost-consciousness by requiring that, in fixing the rate, the court consider the most economical methods of printing and copying.

The amendment to subdivision (d) is technical. No substantive change is intended.

Committee Notes on Rules—1998 Amendment

The language and organization of the rule are amended to make the rule more easily understood. In addition to changes made to improve the understanding, the Advisory Committee has changed language to make style and terminology consistent throughout the appellate rules. These changes are intended to be stylistic only. All references to the cost of "printing" have been deleted from subdivision (c) because commercial printing is so rarely used for preparation of documents filed with a court of appeals.

Committee Notes on Rules—2009 Amendment

Subdivision (d)(2). The time set in the former rule at 10 days has been revised to 14 days. See the Note to Rule 26.

Rule 40. Petition for Panel Rehearing
(a) Time to File; Contents; Answer; Action by the Court if Granted.
  (1) *Time.* Unless the time is shortened or extended by order or local rule, a petition for panel rehearing may be filed within 14 days after entry of judgment. But in a civil case, unless an order shortens or extends the time, the petition may be filed by any party within 45 days after entry of judgment if one of the parties is:
    (A) the United States;
    (B) a United States agency;
    (C) a United States officer or employee sued in an official capacity; or
    (D) a current or former United States officer or employee sued in an individual capacity for an act or omission occurring in connection with duties performed on the United States' behalf — including all instances in which the United States represents that person when the court of appeals' judgment is entered or files that petition for that person.
  (2) *Contents.* The petition must state with particularity each point of law or fact that the petitioner believes the court has overlooked or misapprehended and must argue in support of the petition. Oral argument is not permitted.

Rule 40. Petition for Panel Rehearing

(3) *Answer.* Unless the court requests, no answer to a petition for panel rehearing is permitted. But ordinarily rehearing will not be granted in the absence of such a request.

(4) *Action by the Court.* If a petition for panel rehearing is granted, the court may do any of the following:
  (A) make a final disposition of the case without reargument;
  (B) restore the case to the calendar for reargument or resubmission; or
  (C) issue any other appropriate order.

[The following text of subdivision (b) was effective until December 1, 2016.]

(b) Form of Petition; Length. The petition must comply in form with Rule 32. Copies must be served and filed as Rule 31 prescribes. Unless the court permits or a local rule provides otherwise, a petition for panel rehearing must not exceed 15 pages.

[The following text of subdivision (b) became effective December 1, 2016.]

(b) Form of Petition; Length. The petition must comply in form with Rule 32. Copies must be served and filed as Rule 31 prescribes. Except by the court's permission:
  (1) a petition for panel rehearing produced using a computer must not exceed 3,900 words; and
  (2) a handwritten or typewritten petition for panel rehearing must not exceed 15 pages.

(As amended Apr. 30, 1979, eff. Aug. 1, 1979; Apr. 29, 1994, eff. Dec. 1, 1994; Apr. 24, 1998, eff. Dec. 1, 1998; Apr. 26, 2011, eff. Dec. 1, 2011; Apr. 28, 2016, eff. Dec. 1, 2016.)

Notes of Advisory Committee on Rules—1967

This is the usual rule among the circuits, except that the express prohibition against filing a reply to the petition is found only in the rules of the Fourth, Sixth and Eighth Circuits (it is also contained in Supreme Court Rule 58(3)). It is included to save time and expense to the party victorious on appeal. In the very rare instances in which a reply is useful, the court will ask for it.

Notes of Advisory Committee on Rules—1979 Amendment

Subdivision (a). The Standing Committee added to the first sentence of Rule 40(a) the words "or by local rule," to conform to current practice in the circuits. The Standing Committee believes the change noncontroversial.

Subdivision (b). The proposed amendment would eliminate the distinction drawn in the present rule between printed briefs and those duplicated from typewritten pages in fixing their maximum length. See Note to Rule 28. Since petitions for rehearing must be prepared in a short time, making typographic printing less likely, the maximum number of pages is fixed at 15, the figure used in the present rule for petitions duplicated by means other than typographic printing.

Notes of Advisory Committee on Rules—1994 Amendment

Subdivision (a). The amendment lengthens the time for filing a petition for rehearing from 14 to 45 days in civil cases involving the United States or its agencies or officers. It has no effect upon the time for filing in criminal cases. The amendment makes nation-wide the current practice in the District of Columbia and the Tenth Circuits, see D.C. Cir. R. 15(a), 10th Cir. R. 40.3. This amendment, analogous to the provision in Rule 4(a) extending the time for filing a notice of appeal in cases involving the United States, recognizes that the Solicitor General needs time to conduct a thorough review of the merits of a case before requesting a rehearing. In a case in which a court of appeals believes it necessary to restrict the time for filing a rehearing petition, the amendment provides that the court may do so by order. Although the first sentence of Rule 40 permits a court of appeals to shorten or lengthen the usual 14 day filing period by order or by local rule, the sentence governing appeals in civil cases involving the United States purposely limits a court's power to alter the 45 day period to orders in specific cases. If a court of appeals could adopt a local rule shortening the time for filing a petition for rehearing in all cases involving the United States, the purpose of the amendment would be defeated.

Rule 40. Petition for Panel Rehearing

Committee Notes on Rules—1998 Amendment

The language and organization of the rule are amended to make the rule more easily understood. In addition to changes made to improve the understanding, the Advisory Committee has changed language to make style and terminology consistent throughout the appellate rules. These changes are intended to be stylistic only.

Committee Notes on Rules—2011 Amendment

Subdivision (a)(1). Rule 40(a)(1) has been amended to make clear that the 45-day period to file a petition for panel rehearing applies in cases in which an officer or employee of the United States is sued in an individual capacity for acts or omissions occurring in connection with duties performed on behalf of the United States. (A concurrent amendment to Rule 4(a)(1)(B) makes clear that the 60-day period to file an appeal also applies in such cases.) In such cases, the Solicitor General needs adequate time to review the merits of the panel decision and decide whether to seek rehearing, just as the Solicitor General does when an appeal involves the United States, a United States agency, or a United States officer or employee sued in an official capacity.

To promote clarity of application, the amendment to Rule 40(a)(1) includes safe harbor provisions that parties can readily apply and rely upon. Under new subdivision 40(a)(1)(D), a case automatically qualifies for the 45-day period if (1) a legal officer of the United States has appeared in the case, in an official capacity, as counsel for the current or former officer or employee and has not withdrawn the appearance at the time of the entry of the court of appeals' judgment that is the subject of the petition or (2) a legal officer of the United States appears on the petition as counsel, in an official capacity, for the current or former officer or employee. There will be cases that do not fall within either safe harbor but that qualify for the longer petition period. An example would be a case in which a federal employee is sued in an individual capacity for an act occurring in connection with federal duties and the United States does not represent the employee either when the court of appeals' judgment is entered or when the petition is filed but the United States pays for private counsel for the employee.

Changes Made After Publication and Comment.
The Committee made two changes to the proposal after publication and comment.

First, the Committee inserted the words "current or former" before "United States officer or employee." This insertion causes the text of the proposed Rule to diverge slightly from that of Civil Rules 4(i)(3) and 12(a)(3), which refer simply to "a United States officer or employee [etc.]." This divergence, though, is only stylistic. The 2000 Committee Notes to Civil Rules 4(i)(3) and 12(a)(3) make clear that those rules are intended to encompass former as well as current officers or employees.

Second, the Committee added, at the end of Rule 40(a)(1)(D), the following new language: "– including all instances in which the United States represents that person when the court of appeals' judgment is entered or files the petition for that person." During the public comment period, concerns were raised that a party might rely on the longer period for filing the petition, only to risk the petition being held untimely by a court that later concluded that the relevant act or omission had not actually occurred in connection with federal duties. The Committee decided to respond to this concern by adding two safe harbor provisions. These provisions make clear that the longer period applies in any case where the United States either represents the officer or employee at the time of entry of the relevant judgment or files the petition on the officer or employee's behalf.

Committee Notes on Rules – 2016 Amendment

The page limits previously employed in Rules 5, 21, 27, 35, and 40 have been largely overtaken by changes in technology. For papers produced using a computer, those page limits are now replaced by word limits. The word limits were derived from the current page limits using the assumption that one page is equivalent to 260 words. Papers produced using a computer must include the certificate of compliance required by Rule 32(g); Form 6 in the Appendix of Forms suffices to meet that requirement. Page limits are retained for papers prepared without the aid of a computer (i.e., handwritten or typewritten papers). For both the word limit and the page limit, the calculation excludes any items listed in Rule 32(f).

Rule 41. Mandate: Contents; Issuance and Effective Date; Stay

(a) Contents. Unless the court directs that a formal mandate issue, the mandate consists of a certified copy of the judgment, a copy of the court's opinion, if any, and any direction about costs.
(b) When Issued. The court's mandate must issue 7 days after the time to file a petition for rehearing expires, or 7 days after entry of an order denying a timely petition for panel rehearing, petition for rehearing en banc, or motion for stay of mandate, whichever is later. The court may shorten or extend the time.
(c) Effective Date. The mandate is effective when issued.
(d) Staying the Mandate.
    (1) *On Petition for Rehearing or Motion.* The timely filing of a petition for panel rehearing, petition for rehearing en banc, or motion for stay of mandate, stays the mandate until disposition of the petition or motion, unless the court orders otherwise.
    (2) *Pending Petition for Certiorari.*
        (A) A party may move to stay the mandate pending the filing of a petition for a writ of certiorari in the Supreme Court. The motion must be served on all parties and must show that the certiorari petition would present a substantial question and that there is good cause for a stay.
        (B) The stay must not exceed 90 days, unless the period is extended for good cause or unless the party who obtained the stay files a petition for the writ and so notifies the circuit clerk in writing within the period of the stay. In that case, the stay continues until the Supreme Court's final disposition.
        (C) The court may require a bond or other security as a condition to granting or continuing a stay of the mandate.
        (D) The court of appeals must issue the mandate immediately when a copy of a Supreme Court order denying the petition for writ of certiorari is filed.

(As amended Apr. 29, 1994, eff. Dec. 1, 1994; Apr. 24, 1998, eff. Dec. 1, 1998; Apr. 29, 2002, eff. Dec. 1, 2002; Mar. 26, 2009, eff. Dec. 1, 2009.)

Notes of Advisory Committee on Rules—1967

The proposed rule follows the rule or practice in a majority of circuits by which copies of the opinion and the judgment serve in lieu of a formal mandate in the ordinary case. Compare Supreme Court Rule 59. Although 28 U.S.C. §2101(c) permits a writ of certiorari to be filed within 90 days after entry of judgment, seven of the eight circuits which now regulate the matter of stays pending application for certiorari limit the initial stay of the mandate to the 30-day period provided in the proposed rule. Compare D.C. Cir. Rule 27(e).

Notes of Advisory Committee on Rules—1994 Amendment

Subdivision (a). The amendment conforms Rule 41(a) to the amendment made to Rule 40(a). The amendment keys the time for issuance of the mandate to the expiration of the time for filing a petition for rehearing, unless such a petition is filed in which case the mandate issues 7 days after the entry of the order denying the petition. Because the amendment to Rule 40(a) lengthens the time for filing a petition for rehearing in civil cases involving the United States from 14 to 45 days, the rule requiring the mandate to issue 21 days after the entry of judgment would cause the mandate to issue while the government is still considering requesting a rehearing. Therefore, the amendment generally requires the mandate to issue 7 days after the expiration of the time for filing a petition for rehearing.

Subdivision (b). The amendment requires a party who files a motion requesting a stay of mandate to file, at the same time, proof of service on all other parties. The old rule required the party to give notice to the other parties; the amendment merely requires the party to provide the court with evidence of having done so.

The amendment also states that the motion must show that a petition for certiorari would present a substantial question and that there is good cause for a stay. The amendment is intended to alert the parties to the fact that a stay of mandate is not granted automatically and to the type of showing that needs to be made. The Supreme Court has established conditions that must be met before it will stay a mandate. See Robert L. Stern et al., *Supreme Court Practice* §17.19 (6th ed. 1986).

Committee Notes on Rules—1998 Amendment

The language and organization of the rule are amended to make the rule more easily understood. In addition to

Rule 41. Mandate: Contents; Issuance and Effective Date; Stay

changes made to improve the understanding, the Advisory Committee has changed language to make style and terminology consistent throughout the appellate rules. These changes are intended to be stylistic only.

Several substantive changes are made in this rule, however.

Subdivision (b). The existing rule provides that the mandate issues 7 days after the time to file a petition for panel rehearing expires unless such a petition is timely filed. If the petition is denied, the mandate issues 7 days after entry of the order denying the petition. Those provisions are retained but the amendments further provide that if a timely petition for rehearing en banc or motion for stay of mandate is filed, the mandate does not issue until 7 days after entry of an order denying the last of all such requests. If a petition for rehearing or a petition for rehearing en banc is granted, the court enters a new judgment after the rehearing and the mandate issues within the normal time after entry of that judgment.

Subdivision (c). Subdivision (c) is new. It provides that the mandate is effective when the court issues it. A court of appeals' judgment or order is not final until issuance of the mandate; at that time the parties' obligations become fixed. This amendment is intended to make it clear that the mandate is effective upon issuance and that its effectiveness is not delayed until receipt of the mandate by the trial court or agency, or until the trial court or agency acts upon it. This amendment is consistent with the current understanding. Unless the court orders that the mandate issue earlier than provided in the rule, the parties can easily calculate the anticipated date of issuance and verify issuance with the clerk's office. In those instances in which the court orders earlier issuance of the mandate, the entry of the order on the docket alerts the parties to that fact.

Subdivision (d). Amended paragraph (1) provides that the filing of a petition for panel rehearing, a petition for rehearing en banc or a motion for a stay of mandate pending petition to the Supreme Court for a writ of certiorari stays the issuance of the mandate until the court disposes of the petition or motion. The provision that a petition for rehearing en banc stays the mandate is a companion to the amendment of Rule 35 that deletes the language stating that a request for a rehearing en banc does not affect the finality of the judgment or stay the issuance of the mandate. The Committee's objective is to treat a request for a rehearing en banc like a petition for panel rehearing so that a request for a rehearing en banc will suspend the finality of the court of appeals' judgment and delay the running of the period for filing a petition for writ of certiorari. Because the filing of a petition for rehearing en banc will stay the mandate, a court of appeals will need to take final action on the petition but the procedure for doing so is left to local practice.

Paragraph (1) also provides that the filing of a motion for a stay of mandate pending petition to the Supreme Court for a writ of certiorari stays the mandate until the court disposes of the motion. If the court denies the motion, the court must issue the mandate 7 days after entering the order denying the motion. If the court grants the motion, the mandate is stayed according to the terms of the order granting the stay. Delaying issuance of the mandate eliminates the need to recall the mandate if the motion for a stay is granted. If, however, the court believes that it would be inappropriate to delay issuance of the mandate until disposition of the motion for a stay, the court may order that the mandate issue immediately.

Paragraph (2). The amendment changes the maximum period for a stay of mandate, absent the court of appeals granting an extension for cause, to 90 days. The presumptive 30-day period was adopted when a party had to file a petition for a writ of certiorari in criminal cases within 30 days after entry of judgment. Supreme Court Rule 13.1 now provides that a party has 90 days after entry of judgment by a court of appeals to file a petition for a writ of certiorari whether the case is civil or criminal.

The amendment does not require a court of appeals to grant a stay of mandate that is coextensive with the period granted for filing a petition for a writ of certiorari. The granting of a stay and the length of the stay remain within the discretion of the court of appeals. The amendment means only that a 90-day stay may be granted without a need to show cause for a stay longer than 30 days.

Subparagraph (C) is not new; it has been moved from the end of the rule to this position.

Committee Notes on Rules—2002 Amendment

Subdivision (b). Subdivision (b) directs that the mandate of a court must issue 7 days after the time to file a petition for rehearing expires or 7 days after the court denies a timely petition for panel rehearing, petition for rehearing en banc, or motion for stay of mandate, whichever is later. Intermediate Saturdays, Sundays, and legal holidays are counted in computing that 7-day deadline, which means that, except when the 7-day deadline ends on a weekend or legal holiday, the mandate issues exactly one week after the triggering event.

Fed. R. App. P. 26 (a)(2) has been amended to provide that, in computing any period of time, one should "[e]xclude intermediate Saturdays, Sundays, and legal holidays when the period is less than 11 days, unless stated in calendar days." This change in the method of computing deadlines means that 7-day deadlines (such as that in subdivision (b)) have been lengthened as a practical matter. Under the new computation method, a mandate would never issue sooner than 9 actual days after a triggering event, and legal holidays could extend that period to as much as 13 days.

Delaying mandates for 9 or more days would introduce significant and unwarranted delay into appellate proceedings.

For that reason, subdivision (b) has been amended to require that mandates issue 7 *calendar* days after a triggering event.

Changes Made After Publication and Comments. No changes were made to the text of the proposed amendment or to the Committee Note.

Committee Notes on Rules—2009 Amendment

Under former Rule 26(a), short periods that span weekends or holidays were computed without counting those weekends or holidays. To specify that a period should be calculated by counting all intermediate days, including weekends or holidays, the Rules used the term "calendar days." Rule 26(a) now takes a "days-are-days" approach under which all intermediate days are counted, no matter how short the period. Accordingly, "7 calendar days" in subdivision (b) is amended to read simply "7 days."

Changes Made After Publication and Comment. The Appellate Rules Committee made only one change to Rule 26(a) after publication and comment: Because the Committee is seeking permission to publish for comment a proposed new Rule 1(b) that would adopt a FRAP-wide definition of the term "state," the Committee decided to delete from Rule 26(a)(6)(B) the following parenthetical sentence: "(In this rule, 'state' includes the District of Columbia and any United States commonwealth, territory, or possession.)" That change required the corresponding deletion—from the Note to Rule 26(a)(6)—of part of the final sentence (the deleted portion read ", and defines the term 'state'—for purposes of subdivision (a)(6)—to include the District of Columbia and any commonwealth, territory or possession of the United States. Thus, for purposes of subdivision (a)(6)'s definition of 'legal holiday,' 'state' includes the District of Columbia, Guam, American Samoa, the U.S. Virgin Islands, the Commonwealth of Puerto Rico, and the Commonwealth of the Northern Mariana Islands.")

The Appellate Rules Committee made one change to its proposed amendments concerning Appellate Rules deadlines. Based on comments received with respect to the timing for motions that toll the time for taking a civil appeal, the Committee changed the cutoff time in Rule 4(a)(4)(A)(vi) to 28 days (rather than to 30 days as in the published proposal). The published proposal's choice of 30 days had been designed to accord with the proposed amendments published by the Civil Rules Committee, which would have extended the deadline for tolling motions to 30 days. Because 30 days is also the time period set by Appellate Rule 4 and by 28 U.S.C. §2107 for taking a civil appeal (when the United States and its officers or agencies are not parties), commentators pointed out that adopting 30 days as the cutoff for filing tolling motions would sometimes place would-be appellants in an awkward position: If the deadline for making a tolling motion falls on the same day as the deadline for filing a notice of appeal, then in a case involving multiple parties on one side, a litigant who wishes to appeal may not know, when filing the notice of appeal, whether a tolling motion will be filed; such a timing system can be expected to produce instances when appeals are filed, only to go into abeyance while the tolling motion is resolved.

By the time of the Appellate Rules Committee's April 2008 meeting, the Civil Rules Committee had discussed this issue and had determined that the best resolution would be to extend the deadline for tolling motions to 28 days rather than 30 days. The choice of a 28-day deadline responds to the concerns of those who feel that the current 10-day deadlines are much too short, but also takes into account the problem of the 30-day appeal deadline. As described in the draft minutes of the Committee's April meeting, Committee members carefully discussed the relevant concerns and determined, by a vote of 7 to 1, to assent to the 28-day time period for tolling motions and to change the cutoff time in Rule 4(a)(4)(A)(vi) to 28 days.

The Standing Committee changed Rule 26(a)(6) to exclude state holidays from the definition of "legal holiday" for purposes of computing backward-counted periods; conforming changes were made to the Committee Note.

Rule 42. Voluntary Dismissal

(a) Dismissal in the District Court. Before an appeal has been docketed by the circuit clerk, the district court may dismiss the appeal on the filing of a stipulation signed by all parties or on the appellant's motion with notice to all parties.

(b) Dismissal in the Court of Appeals. The circuit clerk may dismiss a docketed appeal if the parties file a signed dismissal agreement specifying how costs are to be paid and pay any fees that are due. But no mandate or other process may issue without a court order. An appeal may be dismissed on the appellant's motion on terms agreed to by the parties or fixed by the court.

(As amended Apr. 24, 1998, eff. Dec. 1, 1998.)

Rule 43. Substitution of Parties

Notes of Advisory Committee on Rules—1967

Subdivision (a). This subdivision is derived from FRCP 73 (a) without change of substance.

Subdivision (b). The first sentence is a common provision in present circuit rules. The second sentence is added. Compare Supreme Court Rule 60.

Committee Notes on Rules—1998 Amendment

The language of the rule is amended to make the rule more easily understood. In addition to changes made to improve the understanding, the Advisory Committee has changed language to make style and terminology consistent throughout the appellate rules. These changes are intended to be stylistic only.

Rule 43. Substitution of Parties

(a) Death of a Party.

(1) *After Notice of Appeal Is Filed.* If a party dies after a notice of appeal has been filed or while a proceeding is pending in the court of appeals, the decedent's personal representative may be substituted as a party on motion filed with the circuit clerk by the representative or by any party. A party's motion must be served on the representative in accordance with Rule 25. If the decedent has no representative, any party may suggest the death on the record, and the court of appeals may then direct appropriate proceedings.

(2) *Before Notice of Appeal Is Filed—Potential Appellant.* If a party entitled to appeal dies before filing a notice of appeal, the decedent's personal representative—or, if there is no personal representative, the decedent's attorney of record—may file a notice of appeal within the time prescribed by these rules. After the notice of appeal is filed, substitution must be in accordance with Rule 43(a)(1).

(3) *Before Notice of Appeal Is Filed—Potential Appellee.* If a party against whom an appeal may be taken dies after entry of a judgment or order in the district court, but before a notice of appeal is filed, an appellant may proceed as if the death had not occurred. After the notice of appeal is filed, substitution must be in accordance with Rule 43(a)(1).

(b) Substitution for a Reason Other Than Death. If a party needs to be substituted for any reason other than death, the procedure prescribed in Rule 43(a) applies.

(c) Public Officer: Identification; Substitution.

(1) *Identification of Party.* A public officer who is a party to an appeal or other proceeding in an official capacity may be described as a party by the public officer's official title rather than by name. But the court may require the public officer's name to be added.

(2) *Automatic Substitution of Officeholder.* When a public officer who is a party to an appeal or other proceeding in an official capacity dies, resigns, or otherwise ceases to hold office, the action does not abate. The public officer's successor is automatically substituted as a party. Proceedings following the substitution are to be in the name of the substituted party, but any misnomer that does not affect the substantial rights of the parties may be disregarded. An order of substitution may be entered at any time, but failure to enter an order does not affect the substitution.

(As amended Mar. 10, 1986, eff. July 1, 1986; Apr. 24, 1998, eff. Dec. 1, 1998.)

Notes of Advisory Committee on Rules—1967

Subdivision (a). The first three sentences described a procedure similar to the rule on substitution in civil actions in the district court. See FRCP 25 (a). The fourth sentence expressly authorizes an appeal to be taken against one who has died after the entry of judgment. Compare FRCP 73 (b), which impliedly authorizes such an appeal.

The sixth sentence authorizes an attorney of record for the deceased to take an appeal on behalf of successors in interest if the deceased has no representative. At present, if a party entitled to appeal dies before the notice of appeal is filed, the appeal can presumably be taken only by his legal representative and must be taken within the time ordinarily prescribed. 13 Cyclopedia of Federal Procedure (3d Ed.) §63.21. The states commonly make special provisions for the event of the death of a party entitled to appeal, usually by extending the time otherwise prescribed. Rules of Civil Procedure for

Rule 44. Case Involving a Constitutional Question When the United States or the Relevant State is Not a Party

Superior Courts of Arizona, Rule 73(t), 16 A.R.S.; New Jersey Rev. Rules 1:3–3; New York Civil Practice Law and Rules, Sec. 1022; Wisconsin Statutes Ann. 274.01(2). The provision in the proposed rule is derived from California Code of Civil Procedure, Sec. 941.

Subdivision (c). This subdivision is derived from FRCP 25 (d) and Supreme Court Rule 48, with appropriate changes.

Notes of Advisory Committee on Rules—1986 Amendment

The amendments to Rules 43(a) and (c) are technical. No substantive change is intended.

Committee Notes on Rules—1998 Amendment

The language and organization of the rule are amended to make the rule more easily understood. In addition to changes made to improve the understanding, the Advisory Committee has changed language to make style and terminology consistent throughout the appellate rules. These changes are intended to be stylistic only.

Rule 44. Case Involving a Constitutional Question When the United States or the Relevant State is Not a Party

(a) Constitutional Challenge to Federal Statute. If a party questions the constitutionality of an Act of Congress in a proceeding in which the United States or its agency, officer, or employee is not a party in an official capacity, the questioning party must give written notice to the circuit clerk immediately upon the filing of the record or as soon as the question is raised in the court of appeals. The clerk must then certify that fact to the Attorney General.

(b) Constitutional Challenge to State Statute. If a party questions the constitutionality of a statute of a State in a proceeding in which that State or its agency, officer, or employee is not a party in an official capacity, the questioning party must give written notice to the circuit clerk immediately upon the filing of the record or as soon as the question is raised in the court of appeals. The clerk must then certify that fact to the attorney general of the State.

(As amended Apr. 24, 1998, eff. Dec. 1, 1998; Apr. 29, 2002, eff. Dec. 1, 2002.)

Notes of Advisory Committee on Rules—1967

This rule is now found in the rules of a majority of the circuits. It is in response to the Act of August 24, 1937 (28 U.S.C. §2403), which requires all courts of the United States to advise the Attorney General of the existence of an action or proceeding of the kind described in the rule.

Committee Notes on Rules—1998 Amendment

The language of the rule is amended to make the rule more easily understood. In addition to changes made to improve the understanding, the Advisory Committee has changed language to make style and terminology consistent throughout the appellate rules. These changes are intended to be stylistic only.

Committee Notes on Rules—2002 Amendment

Rule 44 requires that a party who "questions the constitutionality of an Act of Congress" in a proceeding in which the United States is not a party must provide written notice of that challenge to the clerk. Rule 44 is designed to implement 28 U.S.C. §2403(a), which states that: "In any action, suit or proceeding in a court of the United States to which the United States or any agency, officer or employee thereof is not a party, wherein the constitutionality of any Act of Congress affecting the public interest is drawn in question, the court shall certify such fact to the Attorney General, and shall permit the United States to intervene . . . for argument on the question of constitutionality."

The subsequent section of the statute—§2403(b)—contains virtually identical language imposing upon the courts the duty to notify the attorney general of a state of a constitutional challenge to any statute of that state. But §2403(b), unlike §2403(a), was not implemented in Rule 44.

Rule 44 has been amended to correct this omission. The text of former Rule 44 regarding constitutional challenges to

Rule 45. Clerk's Duties

federal statutes now appears as Rule 44(a), while new language regarding constitutional challenges to state statutes now appears as Rule 44(b).

Changes Made After Publication and Comments. No changes were made to the text of the proposed amendment or to the Committee Note.

Rule 45. Clerk's Duties
(a) General Provisions.
(1) *Qualifications.* The circuit clerk must take the oath and post any bond required by law. Neither the clerk nor any deputy clerk may practice as an attorney or counselor in any court while in office.
(2) *When Court Is Open.* The court of appeals is always open for filing any paper, issuing and returning process, making a motion, and entering an order. The clerk's office with the clerk or a deputy in attendance must be open during business hours on all days except Saturdays, Sundays, and legal holidays. A court may provide by local rule or by order that the clerk's office be open for specified hours on Saturdays or on legal holidays other than New Year's Day, Martin Luther King, Jr.'s Birthday, Washington's Birthday, Memorial Day, Independence Day, Labor Day, Columbus Day, Veterans' Day, Thanksgiving Day, and Christmas Day.
(b) Records.
(1) *The Docket.* The circuit clerk must maintain a docket and an index of all docketed cases in the manner prescribed by the Director of the Administrative Office of the United States Courts. The clerk must record all papers filed with the clerk and all process, orders, and judgments.
(2) *Calendar.* Under the court's direction, the clerk must prepare a calendar of cases awaiting argument. In placing cases on the calendar for argument, the clerk must give preference to appeals in criminal cases and to other proceedings and appeals entitled to preference by law.
(3) *Other Records.* The clerk must keep other books and records required by the Director of the Administrative Office of the United States Courts, with the approval of the Judicial Conference of the United States, or by the court.
(c) Notice of an Order or Judgment. Upon the entry of an order or judgment, the circuit clerk must immediately serve a notice of entry on each party, with a copy of any opinion, and must note the date of service on the docket. Service on a party represented by counsel must be made on counsel.
(d) Custody of Records and Papers. The circuit clerk has custody of the court's records and papers. Unless the court orders or instructs otherwise, the clerk must not permit an original record or paper to be taken from the clerk's office. Upon disposition of the case, original papers constituting the record on appeal or review must be returned to the court or agency from which they were received. The clerk must preserve a copy of any brief, appendix, or other paper that has been filed.
(As amended Mar. 1, 1971, eff. July 1, 1971; Mar. 10, 1986, eff. July 1, 1986; Apr. 24, 1998, eff. Dec. 1, 1998; Apr. 29, 2002, eff. Dec. 1, 2002; Apr. 25, 2005, eff. Dec. 1, 2005.)

Notes of Advisory Committee on Rules—1967

The duties imposed upon clerks of the courts of appeals by this rule are those imposed by rule or practice in a majority of the circuits. The second sentence of subdivision (a) authorizing the closing of the clerk's office on Saturday and non-national legal holidays follows a similar provision respecting the district court clerk's office found in FRCP 77 (c) and in FRCrP 56.

Notes of Advisory Committee on Rules—1971 Amendment

The amendment adds Columbus Day to the list of legal holidays. See the Note accompanying the amendment of Rule 26(a).

Notes of Advisory Committee on Rules—1986 Amendment

The amendment to Rule 45(b) permits the courts of appeals to maintain computerized dockets. The Committee believes that the Administrative Office of the United States Courts ought to have maximum flexibility in prescribing the format of this docket in order to ensure a smooth transition from manual to automated systems and subsequent adaptation to technological improvements.

The amendments to Rules 45(a) and (d) are technical. No substantive change is intended. The Birthday of Martin Luther King, Jr. has been added to the list of national holidays.

Committee Notes on Rules—1998 Amendment

The language and organization of the rule are amended to make the rule more easily understood. In addition to changes made to improve the understanding, the Advisory Committee has changed language to make style and terminology consistent throughout the appellate rules. These changes are intended to be stylistic only.

Committee Notes on Rules—2002 Amendment

Subdivision (c). Subdivision (c) has been amended so that the clerk may use electronic means to serve notice of entry of an order or judgment upon parties who have consented to such service.

Changes Made After Publication and Comments. No changes were made to the text of the proposed amendment or to the Committee Note.

Committee Notes on Rules—2005 Amendment

Subdivision (a)(2). Rule 45(a)(2) has been amended to refer to the third Monday in February as "Washington's Birthday." A federal statute officially designates the holiday as "Washington's Birthday," reflecting the desire of Congress specially to honor the first president of the United States. *See* 5 U.S.C. §6103(a). During the 1998 restyling of the Federal Rules of Appellate Procedure, references to "Washington's Birthday" were mistakenly changed to "Presidents' Day." The amendment corrects that error.

Changes Made After Publication and Comments. No changes were made to the text of the proposed amendment or to the Committee Note.

Rule 46. Attorneys

(a) Admission to the Bar.

(1) *Eligibility*. An attorney is eligible for admission to the bar of a court of appeals if that attorney is of good moral and professional character and is admitted to practice before the Supreme Court of the United States, the highest court of a state, another United States court of appeals, or a United States district court (including the district courts for Guam, the Northern Mariana Islands, and the Virgin Islands).

(2) *Application*. An applicant must file an application for admission, on a form approved by the court that contains the applicant's personal statement showing eligibility for membership. The applicant must subscribe to the following oath or affirmation:

"I, _____, do solemnly swear [or affirm] that I will conduct myself as an attorney and counselor of this court, uprightly and according to law; and that I will support the Constitution of the United States."

(3) *Admission Procedures*. On written or oral motion of a member of the court's bar, the court will act on the application. An applicant may be admitted by oral motion in open court. But, unless the court orders otherwise, an applicant need not appear before the court to be admitted. Upon admission, an applicant must pay the clerk the fee prescribed by local rule or court order.

(b) Suspension or Disbarment.

(1) *Standard*. A member of the court's bar is subject to suspension or disbarment by the court if the member:

(A) has been suspended or disbarred from practice in any other court; or

(B) is guilty of conduct unbecoming a member of the court's bar.

(2) *Procedure*. The member must be given an opportunity to show good cause, within the time prescribed by the court, why the member should not be suspended or disbarred.

(3) *Order*. The court must enter an appropriate order after the member responds and a hearing is held, if

Rule 47. Local Rules by Courts of Appeals

requested, or after the time prescribed for a response expires, if no response is made.

(c) Discipline. A court of appeals may discipline an attorney who practices before it for conduct unbecoming a member of the bar or for failure to comply with any court rule. First, however, the court must afford the attorney reasonable notice, an opportunity to show cause to the contrary, and, if requested, a hearing.

(As amended Mar. 10, 1986, eff. July 1, 1986; Apr. 24, 1998, eff. Dec. 1, 1998.)

Notes of Advisory Committee on Rules—1967

Subdivision (a). The basic requirement of membership in the bar of the Supreme Court, or of the highest court of a state, or in another court of appeals or a district court is found, with minor variations, in the rules of ten circuits. The only other requirement in those circuits is that the applicant be of good moral and professional character. In the District of Columbia Circuit applicants other than members of the District of Columbia District bar or the Supreme Court bar must claim membership in the bar of the highest court of a state, territory or possession for three years prior to application for admission (D.C. Cir. Rule 7). Members of the District of Columbia District bar and the Supreme Court bar again excepted, applicants for admission to the District of Columbia Circuit bar must meet precisely defined prelaw and law school study requirements (D.C. Cir. Rule 71/2).

A few circuits now require that application for admission be made by oral motion by a sponsor member in open court. The proposed rule permits both the application and the motion by the sponsor member to be in writing, and permits action on the motion without the appearance of the applicant or the sponsor, unless the court otherwise orders.

Subdivision (b). The provision respecting suspension or disbarment is uniform. Third Circuit Rule 8(3) is typical.

Subdivision (c). At present only Fourth Circuit Rule 36 contains an equivalent provision. The purpose of this provision is to make explicit the power of a court of appeals to impose sanctions less serious than suspension or disbarment for the breach of rules. It also affords some measure of control over attorneys who are not members of the bar of the court. Several circuits permit a non-member attorney to file briefs and motions, membership being required only at the time of oral argument. And several circuits permit argument pro hac vice by non-member attorneys.

Notes of Advisory Committee on Rules—1986 Amendment

The amendments to Rules 46(a) and (b) are technical. No substantive change is intended.

Committee Notes on Rules—1998 Amendment

The language and organization of the rule are amended to make the rule more easily understood. In addition to changes made to improve the understanding, the Advisory Committee has changed language to make style and terminology consistent throughout the appellate rules. These changes are intended to be stylistic only.

Rule 47. Local Rules by Courts of Appeals

(a) Local Rules.

(1) Each court of appeals acting by a majority of its judges in regular active service may, after giving appropriate public notice and opportunity for comment, make and amend rules governing its practice. A generally applicable direction to parties or lawyers regarding practice before a court must be in a local rule rather than an internal operating procedure or standing order. A local rule must be consistent with—but not duplicative of—Acts of Congress and rules adopted under 28 U.S.C. §2072 and must conform to any uniform numbering system prescribed by the Judicial Conference of the United States. Each circuit clerk must send the Administrative Office of the United States Courts a copy of each local rule and internal operating procedure when it is promulgated or amended.

(2) A local rule imposing a requirement of form must not be enforced in a manner that causes a party to lose rights because of a nonwillful failure to comply with the requirement.

(b) Procedure When There Is No Controlling Law. A court of appeals may regulate practice in a particular case in any manner consistent with federal law, these rules, and local rules of the circuit. No sanction or other disadvantage may be imposed for noncompliance with any requirement not in federal law, federal rules, or the local circuit rules unless the alleged violator has been furnished in the particular case with actual notice of the requirement.

Rule 48. Masters

(As amended Apr. 27, 1995, eff. Dec. 1, 1995; Apr. 24, 1998, eff. Dec. 1, 1998.)

Notes of Advisory Committee on Rules—1967

This rule continues the authority now vested in individual courts of appeals by 28 U.S.C. §2071 to make rules consistent with rules of practice and procedure promulgated by the Supreme Court.

Notes of Advisory Committee on Rules—1995 Amendment

Subdivision (a). This rule is amended to require that a generally applicable direction regarding practice before a court of appeals must be in a local rule rather than an internal operating procedure or some other general directive. It is the intent of this rule that a local rule may not bar any practice that these rules explicitly or implicitly permit. Subdivision (b) allows a court of appeals to regulate practice in an individual case by entry of an order in the case. The amendment also reflects the requirement that local rules be consistent not only with the national rules but also with Acts of Congress. The amendment also states that local rules should not repeat national rules and Acts of Congress.

The amendment also requires that the numbering of local rules conform with any uniform numbering system that may be prescribed by the Judicial Conference. Lack of uniform numbering might create unnecessary traps for counsel and litigants. A uniform numbering system would make it easier for an increasingly national bar and for litigants to locate a local rule that applies to a particular procedural issue.

Paragraph (2) is new. Its aim is to protect against loss of rights in the enforcement of local rules relating to matters of form. The proscription of paragraph (2) is narrowly drawn—covering only violations that are not willful and only those involving local rules directed to matters of form. It does not limit the court's power to impose substantive penalties upon a party if it or its attorney stubbornly or repeatedly violates a local rule, even one involving merely a matter of form. Nor does it affect the court's power to enforce local rules that involve more than mere matters of form.

Subdivision (b). This rule provides flexibility to the court in regulating practice in a particular case when there is no controlling law. Specifically, it permits the court to regulate practice in any manner consistent with Acts of Congress, with rules adopted under 28 U.S.C. §2072, and with the circuit's local rules.

The amendment to this rule disapproves imposing any sanction or other disadvantage on a person for noncompliance with such a directive, unless the alleged violator has been furnished in a particular case with actual notice of the requirement. There should be no adverse consequence to a party or attorney for violating special requirements relating to practice before a particular court unless the party or attorney has actual notice of those requirements.

Committee Notes on Rules—1998 Amendment

The language of the rule is amended to make the rule more easily understood. In addition to changes made to improve the understanding, the Advisory Committee has changed language to make style and terminology consistent throughout the appellate rules. These changes are intended to be stylistic only.

Rule 48. Masters

(a) Appointment; Powers. A court of appeals may appoint a special master to hold hearings, if necessary, and to recommend factual findings and disposition in matters ancillary to proceedings in the court. Unless the order referring a matter to a master specifies or limits the master's powers, those powers include, but are not limited to, the following:

(1) regulating all aspects of a hearing;
(2) taking all appropriate action for the efficient performance of the master's duties under the order;
(3) requiring the production of evidence on all matters embraced in the reference; and
(4) administering oaths and examining witnesses and parties.

(b) Compensation. If the master is not a judge or court employee, the court must determine the master's compensation and whether the cost is to be charged to any party.

(As amended Apr. 29, 1994, eff. Dec. 1, 1994; Apr. 24, 1998, eff. Dec. 1, 1998.)

Notes of Advisory Committee on Rules—1994 Amendment

The text of the existing Rule 48 concerning the title was moved to Rule 1.

Rule 48. Masters

This new Rule 48 authorizes a court of appeals to appoint a special master to make recommendations concerning ancillary matters. The courts of appeals have long used masters in contempt proceedings where the issue is compliance with an enforcement order. *See Polish National Alliance v. NLRB*, 159 F.2d 38 (7th Cir. 1946), *NLRB v. Arcade-Sunshine Co.*, 132 F.2d 8 (D.C. Cir. 1942); *NLRB v. Remington Rand, Inc.*, 130 F.2d 919 (2d Cir. 1942). There are other instances when the question before a court of appeals requires a factual determination. An application for fees or eligibility for Criminal Justice Act status on appeal are examples.

Ordinarily when a factual issue is unresolved, a court of appeals remands the case to the district court or agency that originally heard the case. It is not the Committee's intent to alter that practice. However, when factual issues arise in the first instance in the court of appeals, such as fees for representation on appeal, it would be useful to have authority to refer such determinations to a master for a recommendation.

Committee Notes on Rules—1998 Amendment

The language and organization of the rule are amended to make the rule more easily understood. In addition to changes made to improve the understanding, the Advisory Committee has changed language to make style and terminology consistent throughout the appellate rules. These changes are intended to be stylistic only.

Appellate Form 1. Notice of Appeal to a Court of Appeals From a Judgment or Order of a District Court.

APPENDIX OF FORMS

Appellate Form 1. Notice of Appeal to a Court of Appeals From a Judgment or Order of a District Court.

UNITED STATES DISTRICT COURT
for the
<_____> DISTRICT OF <_____>

<Name(s) of plaintiff(s)>,
 	
   Plaintiff(s)
 	
v.
 	
<Name(s) of defendant(s)>,
 	
   Defendant(s)
	)
	)
	)
	)
	)
	) Case No. <Number>
	)
	)
	)
	)

NOTICE OF APPEAL

Notice is hereby given that <Name all parties taking the appeal>, [plaintiffs] [defendants] in the above named case <See Rule 3(c) for permissible ways of identifying appellants.>, hereby appeal to the United States Court of Appeals for the <_____> Circuit [from the final judgment] [from an order <describing it>] entered in this action on <Date>.

Date: <Date>   <Signature of the attorney or unrepresented party>

              _____
              <Printed name>
              Attorney for <party>
              <Address>
              <E-mail address>
              <Telephone number>

[The following text became effective December 1, 2016.]

*[**Note to inmate filers:** If you are an inmate confined in an institution and you seek the timing benefit of Fed. R. App. P. 4(c)(1), complete Form 7 (Declaration of Inmate Filing) and file that declaration along with this Notice of Appeal.]*

* See Rule 3(c) for permissible ways of identifying appellants.

Appellate Form 2. Notice of Appeal to a Court of Appeals From a Decision of the United States Tax Court.

Appellate Form 2. Notice of Appeal to a Court of Appeals From a Decision of the United States Tax Court.

UNITED STATES TAX COURT
Washington, DC

<Name of petitioner>,
 	
  Petitioner
 	
 v.
 	
Commissioner of Internal Revenue,
 	
  Respondent
	)
	)
	)
	)
	) Docket No. <Number>
	)
	)
	)
	)

NOTICE OF APPEAL

 Notice is hereby given that <Name all parties taking the appeal>, <See Rule 3(c) for permissible ways of identifying appellants.>, hereby appeal to the United States Court of Appeals for the <_____> Circuit from <that part of> the decision of this court entered in the above captioned proceeding on <Date> <relating to _____>.

Date: <Date>   <Signature of the attorney or unrepresented party>

               _____
               <Printed name>
               <Counsel for _____>
               <Address>
               <E-mail address>
               <Telephone number>

Appellate Form 3. Petition for Review of Order of an Agency, Board, Commission or Officer.

United States Court of Appeals
for the
<_____> CIRCUIT

<Name of petitioner>,	)
	)
Petitioner	)
	)
v.	)
	)
<XYZ Commission>,	)
	)
Respondent	)
	)

PETITION FOR REVIEW

<Here name all parties bringing the petition> hereby petition the court for review of the Order of the <XYZ Commission> <describe the order> entered on <Date>.

Date: <Date>

<Signature of the attorney or unrepresented party>

_____
<Printed name>
<Attorney for Petitioners>
<Address>
<E-mail address>
<Telephone number>

Appellate Form 4. Affidavit Accompanying Motion for Permission to Appeal In Forma Pauperis.

Appellate Form 4. Affidavit Accompanying Motion for Permission to Appeal In Forma Pauperis.

UNITED STATES DISTRICT COURT
for the
<_____> DISTRICT OF <_____>

<Name(s) of plaintiff(s)>,	)
Plaintiff(s)	)
v.	) Case No. <Number>
<Name(s) of defendant(s)>,	)
Defendant(s)	)

**AFFIDAVIT ACCOMPANYING MOTION
FOR PERMISSION TO APPEAL IN FORMA PAUPERIS**

Affidavit in Support of Motion

I swear or affirm under penalty of perjury that, because of my poverty, I cannot prepay the docket fees of my appeal or post a bond for them. I believe I am entitled to redress. I swear or affirm under penalty of perjury under United States laws that my answers on this form are true and correct. (28 U.S.C. § 1746; 18 U.S.C. § 1621.)

Instructions

Complete all questions in this application and then sign it. Do not leave any blanks: if the answer to a question is "0," "none," or "not applicable (N/A)," write in that response. If you need more space to answer a question or to explain your answer, attach a separate sheet of paper identified with your name, your case's docket number, and the question number.

Signed: _____ Date: _____

My issues on appeal are:

1. *For both you and your spouse estimate the average amount of money received from each of the following sources during the past 12 months. Adjust any amount that was received weekly, biweekly, quarterly, semiannually, or annually to show the monthly rate. Use gross amounts, that is, amounts before any deductions for taxes or otherwise.*

	Average monthly amount during the past 12 months		Amount expected next month	
	You	Spouse	You	Spouse
Employment	$	$	$	$
Self-employment	$	$	$	$
Income from real property (such as rental income)	$	$	$	$
Interest and dividends	$	$	$	$
Gifts	$	$	$	$
Alimony	$	$	$	$
Child support	$	$	$	$

Appellate Form 4. Affidavit Accompanying Motion for Permission to Appeal In Forma Pauperis.

Retirement (such as social security, pensions, annuities, insurance)	$	$	$	$
Disability (such as social security, insurance payments)	$	$	$	$
Unemployment payments	$	$	$	$
Public-assistance (such as welfare)	$	$	$	$
Other (specify):	$	$	$	$
Total monthly income:	$	$	$	$

2. *List your employment history for the past two years, most recent employer first. (Gross monthly pay is before taxes or other deductions.)*

Employer	Address	Dates of employment	Gross monthly pay
			$
			$
			$

3. *List your spouse's employment history for the past two years, most recent employer first. (Gross monthly pay is before taxes or other deductions.)*

Employer	Address	Dates of employment	Gross monthly pay
			$
			$
			$

4. *How much cash do you and your spouse have? $_____*

   Below, state any money you or your spouse have in bank accounts or in any other financial institution.

Financial Institution	Type of Account	Amount you have	Amount your spouse has
		$	$
		$	$
		$	$

If you are a prisoner seeking to appeal a judgment in a civil action or proceeding, you must attach a statement certified by the appropriate institutional officer showing all receipts, expenditures, and balances during the last six months in your institutional accounts. If you have multiple accounts, perhaps because you have been in multiple institutions, attach one certified statement of each account.

Appellate Form 4. Affidavit Accompanying Motion for Permission to Appeal In Forma Pauperis.

5. *List the assets, and their values, which you own or your spouse owns. Do not list clothing and ordinary household furnishings.*

Home	Other real estate	Motor vehicle #1
(Value) $	(Value) $	(Value) $
		Make and year:
		Model:
		Registration #:

Motor vehicle #2	Other assets	Other assets
(Value) $	(Value) $	(Value) $
Make and year:		
Model:		
Registration #:		

6. *State every person, business, or organization owing you or your spouse money, and the amount owed.*

Person owing you or your spouse money	Amount owed to you	Amount owed to your spouse
	$	$
	$	$
	$	$
	$	$

7. *State the persons who rely on you or your spouse for support.*

Name [or, if under 18, initials only]	Relationship	Age

8. *Estimate the average monthly expenses of you and your family. Show separately the amounts paid by your spouse. Adjust any payments that are made weekly, biweekly, quarterly, semiannually, or annually to show the monthly rate.*

	You	Your Spouse

Rent or home-mortgage payment (include lot rented for mobile home)
    Are real estate taxes included? [ ] Yes [ ] No
    Is property insurance included?   [ ] Yes [ ] No
	$	$

Utilities (electricity, heating fuel, water, sewer, and telephone)	$	$
Home maintenance (repairs and upkeep)	$	$
Food	$	$

Appellate Form 4. Affidavit Accompanying Motion for Permission to Appeal In Forma Pauperis.

Clothing	$	$
Laundry and dry-cleaning	$	$
Medical and dental expenses	$	$
Transportation (not including motor vehicle payments)	$	$
Recreation, entertainment, newspapers, magazines, etc.	$	$
Insurance (not deducted from wages or included in mortgage payments)		
Homeowner's or renter's:	$	$
Life:	$	$
Health:	$	$
Motor vehicle:	$	$
Other:	$	$
Taxes (not deducted from wages or included in mortgage payments) (specify):	$	$
Installment payments		
Motor Vehicle:	$	$
Credit card (name):	$	$
Department store (name):	$	$
Other:	$	$
Alimony, maintenance, and support paid to others	$	$
Regular expenses for operation of business, profession, or farm (attach detailed statement)	$	$
Other (specify):	$	$
Total monthly expenses:	**$**	**$**

9. *Do you expect any major changes to your monthly income or expenses or in your assets or liabilities during the next 12 months?*

    [ ] Yes   [ ] No   If yes, describe on an attached sheet.

10. *Have you spent — or will you be spending — any money for expenses or attorney fees in connection with this lawsuit?* [ ] Yes [ ] No

    If yes, how much? $ _____

11. *Provide any other information that will help explain why you cannot pay the docket fees for your appeal.*

12. *State the city and state of your legal residence.*

    Your daytime phone number: (___) _____

    Your age: _____ Your years of schooling: _____

    Last four digits of your social-security number: _____

Appellate Form 5. Notice of Appeal to a Court of Appeals from a Judgment or Order of a District Court or a Bankruptcy Appellate Panel.

Appellate Form 5. Notice of Appeal to a Court of Appeals from a Judgment or Order of a District Court or a Bankruptcy Appellate Panel.

UNITED STATES DISTRICT COURT
for the
<_____> DISTRICT OF <_____>

In re
 	
<Name of debtor>,
 	
      Debtor
 	
<Name of plaintiff>,
 	
      Plaintiff
v.
<Name of defendant>,
 	
      Defendant
	)
	)
	)
	)
	) File No. <Number>
	)
	)
	)
	)
	)
	)
	)
	)

**NOTICE OF APPEAL TO UNITED STATES COURT
OF APPEALS FOR THE <_____> CIRCUIT**

    <Name of party>, the [plaintiff] [defendant] [other party], appeals to the United States Court of Appeals for the <_____> Circuit from the [final judgment] [order] [decree] of the [district court for the district of <_____>] [bankruptcy appellate panel of the <_____> circuit], entered in this case on <Date>.

    <Here describe the judgment, order, or decree.>

    The parties to the [judgment] [order] [decree] appealed from and the names and addresses of their respective attorneys are as follows:

Date: <Date>   <Signature of the attorney for appellant>

                                                          <Printed name>
                                                          Attorney for Appellant
                                                          <Address>
                                                          <E-mail address>
                                                          <Telephone number>

[The following text became effective December 1, 2016.]

[***Note to inmate filers:*** *If you are an inmate confined in an institution and you seek the timing benefit of Fed. R. App.P. 4(c)(1), complete Form 7 (Declaration of Inmate Filing) and file that declaration along with this Notice of Appeal.*]

Appellate Form 6. Certificate of Compliance With Rule 32(a).

CERTIFICATE OF COMPLIANCE WITH RULE 32(a)

**Certificate of Compliance With Type-Volume Limitation,
Typeface Requirements, and Type Style Requirements**

[The following text was effective until December 1, 2016.]

1. This brief complies with the type-volume limitation of Fed. R. App. P. 32(a)(7)(B) because:

   [ ] this brief contains <state the number of> words, excluding the parts of the brief exempted by Fed. R. App. P. 32(a)(7)(B)(iii), or

   [ ] this brief uses a monospaced typeface and contains <state the number of> lines of text, excluding the parts of the brief exempted by Fed. R. App. P. 32(a)(7)(B)(iii).

2. This brief complies with the typeface requirements of Fed. R. App. P. 32(a)(5) and the type style requirements of Fed. R. App. P. 32(a)(6) because:

   [ ] this brief has been prepared in a proportionally spaced typeface using <state name and version of word processing program> in <state font size and name of type style>, *or*

   [ ] this brief has been prepared in a monospaced typeface using <state name and version of word processing program> with <state number of characters per inch and name of type style>.

Date: <Date>   <Signature of the attorney>

_____
<Printed name>
Attorney for <_____>
<Address>
<E-mail address>
<Telephone number>

[The following text became effective December 1, 2016.]

1. This document complies with [the type-volume limit of Fed. R. App. P. [insert Rule citation; e.g., 32(a)(7)(B)]] [the word limit of Fed. R. App. P. [insert Rule citation; e.g., 5(c)(1)]] because, excluding the parts of the document exempted by Fed. R. App. P. 32(f) [and [insert applicable Rule citation, if any]]:

   ☐ this document contains [state the number of] words, or

   ☐ this brief uses a monospaced typeface and contains [state the number of] lines of text.

2. This document complies with the typeface requirements of Fed. R. App. P. 32(a)(5) and the type-style requirements of Fed. R. App. P. 32(a)(6) because:
☐ this document has been prepared in a proportionally spaced typeface using [state name and version of word-processing program] in [state font size and name of type style], or

☐ this document has been prepared in a monospaced typeface using [state name and version of word-processing program] with [state number of characters per inch and name of type style].

(s)_____
Attorney for _____
Dated: _____

Appellate Form 7. Declaration of Inmate Filing

[The following text became effective December 1, 2016.]

Appellate Form 7. Declaration of Inmate Filing

_____
[insert name of court; for example,
United States District Court for the District of Minnesota]

A.B., Plaintiff   )
)
    v.   ) Case No. _____
)
C.D., Defendant   )
)

    I am an inmate confined in an institution. Today, _____ [insert date], I am depositing the _____ [insert title of document; for example, "notice of appeal"] in this case in the institution's internal mail system. First-class postage is being prepaid either by me or by the institution on my behalf.

    I declare under penalty of perjury that the foregoing is true and correct (see 28 U.S.C. § 1746; 18 U.S.C. § 1621).

Sign your name here_____

Signed on _____ [insert date]

[**Note to inmate filers:** *If your institution has a system designed for legal mail, you must use that system in order to receive the timing benefit of Fed. R. App. P. 4(c)(1) or Fed. R. App. P. 25(a)(2)(C).*]

Appendix

[The following text became effective December 1, 2016.]

Appendix

**Length Limits Stated in the
Federal Rules of Appellate Procedure**

This chart summarizes the length limits stated in the Federal Rules of Appellate Procedure. Please refer to the rules for precise requirements, and bear in mind the following:

- In computing these limits, you can exclude the items listed in Rule 32(f).

- If you use a word limit or a line limit (other than the word limit in Rule 28(j)), you must file the certificate required by Rule 32(g).

- For the limits in Rules 5, 21, 27, 35, and 40:

    - You must use the word limit if you produce your document on a computer; and

    - You must use the page limit if you handwrite your document or type it on a typewriter.

- For the limits in Rules 28.1, 29(a)(5), and 32:

    - You may use the word limit or page limit, regardless of how you produce the document; or

    - You may use the line limit if you type or print your document with a monospaced typeface. A typeface is monospaced when each character occupies the same amount of horizontal space.

	Rule	Document type	Word limit	Page limit	Line limit
Permission to Appeal	5(c)	• Petition for permission to appeal • Answer in opposition • Cross-petition	5,200	20	Not applicable
Extraordinary Writs	21(d)	• Petition for writ of mandamus or prohibition or other extraordinary writ • Answer	7,800	30	Not applicable
Motions	27(d)(2)	• Motion • Response to a motion	5,200	20	Not applicable
	27(d)(2)	• Reply to a response to a motion	2,600	10	Not applicable
Parties' briefs (where no cross-appeal)	32(a)(7)	• Principal brief	13,000	30	1,300
	32(a)(7)	• Reply brief	6,500	15	650
Parties' briefs (where cross-appeal)	28.1(e)	• Appellant's principal brief • Appellant's response and reply brief	13,000	30	1,300
	28.1(e)	• Appellee's principal and response brief	15,300	35	1,500
	28.1(e)	• Appellee's reply brief	6,500	15	650

	Rule	Document type	Word limit	Page limit	Line limit
Party's Supplemental letter	28(j)	• Letter citing supplemental authorities	350	Not applicable	Not applicable
Amicus briefs	29(a)(5)	• Amicus brief during initial consideration of case on merits	One-half the length set by the Appellate Rules for a party's principal brief	One-half the length set by the Appellate Rules for a party's principal brief	One-half the length set by the Appellate Rules for a party's principal brief
	29(b)(4)	• Amicus brief during consideration of whether to grant rehearing	2,600	Not applicable	Not applicable
Rehearing and en banc filings	35(b)(2) & 40(b)	• Petition for hearing en banc • Petition for panel rehearing; petition for rehearing en banc	3,900	15	Not applicable

Other Books by HSE Publishing Co.

Federal Rules of Civil Procedure (2017 Edition): with Advisory Committee Notes & Recent Cases on ESI Sanctions

Federal Rules of Evidence (2017 Edition): with Advisory Committee Notes & Rule 502 Non-Waiver Templates

Federal Civil Court Rules (2017 Edition): Rules of Civil Procedure, Evidence and Appellate Procedure with Advisory Committee Notes

Florida Rules of Civil Procedure (2017 Edition): with Committee Notes

Florida Evidence Code (2017 Edition): Evidence, Witnesses, Records and Documents

www.ingramcontent.com/pod-product-compliance
Lightning Source LLC
Chambersburg PA
CBHW080659190526
45169CB00006B/2180